Modernity in the Flesh

Kristin Ruggiero

Modernity in the Flesh

Medicine, Law, and Society
in Turn-of-the-Century Argentina

Stanford University Press, Stanford, California   2004

Stanford University Press
Stanford, California
© 2004 by the Board of Trustees of the
Leland Stanford Junior University
Printed in the United States of America

Library of Congress Cataloging-in-Publication Data
Ruggiero, Kristin
    Modernity in the flesh : medicine, law, and society in turn-of-the-century Argentina /
Kristin Ruggiero
        p. cm.
Includes bibliographical references and index.
ISBN 0-8047-4871-3 (alk. paper)
    1. Crime—Argentina—Buenos Aires—History—19th century—Case
studies. 2. Social control—Argentina—Buenos Aires—History—19th
century. 3. Degeneration—History—19th century. 4. Social medicine—
Argentina—Buenos Aires—History—19th century. 5. Body, Human—Social
aspects—Argentina—Buenos Aires—History—19th century. 6. Body,
Human—Political aspects—Argentina—Buenos Aires—History—19th
century. 7. Body, Human—Moral and ethical aspects—Argentina—Buenos
Aires—History—19th century. I. Title.
HV6885.B8 R84   2004

364.982'11'09034—dc21   2003021084

This book is printed on acid-free, archival quality paper.

Original printing 2004
Last figure below indicates year of this printing:
13   12   11   10   09   08   07   06   05   04

Typeset in 10/13 Electra

TO MY PARENTS,

who first introduced me to the fun of history

Contents

Acknowledgments

Generous grants from the National Science Foundation and the National Endowment for the Humanities between 1993 and 1996 made it possible for me to write this book. I am also deeply grateful to the many archivists and librarians who patiently and kindly facilitated my research at the Archivo Nacional de la Nación in Buenos Aires; the Archivo Histórico de la Provincia in Córdoba; the Museo de Policía in La Plata; and the Widener, Law School, and Medical School libraries at Harvard University.

Friends at the many schools and institutions with which I have been associated have been supportive beyond words. These include my colleagues at the David Rockefeller Center for Latin American Studies at Harvard University, the European Law Research Center at Harvard University Law School, the Consejo Superior de Investigaciones Científicas in Madrid, the Universidad Torcuato Di Tella in Buenos Aires, the European University Institute, Cornell University, Keene State College, Holy Cross College, the University of Connecticut, and the University of Cincinnati.

Editors of the volumes in which my work has appeared over the past few years have helped me enormously to conceptualize my work in a wider framework, as have Norris Pope of Stanford University Press and Ivan Jáksić and another, anonymous reader. Many Latin Americanist colleagues have done the same, bringing me into a network that I appreciate more each day. Friends in Argentina added both a scholarly and a human dimension to my research. Among these are Carlos Escudé, Sandra Gayol, Poldy Miskulin, Mariano Plotkin, Andrés Reggiani, and Ricardo Salvatore.

Finally, I want to say a very special thanks to the members of the Department of History, the Center for Latin American and Caribbean Studies, and the Center for International Education at the University of Wisconsin–Milwaukee for their wonderful friendship and support. While it is impossible to single out individuals in this wonderful group of friends and colleagues, there are several people who have been more closely involved in this project than others. These are Mark Bradley, David Buck, Michael Gordon, Howard Handelman, Jeffrey Merrick, Patrice Petro, and Merry Wiesner-Hanks.

I would like to thank the publishers of the following volumes for extending permission to excerpt from my former work. Parts of chapter 1 appeared in slightly different form in *Isolation: Places and Practices of Exclusion*, edited by Carolyn Strange and Alison Bashford (New York: Routledge, 2003): 119-32, and in the *Journal of Family History* (Sage Publications) 17, 3 (1992): 253-70; parts of chapter 2 in *Reconstructing Criminality in Latin America*, edited by Carlos Aguirre and Robert Buffington (Wilmington, Del.: Scholarly Resources, 2000): 149-66, and the *Hispanic American Historical Review* (Duke University Press) 72, 3 (1992): 353-73; parts of chapter 3 in *Documenting Individual Identity: The Development of State Practices in the Modern World*, edited by Jane Caplan and John Torpey (Princeton: Princeton University Press, 2001): 184-96; parts of chapter 5 in *Argentina on the Couch: Psychiatry, State and Society in Argentina, 1880-1970*, edited by Mariano Plotkin (Albuquerque: University of New Mexico Press, 2003); and parts of chapter 6 in *Crime and Punishment in Latin America* (Durham, N.C.: Duke University Press, 2001): 211-32.

Modernity in the Flesh

Introduction

The story told in this book takes place primarily in Buenos Aires after 1880, when the city became the national capital of Argentina, the prize in the political and military struggle over the centralization of the federal government in the first half of the nineteenth century. Political control landed in the hands of liberal democratic elites who promoted European models of constitutional rights and guarantees, modernity, centralism, and urbanism. All this suggested a new era in the rethinking of Argentine nationality and the writing of its historical narrative. National character was in a period of formation, leaving Argentines conflicted over their love/hate relationship with a Latin America that was underdeveloped, and was still living through the chaos from which Argentina had just escaped, and a western Europe that was modern and progressive but in its essence foreign to Argentine identity and in a neo-colonial relationship with Argentina.

The modernization of Buenos Aires brought it more within the realm of European influence and added to Argentines' ambivalence about the Old World. Broad new avenues and spacious parks, modeled after those of Paris, joined the older narrow streets and smaller plazas; restaurants, dance halls, and foreign department stores displayed an elegance in striking contrast to street vendors' carts; the spacious homes of elite landowners and businessmen assured the occupants of the crowded tenement buildings, or *conventillos*, of the working classes that they had come to the right place to improve their lives; government offices and police stations proliferated, symbols of the triumph of increasing centralization, for better or worse, and horse cabs and trams jammed the streets, increasing people's mobility and altering their relationship to their old neighborhoods.

The action of this book originates from mostly lengthy criminal cases—341 of which were examined in detail—and the medical, legal, and criminological commentaries on them. The cases took place in strikingly different locales—the old immigrant neighborhoods of San Telmo and La Boca, which were mostly untouched by modernization; the area around the Congress building; and the newer and more elite area to the north. The changes taking place in the city and nation, reflected in the cases, stimulated discussion about society and modernity, Argentina's relationship to the rest of Latin America and to its models in Europe, and strategies for dealing with the "social question"—social ills such as crime and disease. The discussions, commentaries, and stratagems helped to forge a state consensus about social problems and to create a sense among Argentines of being swept up in a new modern age that no one could escape. An elite home became the place where an illegitimate child, born of a family servant, died. A beautiful plaza turned into a grave for a newborn. An immigrant's room in a boarding house became the scene of a murder by a jealous lover. A dance at a restaurant started the process of a young woman's "corruption," which ended in her incarceration. A diverse population forced the country to negotiate conditions of modernity informed by both foreign and indigenous cultures. During the 1880s, a million immigrants came to Argentina; of the 850,000 who stayed, 60 percent were Italian and 18 percent were Spanish. Their understandings of their rights and responsibilities, of the Argentine national program, and of local customs differed, as did those of people moving into the city from the less-developed provinces. Indeed, the trial records treat people carefully according to their level of exposure to "civilization," education, and moral instruction. The ways in which *porteños*, the inhabitants of Buenos Aires—doctors, lawyers, public officials, newcomers, and the general public—negotiated urban life contribute to an understanding of their intimate and public relationships, behaviors and motivations, needs and desires, successes and disappointments, evaluations of altruistic and delinquent acts, and community solidarity and destructiveness. All of these features intersected in the growth of the republic's capital.

The political backdrop to this history was liberal democracy, which showcased individual rights, yet at the same time, new sciences and a new set of priorities emerged that asserted the precedence of measures to ensure the health and security of the social whole. More than democratic government and respect for individual rights, modernity meant a raised consciousness of the public good and a commitment to science as the warranty of progress. The ideal individual was supposed to be complicit with measures for the social good. In chapter 1, we see wives' individual rights take a back seat to their husbands' authority, reinforced by civil and penal law and concepts such as honor. In chapter 2, we see pregnant women's dire state of health and finances take a back seat to the demands of shame and public interest in the demographic growth of the nation. In chapter 3, we see individual rights give way to identification techniques designed to confront dangers to public hygiene and safety. The dangers ranged from the physical contagions of cemeteries, water supplies, and toilets to the moral contagions of foreigners and political activists, socioeconomic class mixing, and criminals. In chapter 4, we see personal rights give way to a perceived need to search out and make public "degenerative" conditions, including race, hysteria, epilepsy, and neurasthenia, which were thought able to affect everyone and bring down the entire species. In chapter 5, we see individual rights confronted with a drive to actually physically eliminate members of society who were considered morally degenerate. In chapter 6, however, we have an about-face. Passion as an individual right was allowed to take precedence over the needs of society. People recognized that harmful acts committed under the influence of passion were criminal, but also took into account that passion would end up affecting everyone sooner or later, and that these were confusing times, when the passions needed to be more firmly harnessed. On grounds of the supposed dangers of the public's passion, a jury system was never established in Argentina, although specified in the national constitution, and passion was also an issue in the debate over the death penalty. Even though the book focuses on serious medical and legal concerns, however, it also draws on protagonists' ironic and humorous perceptions of the mixed blessings of modernity and liberal democracy, positivism, excessive confidence in scientific medicine and its practitioners, and the pomposity of lawyers.

CARNE

The tensions in liberal democracy between individual rights and the social good were tempered by flesh—*carne*—and articulated by that word. Especially in its relationship to passion, "flesh" communicated these tensions of modernity and was a signifier of the ambivalence felt about modernity in a postcolonial Third World country.

The preference in the sources for the term *carne* captures the sentiment of the times and helps in part to explain this period. The word *cuerpo*, or "body," as in the Foucauldian model, is seldom used, but when it is, it seems to signify a collective wholeness as the total material organism of a man or woman, or as a collective mass, such as the body of policemen, or the "body corporate" or the "body politic." "Body" appears bounded by legalism and by passivity, an object for lawyers and doctors to examine. It is treated as a discrete entity that could be contained by theories and state regulations. *Carne*, on the other hand, expressed more fluidity, immediacy, and life, and reflected more of the essence of the person. The Argentine forensic medical doctor Francisco de Veyga used *carne* in a discussion of the crimes of begging and prostitution in 1904, when he described the perpetrators as being part of "our flesh," rather than real delinquents. These were "aberrant" people who had chosen questionable occupations, but they were still "part of [Argentines'] *carne*." The fact that physical and moral elements were seen as moving from one person to another through their flesh allowed for Veyga's interpretation. Calling in 1899 for a "cutting away" of the gangrene that was consuming the nation, the Argentine jurist and statesman Estanislao Severo Zeballos used the metaphor of the "raw flesh" (*carne viva*) of Argentina.[1] Theories of contagion attributed a kind of intelligence and morality to flesh, which allowed jurists and criminologists to hold people responsible for their acts in certain circumstances. With the development of fingerprinting, flesh also took on the role of identifier. The Argentine policeman Juan Vucetich's method of taking prints of the flesh in the 1890s highlighted the superiority of the flesh over the body as a whole. Flesh prints were the essence of a person, he explained, in a way that body measurements and photographs could never be. "Flesh" might be explained as merely a rhetorical term used by political and professional elites, but to answer the question of why it was preferred to "body," I think that one can assume that it was also a way of thinking.

This was the raw material, the flesh, at hand, and with the aid of the new sciences, a clear commitment to progress, and a strong sense of nationalism, a conscious plan evolved in the republic to create a new character, mentality, and race in Argentina. This book tells the story of the ironies of the state becoming hostage to both the passionate body and the positivist body. The changes were effected both by new medical and legal theories, informed by modern scientific progress and positivism, and by foreign political, cultural, and legal models. As science and positivism began to inform the professions of medicine and law, these professions became useful in attempting to correct for the pathologies besetting Buenos Aires, both those of the modern world and those that the city had inherited from the colonial and indigenous past. Foreign models were imitated and reworked to construct this nation dedicated to civilization and scientific progress. Although professional and political elites debated the advantages and disadvantages of positivism and of imitation, these became the accepted modes of development for Argentina.

Both body and flesh were used to forge a state consensus about social problems. The flesh challenged the body politic. Their struggle articulated the struggle between forces that fought for the social good and forces that fought for individual rights, often engaged in by the same person. Body could be circumscribed, but flesh spilled over. Professional and political elites were constantly trying to rein in the flesh and push it back into the body, whether by means of places of incarceration or by writing excuses for passion into law codes. However, the porousness and vicissitudes of the flesh—such as emanations of gases from the flesh that created miasmas and spread contagion; immoral thoughts and attitudes that were sources of social corruption; and "degenerative" conditions in the population—did not necessarily lend themselves to institutional control. Regardless of the excellence of new penitentiaries, hospitals, asylums, and health regulations, these were ineffective in protecting the innocent and the elite from moral and physical contagion. Social control institutions could be used to teach personal responsibility; they could order the body by surrounding it, disinfecting it, neutralizing it, and isolating it. But they could not really control what medical theories confirmed, namely, the fact that the moral and physical innards of the body spilled out of it through its flesh. Miasmas, contagion, emanations, separation, and excess all had more affinity with *carne* than with *cuerpo*.

In criminal cases, for example, direct personal agency played as much of a role in improving society as Foucauldian social control mechanisms, and the choice of the word "flesh" reflects this thinking. It was not that people were being encouraged to do without the help of institutions—quite the contrary, since more were being built. But within those institutions, and in the prescriptive literature being published, people were being encouraged to do what was right for themselves, which was also what was right for society, in an attempt to merge the commitment to individual rights and the social good. There was a kind of self-sufficient notion to this, not inconsistent with Argentina's self-perception as a global "frontier," a New World place where people from all over could remake themselves and help build a new nation and populace. Much of the public hygienist Eduardo Wilde's advice in the 1880s focused on self-help, and one of his most seemingly outlandish suggestions was that one separate one's own feces and urine for the good of society.[2]

Important social constructs and legal precepts such as honor and passion, on which so much of life hinged, also had more to do with *carne* than with *cuerpo*. Flesh made these constructs more tangible and thus more understandable. Was it X's body that had fired the gun at his co-worker? No, it was a combination of honor—described as a "moral emanation"—with a nervous movement of X's flesh, which became converted without his willing it into an instrument. Should Z be punished with the full force of the law for shooting at his girlfriend's family? No, he should be understood as a man who, because he was in early manhood, had "flesh of passion."

Flesh also better expresses the sensibility of people that connected them more immediately and actively engaged them with society. Flesh was the part of the body that first came into contact with the world. Was Y just a rebellious teenager? No, she was the victim of corrupting miasmas that had penetrated her flesh. Was X guilty of killing Y? Not exactly, since his flesh was afflicted with physical degenerative characteristics passed down through the generations, perhaps beginning with gout and ending with epilepsy.

Flesh was also uppermost in people's minds, too, because of Charles Darwin and the debate about whether man and monkey, disturbingly similar in flesh, were united in other ways. In 1905, Victor Arreguiné scoffed at the idea and wrote that Darwin had "lived and died in a crass error." Darwin's theory was no better, he said, than the Genesis story. "There is the gorilla and chimpanzee, then a great void, and then man on the other bank. No boat links them. Genesis is more logical." A playful cartoon in the weekly *PBT* takes the gorilla's point of view of evolution. When a "wise man" tells a gorilla that he is like the gorilla, only "perfected," the gorilla responds with disdain. "Perfected? Hah. In my family there's no one as ugly as you. Besides, you're not strong and you're a coward. And you think you can have the honor of being my relative? Don't insult me!"[3]

As the state was pursuing positivist science and government, the flesh held out a type of corrective to the focus on scientific and material progress, often to the very same people. The state was a moral community, and progress had to be accompanied by morality, statesmen agreed. In addition, direct personal agency and self-sufficiency, which were consistent with Argentines' perception of their country as a global frontier, were valued. Even if many people in Argentina were not linked to the state through citizenship, they could be linked as a moral community. The flesh held important human qualities, which positivism did not. Positivism was a materialistic doctrine, and people were uncomfortable with the growing phenomenon of materialism. The vision for many of progress in Argentina in the last quarter of the nineteenth century was that cold, hard science was not enough; that progress had to be accompanied by public and private morality.[4] In other words, at the same time that positivists were arguing that men and women did not have free will, the protagonists in criminal cases often seemed to be claiming the reverse.

THE PROFESSIONAL ACTORS

The professional elites who actively engaged social issues through their writings, speeches, and court debates, especially from the 1880s onward, showed a respect for flesh and passion; an appreciation of modernity as well as skepticism; the ability to play politics; a willingness to criticize foreign models as well as to criticize themselves and Argentina; and a developed sense of irony and cynicism. This was the group that set the parameters for legal considerations in Argentina as the national state was coalescing, for how people were judged—such as immigrants facing a foreign justice system, women as a new constituency in court, minors, and the indigenous—and for why people should identify with science and reason and support the common good. These professionals were well educated, had often studied in Europe, frequently were also statesmen and held political power, wrote frequently about the social crisis in Argentina, and often had colorful and volatile life histories.

The jurists responsible for Argentina's initial penal and civil codes, Carlos Tejedor (J.D. in 1837 from the University of Buenos Aires; d. 1903) and Dalmacio Vélez Sarsfield (J.D. in 1823 from the University of Córdoba; d. 1875), shared the dubious honor of being criticized by their contemporaries for authoring "still-born" law codes—Tejedor for not taking into account the important theory of positivism, and Vélez Sarsfield for not taking into account advances in family law and women's rights. On the other hand, Tejedor promoted the study of criminal law before scientific criminal investigation had been incorporated into Argentine customs. He also had a tumultuous political career, being imprisoned for conspiracy to kill the dictator General Juan Manuel de Rosas in 1839, followed by exile to Brazil and Chile. After returning to Buenos Aires in 1852, Tejedor became minister of foreign relations (1870–74), minister to Brazil (1875), and governor of the province of Buenos Aires (1880). His code of 1865–67 became the basis for the first national penal code, sanctioned in 1886. Vélez Sarsfield, who authored the civil code of 1869, also served in public office—in the provincial legislature of Buenos Aires (1850s), as minister of finance (1863), and as minister of the interior (1868–73).[5]

The attorneys in criminal cases had generally earned their degrees at the University of Buenos Aires and followed a variety of careers. Jorge Argerich, for example, who defended a man arrested for attacking President Julio Roca, was a radical who supported the statesmen Leandro Alem and Hipólito Irigoyen; Emilio Gouchon worked for the General Department of Immigration; and Adolfo Cano was a national deputy from 1862 to 1872 and an active supporter of Bartolomé Mitre for president. Lawyers were also writers. Nicolás Casarino, for example, edited *La Opinión* and the *Revista de Tribunales*; Emilio Gouchon wrote for *La Nación* and *El Argentino*, an organ of the Unión Cívica; Luis Vicente Varela wrote for *La Tribuna* and authored a number of law treatises, as did Gerónimo Cortés Funes; and Ernesto Quesada wrote on colonial life and medicine. Most of the judges in these cases had also received law degrees from the University of Buenos Aires and had active political and publishing careers. Ernesto Madero, for example, worked for the Minors' Assistance Office; Norberto Piñero belonged to Argentine and foreign cultural societies, was secretary of the University of Buenos Aires, authored a reform of the penal code in 1890, and served as Argentine minister to Chile; Guillermo Torres was a national deputy for the province of Buenos Aires; Luis F. Navarro was a reporter for *La Prensa*, secretary of *Sud América*, and wrote a *Manual de policia*; and Pastor Servando Obligado, a colleague of Juana Manuela Gorriti's, belonged to the Círculo Literario, wrote about Argentine traditions, traveled extensively, and spoke at Harvard University.

The medical doctors who examined accused persons to assess their physical and mental health and informed the court of any health issues that were extenuating circumstances had generally received their medical degrees from the University of Buenos Aires, although a few had studied in Europe as well. Some had been involved in the era's warfare. Dr. Juan N. Acuña, for example, fought in the last rebellion of López Jordán and opposed Tejedor's troops in 1879; Dr. José Teodoro Baca was in Mitre's army and a surgeon at Pavon; Dr. Lucilo del Castillo was a doctor in the Paraguay War; and Dr. Julián M. Fernández was a military doctor in the War of the Triple Alliance. Some doctors also had political careers. Acuña was a national deputy (1894); Baca was a deputy to the provincial legislature; and Dr. Pedro Antonio Pardo was minister of foreign relations (1874). Baca and Pardo had studied in Europe. Some were active in public health issues, such as Baca, who worked with the Council of Hygiene; Dr. Melitón González del Solar, who was inspector of hygiene during the yellow fever epidemic in 1858; and Castillo, who directed the *lazareto* (leper hospital) on Martín García. Some of these doctors also became known outside Argentina—Francisco Sicardi as a novelist; Juan Antonio Argerich as a student of Ricardo Gutierrez's poems; and Agustín J. Drago, son of Luis María Drago, as a student of Alphonse Bertillon's anthropometric techniques in Paris.

The younger generation of lawyers and doctors were as engaged in the concerns of the end of the century in the courtrooms and clinics and hospitals as the older generation had been on the battlefield fighting for unification of the republic. They fought against classicism and in favor of positivism; they criticized judges for making politically motivated appointments; they criticized one another for lack of professionalism; and they interacted with new constituencies, such as women and women intellectuals, Amerindians, foreigners, and the poor and uneducated. They dealt with the new subjects of the republic. Estanislao Severo Zeballos wrote about gender issues and threats to the Argentine nation; Eduardo Wilde wrote about public health; and Carlos Octavio Bunge wrote about national character. Some of their theories might seem eccentric, but they were representative of the times. José Ingenieros, for example, wrote on degenerative races; Carlos Olivera, on social poisons; Benjamin T. Solari, on the castration of degenerates; Eduardo Wilde, on body fluids; Lucas Ayarragaray and Eusebio Gómez, on passions; and Víctor Mercante, on the degeneration of immigrants in Argentina.

Emerging from three hundred years of colonialism into the 1800s and a world that continued to be dominated by western Europe, Argentina not surprisingly was influenced by European law codes and legal theories and models. Both criminal and civil trial records, reflecting the law codes themselves, tended to cite the law codes of Europe extensively as the basis for decisions. The European legal experts whose works were most often quoted by Argentine legal professionals included Cesare Beccaria (Italian, d. 1794); Jeremy Bentham (English, d. 1832); Adolphe Chauveau (French, d. 1869); Joaquín Escriche (Spanish, d. 1847); and Joaquín Francisco Pacheco (Spanish, d. 1865).

In addition, the European influence on the development of forensic medicine and criminology was strong, and Argentines often cited European forensic doctors and criminologists as authorities, such as Jean Etienne Dominique Esquirol (French, d. 1840); Mathieu Joseph Bonaventure Orfila (Spanish, but on the Faculty of Medicine of the University of Paris, d. 1853); Jean Baptiste Félix Descuret (French, d. 1872); Valentin Magnan (French, d. 1916); Cesare Lombroso (Italian, d. 1909); Gabriel Tarde (French, d. 1904); and Ambroise Auguste Tardieu (French, d. 1879).

As science advanced in the republic, Argentine work became known abroad. Luis Agote's new graphic method of fixing heredity, for example, was adopted by some foreign *alienistas*. Pedro Narciso Arata's numerous articles on medicinal plants of America were translated for European journals of chemistry, and he belonged to foreign academies and institutions in Madrid, Rome, Berlin, Chile, and Paris. Luis María Drago's *Los hombres de presa* was translated into Italian with an introduction by Lombroso, and the Drago doctrine became well known in diplomatic circles. Rodolfo Juan Nemesio Rivarola's proposal for reform of the penal code was well received by foreign jurists. In addition, Argentine professionals were not reluctant to criticize Europeans, as did Ingenieros, an Italian immigrant himself, who said that Lombroso was "crazy," and Samuel Gache who scoffed at Bertillon to his face at an international conference.

POSITIVISM AND CRIMINAL ANTHROPOLOGY

The theories of positivism and criminal anthropology most informed the work of the Argentine medical and legal professionals. Italians such as Cesare Lombroso, Enrico Ferri, Raffaello Garófalo, and Napoleone Colajanni, and the Frenchmen Gabriel Tarde and A. Lacassagne, had firmly established these theories in Europe by the last quarter of the century. In Argentina, the positivist movement was led by José Ingenieros (its most important representative), Antonio Dellepiane, L. M. Drago, E. Gómez, Pedro Gori (an Italian jurist living in Argentina), F. and J. M. Ramos Mejía, Osvaldo Piñero, R. Rivarola, J. N. Matienzo, Cornelio Moyano Gacitúa, Francisco de Veyga, Juan Vucetich, and the editors of *Criminalogía Moderna* (a phrase coined by Raffaello Garofalo meaning the study and knowledge of crime). The opposition to positivism, a smaller but vocal group, was led by Godofredo Lozano, Manuel Obarrio, and Emilio B. Prack.

The movement toward a society more informed by positive science in the second half of the nineteenth century was steady, but uneven. First, the regent law code, which had come to be used throughout much of Argentina, beginning in 1877, when the province of Buenos Aires was the first to adopt it, with the capital following in 1881, was not based on positivism, but rather on an older vision of law known as "classical" law. The philosophy of the classical school was based on the eighteenth-century Enlightenment principles of rationality, liberalism, humanitarianism, and science. Formulaic classical law viewed crime as a single, discrete act, an abstract entity produced exclusively by free will and moral responsibility. It viewed punishments as fixed and proportional to the crime, and as focused on the crime rather than on the criminal. In addition to being classical, the code cited laws from the colonial period—such as the Siete Partidas of Alfonso X, published in 1265 and in effect in Spain until 1831, and the Nueva Recopilación—as authorities. The code was also foreign. The two principal influences on the Tejedor code, which contained four hundred and fifty articles, were the Spanish code of 1850, edited mainly by Joaquin Francisco Pacheco, and Von Feuerbach's 1813 Bavarian code. Moreover, the literal translation of articles from foreign codes often made little sense in Spanish, and the Germanic origin of much of the code convinced many people that it was inappropriate for a Latin nation.[6] Tejedor also drew on the French code of 1810, the Peruvian code of 1863, and the Louisiana code. Eventually, Argentine case law also came to be used, especially after the first major collection of sentences was published in 1885.[7] Basically, Argentine law was a hybrid of diverse and contradictory doctrines — from Spanish colonial law, classical law, Tejedor's code, and collections of sentences — that seemed to have been put together like "someone [randomly] picking flowers" and that had little to do with Argentine identity.

The major issue of contention in the code of 1886 was the absence of the positivist principles and philosophy that had been growing in popularity in the second half of the nineteenth century and were becoming the philosophical basis for the new field of criminology. The debate flourished in trial briefs and legal theaters, but its principles were not incorporated into any Argentine penal code for several more decades, until the code of 1921. Argentina's need to construct its own identity and disentangle itself from a colonial power and from foreign influence informed the debate. The challenge was well reflected in the areas of law and forensic medicine, where legal practitioners shifted between traditional, "classical" law and progressive, "positive" law and often disagreed during court cases over which law to use. Legal professionals continued to cite the colonial law codes and European authorities throughout the nineteenth and early twentieth centuries, at the same time as they were citing the newer school of positivist law. The code could not deal with such social problems as crime and disease.[8] All the old legal issues were being reargued in the light of positivism. These included the right to punish; the nature of punishments; the death penalty; free will; and the nature of criminals. Just about every legal professional had an opinion on positivism and the science of criminology that it infused. The Argentine jurist and statesman Luis María Drago, an enthusiast for positivism, wrote in 1888, for example, that he was pleased that the "repercussions of this movement ha[d] even reached Argentina," because it founded and sustained a society whose main object [was] to promote progress in the penal sciences. To Pedro Gori, positivism, as he wrote in 1898, meant a "rejuvenation," a "more modern concept of the phenomena of life, which moved jurisprudence closer to the physical sources of life itself, and away from crime as a juridical abstraction." He might have said closer to "flesh." This modern way of confronting crime explained criminal acts as real facts, he wrote, as pathological expressions of illnesses that were either sporadic or epidemic, or contagious. The causes of crime were alive; they were found in the individual and in the environment. As the editors of *Criminalogía Moderna* wrote, crime had to be judged "not with the metaphysical aridness of austerity, but with the lover's eye of the studious [scientist] in the social clinic." This would lead to the discovery of the "average morality" of the Argentine people and of the negative index that was their criminality.[9] Scientists seemed almost to celebrate the abnormal—the degenerates, *alienados*, and neurasthenics. Their rejection of the abstractions and aridness of classical law help explain why they seemed to embrace the immediacy of the flesh.

Although Argentine positivism took a great deal from European positivism, especially from Italian legal and criminological/penal positivism, it also developed along independent lines. There were even some areas in which Argentina's commitment to positivism was uniquely outstanding. For example, in 1888, while Argentina was still in the early stages of adopting the new sciences, F. and J. M. Ramos Mejía, N. Piñero, L. M. Drago, R. Rivarola, and J. N. Matienzo, among others, founded the first scientific society in the world dedicated to the positivist study of delinquents, the Sociedad de Antropología Jurídica. The turn of the century witnessed a surge of publishing in the sciences in Argentina. Important journals were founded, like *Archivos de Psiquiatría, Criminología y Ciencias Afines* in 1902. New techniques of criminal identification were developed, such as Juan Vucetich's system of fingerprinting in the 1890s. Foreign visitors praised Argentina's modern asylums as "scientific and even elegant." The *asilo* in Luján was the envy of European public health doctors and was honored at the Medical Congress of Paris in 1900. Institutes were established, such as the Instituto de Criminología at the National Penitentiary in 1907, which was perhaps the first in the world to study prisoners scientifically. A French medical journal applauded the institute as a "model establishment," which functioned as both a laboratory and a clinic, investigating the biological and environmental origins of criminality, proposing various methods of curtailing crime, and recording detailed data on each clinic patient.[10] Knowledge of Cesare Lombroso's work was widespread in Argentina, especially his *L'uomo delinquente* (1876) and *La donna delinquente*, written with Guglielmo Ferrero (1893), and there was personal contact as well, in that Lombroso sent photographs from his collection of craniums to his Argentine colleagues. Although Lombrosian theories were not universally commended in Argentina, there was a great deal of enthusiasm among certain Argentine criminologists, whose acceptance of positivism earned the compliments of Lombroso's daughter Gina. In a letter to her father published in a journal in 1908, Gina wrote that Argentine society was more receptive to Lombrosian ideas than even Italy itself.[11]

Positivism was constantly being debated, and legal practitioners regularly attacked it in their publications. The issues of free will and the right to punish were integral to the debate. Two of the last representatives of classical penology, Manuel Obarrio, writing in the 1870s, and Enrique B. Prack, writing in the 1890s, argued that the right of a state judicial system to punish was based on a person's free will and moral responsibility alone, and that if positivism were taken to its logical conclusion, it would result in the abolition of all criminal responsibility, in the reclusion of all criminals in asylums, and in the disappearance of penitentiaries. For Prack, the absurdity of denying man's free will was highlighted by a remark made at the Congress of Criminal Anthropology in Rome in 1886 to the effect that the "criminal, far from being an abnormal being, was the true normal man, and that honest men were the only abnormal beings that existed in nature." In light of this and other "heretical and subversive" ideas, Prack and others labeled positivism scientific nihilism. By denying free will, Prack wrote, the new doctrine annihilated morality and disregarded individual responsibility for criminal acts. It was like making man into a "machine." If a person's act was merely the result of his nature and did not earn him either merit or demerit, Prack argued, then all human acts would be equal and the world would not be able to establish the difference between virtue and vice. The positivist stance that free will could not exist because it would be in conflict with the law of causality was wrong, Prack argued. An action was more than just a force or a manifestation of force, and it was more than just the manifestation of a person's nature.[12]

In the field of criminology, as in many other fields, positivism became the dominant ideology. Providing a new starting point, the Italian school built Charles Darwin's and Herbert Spencer's work on the natural history of man and woman into a theory of the natural history of delinquents. The new science was based on the idea that criminals "originated" in the primitive "races," and that these "born criminals" had certain somatic and psychic characteristics by which they could be recognized in the flesh. The term "criminology" began to be adopted by international congresses in the 1880s to mean the total complex of individual, biological, and sociological factors related to crime and criminality. Lombroso had followed the conclusions of the French medical philosopher Prosper Despine, writing in the 1870s, on the psychic anomaly of certain delinquents and had added his own somatic degenerations to Despine's scheme in 1876. Lombroso's classification of criminals included an extensive package of hundreds of characteristics of the cranium and face, and the presence of anesthesia, color blindness, muscular agility, tensions, reflexes, reflections, cardiac defects, and moral "defects."[13]

In detail, criminals' craniums were seen to exhibit such characteristics as

flatness or pointedness, numerous furrows between the skull bones, protrud-
ing jaws, with an overly developed lower jaw, overly developed cheekbones,
and a depressed forehead. The brain mass of criminals was characterized by
an abundance of folds and furrows, increased weight, an adherence of the
connective tissue of the brain and spinal cord to the gray matter, spots of congestion, and cerebral softening. The head itself was characterized by a great
deal of facial asymmetry, the absence of a beard, bronze-colored skin, a
prominent monosymmetrical eyebrow, irregular, jug-handle ears, a curved
nose, and black, stiff, abundant hair. Particular to assassins was a glassy, gla-
cial, fixed, and penetrating look. Criminals were said to be heavier and taller
than normal, and either ambidextrous or left-handed. They squinted, had
either exalted or depressed reflex movements, and a reduced vascular-motor
reaction. They had altered tactile and pain sensitivity, which explained why
criminals easily tolerated tattoos. Criminals were "disvulnerable," or as was
reported in Buenos Aires, they had good *carnadura*, or thick flesh.[14]

The Lombrosian School came under attack immediately. First, it was criticized as being just a new form of the older science of phrenology, which was
based on palpating the cranium to determine a person's intelligence and emotions. Second, the new school could not come up with a set of characteristics
that was fixed or uniform and that could consistently distinguish criminals
from noncriminals. Moreover, the indices of criminality, that is, the propor-
tion of congenital anomalies in a given group of criminals, were criticized as
too vague. Third, there were also strong challenges to the contention that
man did not have free will. The major player in the opposition to positivism,
Godofredo Lozano, went after Lombroso. In his 1889 book *La escuela
antropológica y sociológica criminal*, Lozano questioned the Lombrosian
assumption that crime was merely a manifestation of a tendency in a person's
body. This could not be proven, Lozano argued, because no science had yet
figured out the relationship between the brain, psyche, and character, never
mind the relationship between these and anatomical structure. The issues of
modernism and materialism arose especially in the context of free will, as did
the abandonment of traditional values, such as the moral responsibility of
delinquents.[15] There were other Argentine critics as well, but most criminologists were equally unwilling to give up on the general new approach to criminality represented by the Lombrosian school. The point was that, like it or
not, because of the increase in crime, the new school could not be ignored.
Moreover, journals of legal medicine, psychiatry, and sociology that promoted the new doctrine proliferated. Courses in criminal anthropology appeared
in Italy and France. Students began making penitentiary visits to study living

criminals. A wide variation of theories developed from these investigations, but they were for the most part variations on a common theme. Coming to this somewhat later than their European colleagues, Argentines adopted an eclectic approach (hence their liking for flesh) that allowed them to take from different schools and avoid having to side completely with either the Italian school, which focused on the biological causes of criminality, or the French school, which focused on environmental causes. José Ingenieros, the most important representative of positivism in Argentina, and a prolific writer, followed Lombroso on the need for the medical study of criminals, and his classification of delinquents in 1900 was predominantly biologically based. Ingenieros criticized Lombroso's focus on morphology, however, and argued for more attention to psychology and culture.[16]

Argentines had their own special context for positivism, as well as their own aggregation of versions. In 1898, for example, the Argentine criminologist Manuel Carlés applied Lombroso's theory of atavism—the appearance of characteristics of one's primitive ancestors in the current generation—to the Argentine pampas. Atavism, wrote Carlés, took on special aspects in Argentina. The typical South American man, that is, the gaucho, was described as a unique type physically and morally. "He has a homogeneous constitution," Carlés wrote, "and an intimate relationship between his temperament and the environment." All individuals on the pampas supposedly had what Carlés called a moral and physical "air of [being from the same] family" from generations back. Take any gaucho, Carlés said, and you would find that he was thin, tall, strong, well-constituted; agile, nervous, with permanent features and curved lines without angles; a narrow forehead; big, round eyes, roguish and deep; a pronounced and spacious nose and mouth; and a beard and moustache.[17] Typical of contemporary criminologists, Carlés's list included such psychic features as nervousness and roguishness along with physical ones. Carlés and Argentina transformed the gaucho into a noble figure who did not succumb to the temptations and flaws of modernity.

Carlés put his interpretation of the Lombrosian theory of atavism to work in analyzing the cruelty of a criminal in a judicial case with which he was involved in or around 1899. He described the criminal as "vain and lascivious," saying, "like any person who had been raised far away from social culture, he told us of his loves." In other words, Carlés judged this man harshly because he seemingly could not control his feelings and easily disclosed them to outsiders. He was a sheepherder and had set his mind on conquering the heart of a young woman on the *estancia* where he worked. He was quite smitten by her, but apparently she was attracted to another man or was just unfaithful. When the lover surprised his girlfriend "in the act of infidelity," he hid his anger, but he later stabbed her in the chest. When he told Carlés that he had planned to stab her for some time, but that the act was not one of jealousy or vengeance, Carlés concluded that the lover was a truly cruel person. Killing in an act of jealous rage or because of an offense to honor was understandable, but not calculated, cold-blooded killing. Because of this barbarous act, the lover had to flee and became a fugitive. He later killed two other women. The similarity of Carlés's clinical gaucho to the literary outlaw gaucho Martín Fierro cannot be missed. Rather than reproaching the man for his crime or acting as a "moral evangelist," Carlés wrote, he had chosen to take the route of scientific inquiry in the interest of truth and also to gain the man's trust. Trust, he wrote, was rarely reached through dogmatism, especially because delinquents had "only a thin skin covering their egoism." This was a man, in Carlés's analysis, in whom the scientific observer could see the influence of his ancestors, the links that connected the remote past to the present and future. Caught in the chain of a semi-barbarous lineage, such men were endowed with cruel instincts, bloody passions, and a perverse indifference even to killing their own offspring.[18]

THE JUDICIAL PROCESS

We can imagine how the gaucho's trial went. While there had been some progress in standardizing law codes and the judicial process in Argentina, there was much in the system that seemed outdated to professionals, including even some of the era's products, such as the 1886 penal code. Just as this code was being criticized as outdated, so was Argentina's court procedure. The Argentine judicial system was characterized first by the importance of the judge and his dominance in the courtroom. The "secret and written nature of the procedures," "the almost compulsory 'confession' of the accused, and the immediate detention of the accused," in particular, seemed more appropriate to the colonial period. As described by a legal practitioner in 1872, the Argentine courtroom resembled the infamous institution of the Inquisition. After being detained, one was immediately sequestered, interrogated, "sometimes capriciously and always terrifyingly," to get a confession, as if it were certain that one was guilty. The *sumario*, or instruction stage—the indictment, which proved the existence of a punishable act—also took place in secret. This was the fact-finding stage, and the stage when the declaration was taken, and has sometimes been likened to the grand jury in the Anglo-Saxon system.

At this stage, the accused were without legal representation and could not question witnesses. Only the judge heard the witnesses' testimony. Because of the secrecy, the accused could not defend themselves. Forming the indictment usually took at least six months and could take up to two years or more, during which time the accused were often kept in preventive detention, which the jurist Raimundo Wilmart argued in 1899 was a violation of personal liberty and, in reality, a punishment.[19] Many defendants and their lawyers agreed.

Only once the plenary stage of the case had been reached, after the indictment had been drawn up and the case went to the sentencing judge (*juez de sentencia*), could the accused finally be questioned in the presence of his or her lawyer and learn all the charges. At this point, all means of defending the accused had often disappeared, though, because the witnesses had disappeared. Often, the judge at this stage was the same one who had framed the indictment, who now became the *juez de crimen*. The trial continued by means of written documents, with the defense lawyer now acting in behalf of the accused. However, the judge heard the proofs and the witnesses in secret. The accused and his or her accuser and the witnesses never were in one another's presence, although the accused person had the right to have a face-to-face meeting (*careo*) with the witnesses who had testified against him or her. Often the witnesses were not even recalled at the plenary stage, and if they were, it was just to repeat their testimony from the indictment stage and then have them confirm it.[20]

Did Carlés's clinical gaucho have extenuating circumstances, such as passion, which was part of the discourse in over half of the cases involving violent crime? Was police practice legitimate? Were procedures such as anthropometric measurement used to see if he was a recidivist? Was there anything at all that could be used to allow a sympathetic judge to lessen the man's sentence? Disease perhaps? Did he have one of the fashionable new diseases, such as neurasthenia? Did he show signs of atavism? What about his class and background? Was he an Amerindian, and thus not as responsible for his acts? Did the fact that he was less cultivated make him more vengeful? Obviously, he was convicted, but did society have the right to punish such a man, who had merely been reacting under the influence of his savage ancestors? Traditionally, the right of the state and society to punish one of its own was based on a set of Enlightenment philosophies, which included Rousseau's social pact between the state and its citizens, Bentham's equation of utility with interest, and Kant's theory of an evil for an evil. These were greatly modified in the late nineteenth century. Argentine penal cases usually cited the

Spanish jurist Joaquín Escriche when discussing the right to punish. To Escriche, writing in the mid 1870s, punishment was an evil of passion that the law carried out against a person for the evil of something he had done: a *mal de pasión* that the law imposed for a *mal de acción*. Even though punishment was not fully a good, it did produce more good than evil, Escriche argued, because its goal was to repair the evil caused by crime; to remove the person's will or power to offend again; and to stop other people from committing crimes through fear.[21] In the last part of the nineteenth century, legal practitioners and theorists began to develop the theory of "social defense." This theory, developed by the Italians Enrico Ferri and Raffaello Garófalo, held that society had the right to punish because it had the duty of preserving itself, that is, of its own social defense. Societies, like individuals, were being encouraged toward the vision of self-help.

Carlés was examining the gaucho either in the penitentiary or at an asylum; we do not know which. How should this man be punished? Should the death penalty be imposed? Or exile to the prison in Patagonia from which prisoners did not return, or a mental asylum? Should the prisoner be assigned to the National Penitentiary, and should methods of public shaming be employed? Judges who imposed the death penalty in this period would likely be drawn into the debate over the use of capital punishment, and although judges still called for it, it was most often commuted into a prison term. Likewise, there was a gradual trend away from imposing degrading or shaming penalties. Instead, incarceration, work, and education became important substitutes. In the thirty-two fully sentenced cases between 1871 and 1906 examined in the National Archives by the author that involved wounding, homicide, or attempted homicide, five people were sentenced to twenty or more years' imprisonment, nine to from ten to twenty years, two to from five to ten years, six to less than five years, and six to an undetermined period. Two were absolved, and two were declared insane. On the other hand, there developed the conviction that delinquents designated as "born criminals" could not be rehabilitated. Incarceration for them was often for life. If some of the new scientists had had their way, methods such as sterilization and elimination might also have been applied. In the chapters that follow, the tensions between moral condemnation and exemplary punishment of cruel acts, on the one hand, and scientific distance and measured medical examination and analysis of the criminal, such as Carlés had engaged in, on the other, will become familiar.

Other features of trials in this period that will become apparent in subsequent chapters are the large number of witnesses called; legal practitioners' often flowery rhetoric and literary and cultural references; the frequent appointment of medical doctors to examine the accused and make reports to the court; the appearance of new techniques such as anthropometrical measurements in these medical reports; the frequent appearance of members of a more professionalized police force in court, along with references to innovations such as a police museum and library; the appearance of new institutions such as the morgue, the autopsy amphitheater, and the new National Penitentiary, designed as a radial system with a central tower, Bentham's famous panopticon, in 1877. In addition, a large number of immigrants appear in the cases, commensurate with their high representation in the general population, as well as European theoretical models in the medical and criminological fields. Finally, the word and concept of "flesh" also frequently appear. While some of these features were common to many Latin American countries, others, such as the flowery briefs and the medical reports, were unique to Argentina, or at least uncommon elsewhere in Latin America.

THE PRICE OF SCIENCE IN SOUTH AMERICA

The larger context in which Carlés and others worked was bounded by a post- or even neocolonialism, an ambiguous relationship to European culture, and a feeling of inferiority that showed up in many ways besides the penal code. Argentines generated their own sense of inferiority, but the response of Europeans to South American culture exacerbated it. Buenos Aires, with its large urban population and all the difficulties that went with urbanization, foreign immigration, and rural-to-urban migration, shared the problems of most world capitals and adopted strategies and theories that were being worked out in European cities. In a way, Argentine intellect was taken hostage by European theories about contagion, degeneration, and the body. Some people argued that a scientific Argentina was gained at the expense of its honor and sovereignty. Side by side with Argentine professionals' admiration for modern Western civilization was their often-biting criticism of the "retrograde" custom of Argentine "imitation" of foreign philosophical, institutional, and cultural models. The apparent contradiction led to lurid, amusing exchanges. The situation was exacerbated by the new fear of immigration, but it also went back to the period of national independence. The Argentine jurist and statesman Vicente F. López picturesquely noted in 1870 in reference to constitutional reform that Argentina had been imitating Europe since 1810, "sleeping alternatively for sixty years with the sheets of the French Revolution and those of the Viceroyalty," and suggested that it was time that they "at least

[be] wash[ed]." The discussions that took place in professional journals and in court documents show that the criticism was closely linked to the issue of sovereignty and national sensitivity to character. Imitation was labeled "servile" by the Argentine medical doctor Antonio Dellepiane, writing in 1895, and an "unpardonable offense" by the Argentine journal editor José Luis Cantilo, writing in 1898. It was like making "grotesque dolls like the monkey, in the passion of the copy," the Argentine obstetrician and journal editor Juan Ramón Fernández wrote in 1899. Modernity was also part of sovereignty, and imitation was labeled unmodern. Modern science relied on study and investigation of the subject at hand. Legal precepts "must arise from the entrails of the social body themselves," Dellepiane argued. It was "inappropriate" to do anything else.[22]

The entire notion of "imitation" was being reformulated in terms of the ever-present social Darwinism. The Argentine Carlos Octavio Bunge, writing in 1900, favored the French sociologist Gabriel Tarde's theory that imitation performed an important function in social development, because it was the usual form of adaptation, and that it was just as valuable as invention. Tarde folded in the idea of "vibration," that is, that because of molecular vibrations, there was universal repetition. While doubting the power that Tarde attributed to imitation, Bunge still favored it and wrote that imitation could find fertile soil in cosmopolitan Argentina. Foreigners often agreed. Walter S. Logan, a North American jurist who knew Argentina well, wrote in 1899 that the only hope for the future in the Latin nations was in their continuing to imitate foreign models.[23]

The dilemma of whether to imitate—one of the most important issues of the period in Argentina—also became part of criminal court cases. The exchange between judge, prosecutor, and defense lawyer in a case of theft from 1882, for example, shows this well. The prosecutor roundly criticized the lower court judge for invoking two foreign authorities in his sentence, Adolphe Chauveau and Faustin Hélie, the authors of the eight-volume treatise *Théorie du code pénal*, published in Paris between 1834 and 1842. Because the judge had used foreign sources, the prosecutor argued, the sentence was not valid. The defense lawyer argued, on the other hand, that he was surprised by the prosecutor's "passion and scorn" for two authorities who were cited frequently in the Argentine penal code itself. "The *fiscal* can't do this to authors upon which our penal code is based, because it is like repudiating the [whole] doctrine of the code."[24] It was well known that the Argentine code relied on foreign sources; nevertheless this prosecutor and other lawyers continued to complain about the fact.

The charge of using foreign authors and codes came up often in Argentine court cases, as did charges that when a lawyer could not find the support he needed to defend his client in Argentine law, he resorted to foreign codes. Jurists questioned where Argentine law should come from. If the answer was that it should come from the collectivity, then the problem was that the state was engaged in a program to transform the collectivity. At what point in this process did a state compile a code? Moreover, writing a law code that did not cite foreign codes and previous legal history seemed like an impossibility. In spite of the logic of these arguments, the editors of the *Revista de Lejislación y Jurisprudencia* argued in 1876 that even if Argentine law was sometimes in conflict with foreign codes and commentators, it should still be respected, and it should be remembered, moreover, that foreign laws and commentators were not those of Argentina.[25]

Objections to the copying of foreign models focused on the harm this did to the Argentine character and nation. It indicated, professional and political elites wrote, that Argentines did not have confidence in themselves. This meant that Argentines could not do "great things" and that they did not have "patriotic vigor." Copying led to uncritical, unreflective thinking, to accepting other societies' errors. It produced weak, incapable men, without faith, without a flag, who had been induced to restrict their initiatives and aspirations. Imitation also led to Argentina being measured by Europe with the criteria of the European experience, which would always place the republic in an inferior position. Argentines blamed any failure of the models, the Argentine jurist Carlos Aldao wrote in 1898, on their (Argentines') "bad understanding," thus perpetuating their inferior position.[26] Argentines' understandable sensitivity to how their country was seen in the postcolonial world was captured by many authors of the period. The Argentine medical and legal professional, public hygienist, and statesman Eduardo Wilde wrote, for example, about his experience as an Argentine abroad in 1896. While in Europe collecting brains for his clinical studies, Wilde had had the opportunity to talk with many locals. One of them, the director of a shop that made wax body parts was impressed by Wilde's knowledge of anatomical details, Wilde reported, not expecting such depth of knowledge in a South American, that is, Wilde wrote, from a "savage, in the opinion of many Europeans."[27]

The national character was in a period of formation in the last decades of the nineteenth century, as were most national institutions. What would it be? A balance between European civilization and Argentine identity? A gain of population and, at the same time, a loss of identity? Argentina, observers wrote, was falling into the "hands of the indifferent and foreigners, who [bought] and [sold] in the plazas without their lips [ever] intoning the national anthem or gratitude to the founders of Argentina." Argentines were giving themselves up to "European demagoguery and Yankee utilitarianism and doctrinaire cosmopolitanism," according to the Argentine jurist José Manuel Estrada, writing in 1896. European demagoguery appeared in the sector of politics, and Yankee utilitarianism surfaced in the morals that governed those politics. Supposedly, Argentines wanted to change the "political fiber" of the population, yet they bought into an "idolatrous veneration of another people, eager for gold, whose good sense [was] calculated, and whose heart [would] never understand the palpitations of an Argentine heart." Abdicating "its initiative, customs, and at times . . . honor," Argentina would find itself without a "robust social body."[28]

1 Liberalism and the Ego

From early in the new Argentine republic, liberalism, which was one of its important values, was circumscribed by the call to sublimate the individual, the ego, for the well-being of the whole. This was especially true of society's main integrating unit, the family, which needed to work in harmony and avoid conflict. The emergence of scientific justifications of traditional notions of women's inequality and immorality helped reinforce this harmony. Scientific authority, political and professional elites hoped, would reconcile women to accepting male authority as an ordering principle that was conducive to progress. They encouraged women to become knowledgeable about the new sciences, retreating to patriarchal and religious notions of female inferiority, now buttressed by scientific evidence. Modernity could not then be conflated, at least for women, with liberal democracy and secularism. In the view of state planners, social stability depended on the success of marriage, which engendered habits of "order, economy, planning, morality, and responsibility." Only within marriage, the public hygienist Eduardo Wilde wrote in the 1880s, did the "sentiments of family and the instincts that linked man with his race and the world" develop. Learning to sublimate one's ego within a family curtailed "selfish individualism" in the outer world. Married couples engendered conservativeness and greater stability and order, Wilde argued, while the unmarried population proceeded as if they had "nothing to lose, which made them irresponsible, intemperate, and sometimes revolutionary." Even though Wilde admitted that some unmarried people were exceptions and simply lacked the aptitude for marriage, he blamed them on the "indecent books" and "corrupted reproductive instincts" that "poisoned morality." Leisure time spent outside the family was what "destroyed shame and modesty."[1]

The key to a marriage's success was a wife who put the interests of her husband and children first, which consisted largely in the careful management of her honor. The effective functioning of a family depended on the mother's reputation, and society, helped by the law, gave men the right to judge women's honor and to declare a woman unworthy of her husband's name and companionship if she offended him. Any aberration in a wife and mother's body that undermined her role and prevented family harmony was thus a problem at the highest levels of society. Women were complicit in monitoring these "aberrations," competing for awards for the most virtue and participating in extravagant praise of the maternal. Although by the turn of the century more progressive views on the role of women received more coverage in print and in court, some version of the traditional view usually dominated in court cases, backed by scientific reasons for what were formerly just suppositions and prejudices.

SCIENTIFIC INEQUALITY

According to the new sciences, men and women had natural biologically based roles, which it was "egotistical" to transgress. As the Argentine jurist and statesman Luis María Drago explained in his thesis of 1882 on marital authority, Herbert Spencer's experiments in recent years had shown that women exhaled less carbonic acid relative to their weight than men. This explained the fact that women had less developed nervous and muscular systems, which meant that their limbs and brains were smaller than men's. Moving from the physical to the mental, Spencer concluded that a smaller brain mass meant that women's intellectual and affective faculties were less than men's, so that women had a reduced capacity for abstract reasoning and abstract emotions, as well as for notions of justice. "Women do not meditate," he wrote. Rather, "thinking for them is a happy accident more than a permanent state." Society did have the dubious advantage, however, that because women's decreased mental abilities put them in an intermediate category "between man and child," they were able to "make the adult male world comprehensible to the child."[2]

Since men and women were unequal, Drago argued, they could not possibly have the same rights, because "their organic formation had destined them for different goals." Although later in his life, as a deputy, Drago became a spokesperson for women's equality, in his thesis of 1882, he maintained that women's inferiority to men was an actual fact, and not a legal fiction, as feminists of the period were trying to assert. Science had shown that special organs had created special functions in nature, and the same organ was not equal in men and women. For example, after puberty, men continued to develop, but women stopped for thirty years while they became totally focused on their maternal functions. Science had proven that men's intellectual and physical power surpassed women's. This made it "insane" for women to want to transgress these scientific laws. Attempts to do so endangered family and society, and now they had been found to be anti-scientific as well.[3]

Because of physical and mental differences between men and women, women had a different mission in life from men and had to submit to them. While woman was morally the equal of man, Drago explained, she had received all the freedom that was possible; she had another mission to fulfill and "had to submit to a law that took this mission into account."[4] Moreover, merely as women, wives fell under the rule that inferior members of society owed passive obedience to the superior in all cases, such as children to parents and servants to employers.[5]

Law codes and the legal system incorporated the principle of the marital power of the husband, *potestad marital*, in tangible ways. For example, the penal code gave a husband the power to have his wife arrested and incarcerated if she violated any of the clauses contained in the civil code, such as the stipulation that a wife live with her husband. In this system of incarcerating, or "depositing," women, state and Church cooperated with the husband's marital power to put difficult and deviant women in reclusion, without this being considered an attack on women's liberty. It is important to note, too, that such depositing occurred in long and "stable" marriages, and among the middle and upper classes. Husbands' preferential treatment in adultery laws also reflected their marital power. Male infractions of the marriage vow, for example, were described in 1861 by Severo Catalina del Amo, a Spanish author popular in Latin America, as mere instances of rakishness. After all, men were strong. Since women were weak, however, female infractions were *delitos*—offenses or crimes. The least flaw or mistake on the part of a wife could dishonor her husband, but his own sexual follies did not. That is, the honor of the couple was concentrated only in the wife. Depositing had to do with where honor lay. Explaining that Spanish law was original on this point, Catalina del Amo wrote that, "the part of honor that the husband loses is not his. It belongs to the honor of his wife, which he has on deposit." A husband could only lose his honor through his wife's immorality in terms of sexual honor. Of course, there were other ways that he could lose honor, and dueling was a popular restorative of honor.[6]

Some political elites did not miss the essential contradiction between a state that purported to be a democracy and laws that treated citizens inequitably. In his criticism of the Argentine civil code of 1869, the statesman Juan Bautista Alberdi, author of the nation's 1853 constitution, argued that the republic could not have a "revolutionary constitution," or state, or personal democracy, as long as it had outmoded civil laws that permitted "autocracy in the family" and "absolutism in the male." The Argentine socialist Mario Bravo, writing in 1927, criticized the Argentine civil code for the profound inequalities between men and women embodied in it, and for being as restrictive as a "Chinese shoe" for married women. In this code, married women lost their autonomy and capacity, Bravo charged, and the rigor of the law was increased against them precisely at the moment of the "greatest act of their lives," that is, marriage, when a woman began to fulfill her human functions and have a consciousness of her mission. A wife's status was reduced to that of incapable persons, such as minors, the mentally ill, and the deaf and mute. This was true for all acts of her civil life. She could not generally, for example, file a lawsuit or enter into any contract without her husband's consent. She also could not administer property, irrespective of whether she had brought it to the marriage or acquired it afterward, except by prenuptial agreement. For a woman to receive goods that were already specified as under her control, she needed her husband's permission. A husband could revoke at will any authorization he had given his wife. Furthermore, a violation of or attempt on the modesty of a married woman could not be pursued except by her husband.[7] Clearly, the goal of the civil code was to consolidate the Argentine family on a very conservative basis.

Even reformers of a later generation than Vélez Sarsfield, who cast their observations and theories in new scientific terms, in the end espoused similarly restrictive views of women. One of Argentina's most noted jurists and statesmen, Estanislao Severo Zeballos, who was both a scientist and reformer, linked woman as servant to man and woman as an educated contributor to modern society. In a speech delivered in 1902 at the Politeama Theater on becoming an honorary member of the Sociedad Científica Argentina, Zeballos praised women's ability to bond mysteriously with their children. Mothers could "penetrate their [children's] organism[s] like an X-ray," which made them into valuable handmaidens to medical doctors, who were often baffled by the "enigma[s] of positivist science." Zeballos's point was progressive, that the family needed both moral mother and positivist scientist, and that society would do well to teach women more science so that they could be of more help to doctors and be happier in their homes. His plea that because women carry "our name, are the depository of our honor, and have given us their honor and blood, they should be given the discretion necessary to govern themselves, so as not to live as a permanently protected child," was perhaps an intentional way to enlist the support of more traditional members of the audience.[8]

Traditionalists in the audience would also have been comfortable with Zeballos's picture of woman's sublimation of her ego in the interests of the family. She was the "supreme expression of being; the inexhaustible source of all tenderness, of the most exquisite susceptibility, of the most intimate happinesses, of the deepest foresight and the most delicate fears." She was the "strongest creature of the universe in the weakest organism, as strong as the cold, thirst, hunger, and fire that did not stop her when she renounced and resisted everything to devote herself to or defend the loved child." The mother was the "supreme abnegation who suppressed her own person, who saved the soul from the passions, who had no self-love, who ignored vanity, and who gave herself to the pleasures of infinite pardon, even for the ungrateful child." "If I had to say it in two words," Zeballos wrote, "the mother, as I conceive her, I would say—she is God himself transformed into a woman, scattering his benedictions in every home."[9] Woman was the supreme abnegator, like God himself, unstopped by cold, thirst, hunger, and fire, humble, without any ego or vanity, who saved the soul from passion and provided infinite pardon.

Perhaps Zeballos's effusiveness was necessary in order to win over his audience to his point that women needed to be brought more fully into the national project of fostering a scientific culture through government and the home. Research had already shown that in countries where women had "strong characters and where their sensitivity [was] balanced by scientific culture," there was an "undeniable superiority in the governing class, and that it [was] a statistical fact that most famous men [had] superior mothers." A good home could lead to governments that were "freer, more moral, and more moderate." There ought to be an end to the oppression of women as embodied in the civil code. Women needed to become educated, Zeballos said, so that they could fulfill their "social mission of helping man with greater efficacy, because regarding business and family interests, women could foresee disasters, while man just ran blindly into them." In the early twentieth century, political and professional elites were ruing Argentina's inferiority to Australia, New Zealand, and Canada, countries with which the republic had once been favorably compared. The main difference between these countries and Argentina was their scientific government, Zeballos argued, and it was not, as many people considered, a question of race. Zeballos ended his speech with a call to "mothers of family" to educate new generations of Argentines with these fundamental and scientific ideals.[10]

SCIENTIFIC IMMORALITY

Of course, part of the new scientific climate was what criminologists had contributed to biological theories about women's natural immorality. These theories helped justify the depositing of women to protect them and their families from their natural immoral proclivities. The call to women to help build a moral state was accompanied by the upfront message that they were especially susceptible to immorality. With potentially profound consequences for the state and society, criminologists argued that all women had an "internal, latent, and thus largely unnoticed fund of immorality," thus linking them to criminals. Motherhood perhaps tempered this, but in the Lombrosian School, even motherhood was problematic. In its explanation of crime, this school, which posited that all criminals were linked to "others," located women (as woman) among those "others," along with "apes, children, prehistoric men, and contemporary savages." Children could be recuperated (although apes and savages could not), but women's weakness led to moral contagion that prevented the species from advancing. Delinquent women, according to Lombroso, writing in 1893, acted out of "blind and innate evil," and "out of a passion of evil for the sake of evil." In addition, they had a propensity to lie. These were also characteristics of born criminals, epileptics and hysterics.[11] Female delinquents had little chance of rehabilitation. Although the Church and the Argentine Beneficent Society promoted the notion that women deviants could be reformed, criminologists and police adhered more to statistics that showed that women had a high rate of recidivism. This was explained by the Lombrosian School as due to women's psychic organization and the weakness of their constitutions, which made their punishment ineffective. Moreover, women's moral condition was thought to deteriorate in jail, because they were inordinately affected by their contact with other prisoners. Their impressionability developed into an almost pathological state of weakness that was insensitive to moral reaction. Moreover, they often could not find honest work after they were released from jail, which also contributed to their recidivism.[12]

The two special characteristics of the delinquent woman's physiognomy were precociousness and a virile appearance, Lombroso argued. As a woman's maternal feelings and modesty decreased, a space was left for the invasion of virile characteristics like audacity, exaggerated sexuality, and a taste for violent exercise, weapons, politics, and even men's clothing. The list alone is interesting in its attribution of exercise and politics to men. Toward the turn of the century, Argentine women were in fact engaging in exercise and politics, occasionally using weapons in blood crimes, and perhaps even dressing as men, as some European feminists were doing. To these virile characteristics were then added the worst qualities of the female psyche, Lombroso explained, that is, vengeance, cunning, and cruelty. These women even grew to resemble men physically, Lombroso argued, with overdeveloped jaws and neck muscles. The loss of good female qualities, assumption of masculine qualities, and emergence of bad female characteristics resulted in particularly evil criminals.[13]

Especially striking, according to Lombroso, was the fact that women's underdeveloped moral sense predisposed them to commit acts of extreme cruelty. Lombroso used the adjective "diabolic" to underscore the evil nature of women's cruelty. Women were not satisfied with merely killing their enemies, he explained. No, they wanted to torture them, even when they were their lovers or their own children, and "make them know the full taste of death." He cited examples of women who had blinded their victims with ground glass, torn away human flesh with their teeth, and driven sharp instruments into their victims' brains through the ear. He attributed this cruelty to women's lesser "sensibility," their lack of genuine sentiment, and their submission to "morbid psychic activities," which intensified their bad qualities as women and induced them to seek relief in evil deeds. The innocuous semi-criminal present in the normal woman could thus be transformed into a born criminal more terrible than any man. As the double exception of woman and criminal, the criminal woman was, Lombroso argued, truly a "monster."[14] Man—by his nature and his need to earn a living, by the "energy of his passions" and his "robust physiological organization"—committed crimes of blood or against property. In contrast, when a woman's moral sense was not sufficiently developed, she made perverse uses of her own flesh, in addition to committing cruel acts on others' flesh, through prostitution, or, "when her sexual passions were quenched, by serving strange passions, or performing analogous acts such as abortions and infanticides." This was woman's "natural and characteristic delinquency."[15] Added to this was the troubling "fact" that women with latent criminal tendencies, unlike men, had no visible anomalies in the slope of the forehead, the shape of the ears, and so on. Women could not have invented a better form of betrayal of men and society than to disguise their flesh so that it did not reveal its criminality.

Women's nervous systems contributed to their succumbing easily to moral contagion. Women, and nervous people in general, were like "sponges," absorbing contagion and spreading it. Corruption came from the environment, true, but, more important, it came from a woman's essence as woman.

Women's flesh exuded their essence, which was corrupt. Trial records contain nasty, libelous diatribes against women. Women's seduction of men, for example, which was part of their nature, brought men into contact with licentious vapors. A woman on trial for adultery in 1891 was described by the prosecutor as a "demon and Satan," a "reptile who with infernal arts knew how to extract the pure heart, the virgin heart of a man." Women, wrote the prosecutor, knew the "politics of the heart" and used magic to "strangle and dominate" the will of men, whose "mouths vomited bile" and whose "hearts oozed blood" in torment.[16] Women were described as "monsters of perversity," in competition with Machiavelli. Their hatred was great. While men led by calculation, women worked through passion and sentiment. "If you ask a woman for advice," as a lawyer argued in another criminal case from 1891, "she responds immediately with a yes or a no: she has no reflection and only judges by instinct." "Such [is] woman," he commented, "studied in the light of a sane philosophy. Woman [is] man's enemy. Though weakened by her sex, woman [is] strong and implacable in her vengeance in exchange."[17]

INEQUALITY IN THE LAW

Scientific evidence of women's inequality and immorality lent support to Argentina's narrow definition of divorce and its unequal law on adultery. Divorce at this time was the permanent "separation of bodies," or "separation from bed and table." Spouses had the right to perpetual separation but not the right to remarry. Separation was provided for in the 1869 civil code, and either spouse could sue for it. Vélez Sarsfield and others supported this definition of divorce and argued that any other interpretation was alien to Argentines and to Catholicism. After all, Vélez Sarsfield argued, according to biblical teaching, woman was made from the rib of man, so that man and woman made a whole. Nothing should be allowed to break that whole, not even a husband's extreme cruelty to his wife, who was technically part of his own flesh. Divorce was also considered conducive to social breakdown that reached beyond the family: it was anti-social, in that it produced class struggle, and anti-patriotic, in that it destroyed families, led to cosmopolitanism, and wounded the sentiments of the national soul, Vélez Sarsfield maintained.[18] This is a striking series of effects. The destruction of families is obvious, but class struggle, cosmopolitanism, and a hurt national soul may be less so. "Class struggle" referred to the "evils" of anarchosocialism and communism; "cosmopolitanism" referred to the mixed benefits of immigration; and the "national soul" referred to the loss of Argentina's national essence and identity. What connected these is that they were all "alien." In the Argentine jurist and socialist Enrique del Valle Iberlucea's 1902 critique of the civil code, he explained that the conservative nature of the code stemmed from the fact that the codifier was guided by what he considered to be an ideal marriage, that is, the type cultivated by the aristocratic families of the parishes of San Telmo, San Francisco, and Santo Domingo. The fact that almost all the basic material that informed the code came from Europe may also have made a difference. For example, Vélez Sarsfield had been working with a French translation of a work by the Roman law scholar Friedrich Karl von Savigny, but when the German original arrived in Buenos Aires, he switched editions and had to modify much of what he had already written.[19]

Couples who filed for separation usually received it, although not always. Courts granted separation for a limited period, such as several months, during which the legal office of the Catholic Church worked to try to preserve the marriage if the couple were Catholic. In reality, many separations ended up by becoming permanent, or spouses abandoned each other without going through the legal process of separation. Many separation/divorce cases ended up in criminal court because of the allegation of adultery. Adultery was classified as a "crime against honesty" in Argentina for three main reasons. First, marriage was a sacrament and preserved the family's strength and integrity, whereas adultery affected the conjugal link and maternal love, and engendered jealousy, hatred, vengeance, and sometimes crime. Second, adultery was considered an "injury" that discredited and dishonored one's spouse. Third, a clause in the law of civil marriage obligated fidelity, because it stimulated trust between spouses that was needed to maintain and dignify conjugal love. Fidelity allowed spouses to develop their productive activities within and outside the home with inner peace. Since fidelity was judicially mandated, adultery was thus a crime.[20]

Adultery committed by women was much more severely treated than that committed by men. This was partly because a woman's honor reflected on her husband's, and also because of the innate immorality ascribed to women. The skewed system remained in the law under the liberal state in part also to curb personal violence against spouses. Although both the penal code of 1886 and the Tejedor code before it had liberalized the punishment for women's adultery, reducing it to two years' imprisonment from the punishment of perpetual reclusion and even death called for in previous codes, the law continued to define the crime of adultery differently for men and women. Although it punished a wife who engaged in any sexual act with a man who was not her husband, it punished a husband only for habitual intercourse with one particular

woman other than his wife—that is, when he had a "concubine inside or outside the conjugal house."[21] Judging from the practice in criminal court cases
though, husbands who cohabited with their mistresses for several days running, even "publicly and scandalously," argued successfully in court that this
could not be considered *mancebía* (licentious living with a mistress), but
rather simple fornication, not punishable in a man. In contrast, wives who disappeared for as little as an hour behind closed doors with another man could
be successfully prosecuted for adultery, even though no more proof existed
than the closed door. Whereas judges tended not to punish husbands for intimate friendships, hugs and kisses, and licentious acts with other women, they
did punish wives for these and much less offensive acts. The questions that
were drawn up by husbands, and that judges then posed to the men's wives
concerning their relationships with other men—such as, Did you eat at the
same table with him? Did you walk arm in arm with him? Did you address
him as *tu?*—indicate that the courts took husbands' authority over their wives
very seriously. With husbands, evidence of their having shared a meal with
another woman, been seen in public with her, and so on, was not enough to
make a judge rule that adultery had occurred. For example, one judge refused
to admit the evidence that a husband had been seen with a woman not his
wife in a compromising situation, with both of them dressed in "light clothing," because of the excuse that it was summer. Another judge declined to
admit the evidence that a husband had been seen hugging a woman not his
wife because it was a personal judgment and thus unreliable.[22]

This skewed approach to adultery was based on the notion of male honor.
Even in this scientific and progressive age, the concept of honor continued to
evolve, although definitions of it remained largely in accord with the colonial
view that *honor* referred to the status of an individual, and *honra* to the person's reputation. As the Spanish jurist Joaquín Escriche, who was often cited
in Argentine legal sources, wrote in the mid 1870s, a wife's adultery destroyed
her husband's "illusion that he alone possess[ed] [her] heart." In addition, it
profoundly "wounded his honor" and made him an "object of scorn." Finally,
it introduced the threat of another man's child. The problems of love/affec-
tion, honor, and lineage created an effective block to the equal treatment of
wives' adultery. In contrast, a husband's adultery created none of these problems. Moreover, while "shame and chastity" were a wife's primary virtues,
these were only secondary virtues for men. Thus, a man could be unchaste
and commit shameful acts without serious consequences, because no one
expected his virtue to take this form. On the other hand, when a woman
renounced these virtues, "it was taking depravity to a high point, because if a

woman violated shame, it was as if she had renounced *all* her virtues"—such was the importance of female shame. Thus, an adulterous woman could be expected to go on to commit more heinous acts, even murder. The legal maxim "Adultera, ergo venefica," "Adulteress, therefore deadly," reflected this.[23]

The law also defined adultery differently for men and women for reasons that had to do with wives' motives. Wives supposedly committed adultery because of their "sensuality or greed," rather than to take revenge on an adulterous husband. A wife's adultery was the "fruit of an exasperated sensuality to the point of being unhealthy, or the consequence of a greed that expressed the most brutal egoism." Such a woman, who, to satisfy her sensuality or greed, sacrificed her husband's esteem, her own reputation, the stability of the home, and her children's welfare, was considered a dangerous person who required punishment. If a woman argued in court that she had committed adultery in response to her husband's infidelity, the judge did not have to accept it as an adequate excuse. No matter what "sin" a husband had committed, it was argued, it did not excuse his wife's adultery, because, while a husband's sin could be considered as the cause of his wife's hatred of him, it could never be considered a cause of her loving a third party.[24]

In the late nineteenth century, the judgment and punishment of wives' adultery remained harsh in spite of liberal theory, because the state was assuming more responsibility for questionable behavior in order to curtail instances of private vengeance and was concerned with the order needed to keep the expanding population safe. By creating confusion, so that the injured husband could never be tranquil in his home again, a wife's adultery potentially threatened social order. Giving husbands the authority to kill their wives and accomplices was to return to a lawless state of individual vengeance and allow husbands to be the judges of their own cases. Thus, by refining control of women's behavior by linking modernity and state-building back to traditional views of honor and male authority, the state could avoid the anarchy of passionate husbands' criminal acts. Even people who in general did not believe in punishing adultery, still believed that *women*'s adultery should be punished, and that it should be done publicly, because it was a manifestation of a deeper social evil, namely, prostitution, toward which it was usually the first step. Lombroso argued that prostitution was women's natural form of criminality. Thus, in punishing adultery, which was against the law, police and judicial forces were indirectly fighting prostitution as well. This was argued to be more effective than legislating against prostitution itself, since besieged prostitutes would only go underground. Punishing adultery was not easy to do, however, because support for the skewed law on adultery and pressure on women who tried to seek divorce was counterbalanced by a movement to decriminalize adultery and legalize divorce. Nonetheless, although ambivalent about Argentina's outmoded laws on adultery and divorce, some politicians and professionals also saw a need for the state to become more involved in the punishment of women's adultery.

A new generation of Argentine lawyers argued in the last two decades of the century, however, that the outmoded laws on adultery and divorce in Argentina "dishonored" the liberal and progressive tradition of Argentine legislation. They saw divorce as a necessary corollary of the civil, positive, and lay concept of marriage and noted its legality in highly civilized countries.[25] A cosmopolitan country such as Argentina, which had benefited from foreign influence, they argued, should have been following the example of the English, Germans, and even several Latin American countries, namely, Cuba, Santo Domingo, Costa Rica, Guatemala, Nicaragua, Honduras, Panama, Mexico, Venezuela, and Uruguay, which all had absolute divorce.[26] Conceiving of the issue as a race, Enrique del Valle Iberlucea challenged jurists in 1902 not to stop in the middle of the competition, but rather to "imitate the examples that [had] given Argentina a cultured and progressive people." Divorce should be adopted, then, in the interests of maintaining Argentina's cosmopolitan character. This was also part of an interesting modern drive at the time to universalize legislation and champion what might be called a more human and global approach to such issues, rather than a national one. The goal, as Iberlucea put it, was to "impose on nations a community of law." Approval of divorce was by no means a dominant tendency, however, and Iberlucea recognized that quick approval of it was probably a utopian idea.[27] Reformers advocated divorce as an escape valve to avoid greater misfortunes, because the harm done to children was not the legal rupture of marriage, they argued, but rather the discord, hatred, and violence of unhappy unions.

Iberlucea argued that at the time when the civil code had been written in the 1860s, there had not been many foreigners in Argentina, but that a few years later, this had changed. Foreigners had broken the tradition that the national family had followed and the Argentine nation had to hurry to catch up. In reference to Vélez Sarsfield's fear of cosmopolitanism, Iberlucea replied, "What do we have to fear from cosmopolitanism anyway?! Foreign influence has always been beneficial for Argentina." Argentina should accord its immigrants the same rights as they received in their own countries, including the right of divorce. Argentine society had become that of a country with many nationalities, which "daily change[d] [Argentine] customs and character."[28]

Supporters of divorce, such as Luis Campos Urquizi in 1901, argued that fully legalizing divorce would actually facilitate the formation of legitimate families and "enrich the state." The drawback of the separation of bodies principle was that it made people fall either into "licentious habits or into celibacy, which was contrary to natural laws and deprived society of healthy families." In spite of these arguments, many people felt that the end of the century was not the time to make fundamental reforms in divorce. "We cannot institute reforms through the simple individual spirit of initiative," Miguel F. Rodríguez wrote in 1900, "when the environment cannot receive the innovation."[29]

PRIVATE JUSTICE, HONOR, AND THE STATE

As committed in theory as the elites were to progress and civilization, they were supportive of and complicit in keeping alive a sphere of private justice based on renewed respect for and concern for honor, or perhaps they did not see the contradiction that modern audiences might see in this, because in fact both were considered modern. In a way, this was a new contribution to popular conceptions of justice. Historians have noted this and argue that male honor actually became more valuable with the process of modernization, and that dueling, which flourished in Argentina at the end of the nineteenth century, filled a gap in legislation.[30] This was new, and so was the state's concern about the growing affronts to marriage and to husbands, what with feminists making themselves heard and women suing their husbands for divorce.[31] Two late-nineteenth-century cases illustrate how tolerated acts of private justice sometimes found their way into court to be resolved: the alteration of a photograph in 1886 and the cutting of a woman's hair in 1899, both done by disappointed lovers.

The first case concerned a middle-aged married couple, who, horrified by a disfigured photograph that denigrated their honor and reputation, decided to take their complaint to court.[32] In 1886, Gerardo and María Arciello, residents of the San Telmo section of Buenos Aires, had had a family portrait of themselves and their son taken by a local photographer, hardly imagining what the consequences would be. One day, however, they received a doctored print of the photograph in the mail that seriously insulted and injured them, picturing María with the "San Benito [stigma of infamy] of her supposed prostitution [hanging around her neck], calling her the Great Whore" and showing Gerardo with horns as a symbol of his moral degradation, calling him the Great Cuckold. A message on the back of the photograph read: "This is the true photo of yourself that we're sending you to make you see what all your friends and enemies, relatives and countrymen [have already seen], and if you want to know who did this to you just ask in the photograph about the prick that you have up your ass [meaning that Gerardo had only himself to blame]. Good-bye Turd."

Here, the honor that was involved was not only that of the couple themselves but that of the Italian community in Buenos Aires collectively. Horns were the symbol of the devil and represented an excess of virility. For a cuckolded man, however, the horns signified the reverse, that is, a lack of virility. The horns were not a "punishment or a moral condemnation," it has been argued, "but rather a sign of a state of contamination that the man had reached from allowing himself to be deprived of a privilege and of eluding a duty." Furthermore, this was a "ritual state of contamination, so that others stayed away from him."[33]

Gerardo and María charged that one of their friends had attempted to seduce María and, when she refused him, had vowed to take revenge on her and "bring about the most complete ruin and scorn for her and her husband, before the public [of] their friends and the Italian community." The friend and the photographer, who was accused of complicity, denied this, and in the end the case was dropped for lack of evidence. But the harm had been done. A dishonoring public act had taken place. The disfigured photo was distributed widely at local cafes, "ridiculing the sacred right that guaranteed Gerardo the defense of his honor," said his lawyer, as it made public his defamation. The photo "endangered their marriage and implied the tolerance and complicity of the husband in his wife's impieties."

Undermining conjugal fidelity by calling a husband's dignity into question and making him an object of public derision was no mere prank, the lawyer argued. The effect of this social stain was permanent, even if the person's conduct was irreproachable, and the act could never be punished sufficiently, because it would affect the family for generations to come. The photograph was the public part of the offense, damaging Gerardo's *honra*, his good name, the favorable opinion that he had hitherto enjoyed, and the invaluable reputation that he had acquired by reason of his virtues. But Gerardo also received a personal letter that challenged him to "do something cruel to this whore, if you are a man of honor." This "honor" was inherent in Gerardo, as it was in every individual. It emanated from him and existed without external opinion recognizing it. It was a sentiment that gave people their self-esteem. Gerardo was enjoined to do what another *paisano* had done to his wife: that is, to cut off her hair while she was sleeping. "So what kind of a man are you," asked the letter writer, "that you haven't dealt with a woman who has dishonored you. Listen to me," the author wrote. "The cuckold scale [*cornuteria*] has four levels. There's the husband who doesn't know anything, the *becco*; the husband who begins to know it, but not to attend to it, the *rebbecco*; the husband who knows who eats, drinks, and sleeps with his wife, the *rebbeccone*; and finally, the husband who takes the guy by the neck and delivers him to his wife, the *casparino*. So pay attention, Gerardo; you're now at level three and you're on your way to level four." (The four Italian sobriquets roughly translate as "pecked," "pecked again," "really pecked again," and "really stupid bumpkin.") Rather than cutting off his wife's hair, challenging the suspected culprit to a duel, or taking the matter into his own hands in some other way, however, Gerardo chose to take his offense to court. If he had placed his wife in deposit, it would have had the effect of "repairing" his honor, even in the probable event that his wife was wholly innocent of having committed adultery. The case was dismissed for lack of evidence.

In the second case, from 1899, a disappointed lover revenged himself on a girl who had rejected him by cutting off her tresses with a knife.[34] Instead of taking a more personal approach outside the law, the girl's mother accused the lover of having committed a *lesión*. This was clearly a novel case in the legal arena, because it became the center of a legal debate over whether haircutting was a *lesión* or merely an injury. The penal code of 1886 provided for the punishment of "wounds, blows, the administration of harmful substances, and any other *lesiónes* willfully committed," whereas injuries were verbal and written acts that dishonored, discredited, or scorned. *Lesiónes* included blinding and castration, mutilation of a principal member or organ of the body, and any injury that left a person demented, unable to work, impotent, or with a major member crippled or notably deformed.[35] Instrumental in this debate was the prominent prosecutor Ernesto Quesada, who argued in 1899 that haircutting was in fact a *lesión*. The police decision to drop the case because they did not consider haircutting a *lesión*, he wrote, was wrong and reflected an overstepping of police authority. "[C]abello es pelo," Quesada declared, meaning that the hair that grows on the head forms part of the body. What Quesada was saying, one might argue, was that hair was like "flesh." Haircutting, since it deprived the woman of an integral part of her body, was a crime of corporal *lesión*, just as if she had lost a finger or a leg. Glosses on what constituted the crime of *lesión* included Tejedor's criterion that it had to "alter health" and Rivarola's that it must produce "extraordinary effects and an incapacity for work."

ISOLATION OF WOMEN IN HOUSES OF DEPOSIT

Poignant pleas by women sent by men and the legal system for incarceration in houses of deposit added to the array of areas of tolerated private justice. Somehow, though, the system of depositing was accepted as appropriate for a liberal democracy. Depositing was part of the state bureaucracy, of a state-level structure, to which the Beneficent Society also belonged, that attacked the social issues of the new democracy in a patriarchal and patronizing way. It is noteworthy that there was no parallel institution like a house of deposit for men, or any parallel power of deposit. Women, as walking vessels of possible immorality, were apparently more legitimately confineable than men. Nevertheless, women resisted being deposited in their court testimony, and they had the support of the occasional official or professional who broke the chain of male/state/Church coercive power. As more cases of adultery and divorce began to be heard, women's resistance appeared more frequently in the court records, making cases of adultery and divorce more contentious as husbands fought to keep their marital authority intact and as wives fought to circumscribe it.

The uniqueness of houses of deposit at the turn of the century arose first from the fact that in an age of increasing secularism, they depended on an anachronistic combination of civil judicial and penal authorities, federal subsidies, and Catholic religious orders. Second, while political and professional elites were trying to centralize judicial and penal authority in the state, they were also giving men a substantial degree of judicial and punitive control through the system of depositing women against their will. Third, while the models of government being developed in Argentina held individual rights and personal liberties to be sacred and modern, houses of deposit denied their inmates these same rights and liberties. Instead, the law and tradition gave the state and individual men wide latitude to manipulate access to these rights. Finally, while feminists such as the Frenchwoman Luisa Michel were invited to speak publicly in Buenos Aires and challenges to the inequities of the adultery law were openly being made by legal professionals, women were regularly consigned to houses of deposit for disobedience to fathers, for "scorning" and "dishonoring" husbands, for "irascibility," and for suing adulterous husbands for divorce.

THE TRADITION OF DEPOSITING WOMEN

Houses of deposit had a long tradition, going back at least to the seventeenth century, and they continued to be used in nineteenth-century Argentina. In their most benign form, they served as schools and asylums for girls, places of worship for the neighborhood, and refuges for widows and other women in need of "family." Often, though, the system of depositing resembled public displays of private vengeance that were inconsistent with Argentina's liberal democratic state. At the same time that women were isolated, they were also put on public show. And their institutionalization affected the presumption of their guilt. In this form, houses of deposit isolated and excluded women from society at the request of husbands and fathers, police and judges, employers, the state agency for minors, and charitable groups. Male friends counseled offended husbands to send their wives away to houses where they would be "deprived of [their] freedom."[36]

In the later nineteenth century, houses of deposit served primarily as institutions of incarceration and correction and developed particularly contradictory rationales, unique to the history of state formation and modernism. The liberal state, which guaranteed the individual freedoms spelled out in the constitution of 1853, somehow made elements of society accept the necessity for the incarceration of women in houses of deposit who were often only guilty of irascibility. Depositing then fitted into the state's plan for controlling men's offended honor and anger by controlling its fleshly source, namely, women.

A husband's marital authority included depositing as a legal right. It resonated with sixteenth-century canonical theory that held that the amount of time needed for a wife's reform was two years. Only then would it be as if "she had not sinned, enabling her marriage to regain its vigor and viability."[37] Depositing was a tradition in Spanish law and custom, well explained by Joaquín Escriche in the mid 1870s, that had been inherited by Argentine law and custom. By tradition, temporary separation of a wife from her husband, for whatever reason, necessitated her placement under a *depositario*, or trustee, which meant actually residing in that person's house. According to Escriche, only a civil judge could decree deposit, and only in five circumstances. First, he could decree the deposit of a married woman who had tried or wanted to try to initiate a *demanda* for divorce or to charge adultery. A woman in this situation might welcome deposit in order to have the freedom necessary to initiate or continue judicial action, or to avoid bad treatment from her husband. The deposit had to be solicited in writing by the wife, because she was in the best position to know whether there was danger from her husband. In this type of provisional deposit, the judge took into account the husband's will concerning the location of the deposit but did not necessarily accede to his wishes unless the reputation or the interests of the family were at risk. If the judge refused to comply with the husband's desires, the husband had the right of appeal. If the plaintiff wife delayed pursuing her case longer than a month, if she had problems obtaining counsel, or if she changed her mind, the judge remitted her to the conjugal home. The one-month limit meant that the system could not be misused by couples who just wanted to live apart, which was considered morally unseemly and destabiliz-ing for public order. If a couple gained permanent separation, the wife could take charge of her own deposit even if her husband opposed it. However, if he subsequently decided to charge her with adultery or some other offense, such as defaming him, he could obtain her relocation to another house of deposit. Agreements between husband and wife about the details of the personal goods that she took with her when she went into a place of deposit could be verbal, but the deposit arrangement with the trustee was written. Judges instructed husbands not to disturb their wives or trustees.[38]

The second case in which deposit occurred was when a wife was charged by her husband with divorce or was accused of adultery. Concerned that the husband might abuse his wife or deprive her of the freedom necessary for her defense, and that having to live with one's accuser constituted "torture," the judge imposed deposit for the wife at the request of either spouse. After the legal suit was accepted, the judge went to the husband's house . . . to try to come to an agreement with the wife about the deposit . . . if they did not agree, the judge would follow the wishes of the husband.[39] The third case that called for deposit was when a single woman wanted to marry against the will of her parents or grandparents. If she was of age, she had to wait three months before she could marry, during which time she could deposit herself for secu-rity. The last two categories concerned the deposit of mistreated children, and of abandoned orphans and incapacitated individuals.

In a limited way, depositing was an advance for women. The argument that wives should have the option of leaving the conjugal home if their hus-bands were abusive, or if they had been accused of adultery and did not want to live with their accuser, was progressive. At one time, the courts had only been able to relieve a wife from the obligation to live with her husband if her life was in danger. If her husband had a concubine living in the conjugal home, for example, the wife did not have the right to leave, unless she sued for divorce. Not all wives, however, wanted to pursue divorce cases. Giving the civil judge the power to declare a separation of bodies "in urgent cases" was an advance. Undoubtedly, there were judges who interpreted "urgent" to mean only when the wife's life was in danger, but the clause left space for a much wider interpretation. Houses of deposit were also more appropriate for women than the alternative police-run depository on Calle 24 de noviembre, which was described as immoral and unhygienic, and where force was used to control inmates.[40]

Depositing was a legal right contained in both civil and ecclesiastical law. According to the civil code of 1869, once a suit for divorce had been initiated, or even before this in urgent cases, the judge could decree the separation of the spouses and the "deposit" of the wife in an "honest house." Also justifying depositing and indirectly recommending it was a law that obliged spouses living separately during divorce proceedings, as well as when divorce was decreed, to be mutually faithful, or else to be criminally accused of adultery. Although it seems that this law was seldom respected, it did behoove spouses, especially wives, to accept or even seek a house of deposit in order to protect themselves from the accusation of adultery.[41] Civil judge and ecclesiastical judge usually worked together in cases of adultery and divorce. If the spouses were Catholic, they usually went first to the ecclesiastical judge for counseling, who researched the case and tried to bring about a resolution. The secular judge assigned the place of deposit, fixed the amount of the wife's support, and made provisions for the care and education of the children.

There were several gray areas, however, where conflict could occur. Although ecclesiastical judges were only authorized to intervene in cases of divorce, and then only to gather information about the divorce being sought, they in fact intervened in all kinds of cases that did not involve divorce and decreed the deposit of women. By law only a secular judge could solicit police force to put a woman in deposit. However, it was not at all uncommon for ecclesiastical judges to request the use of force by the police and for the police to comply with their wishes. Secular judges often upheld decisions made by ecclesiastical judges, but occasionally they challenged the authority of the ecclesiastical court, as well as of the husband. After a frustrating dispute in a case from 1885, for example, the secular judge decreed that neither the husband nor the ecclesiastical authority had the right to deprive a woman of her freedom, and that deposit had to be at the wife's request, not against her will, and not in known houses of "correction" like the Spiritual House, that is, the Santa Casa de Ejercicios Spirituales, which advertised itself as a house of spiritual retreat.[42]

On the surface, depositing might appear to have been the equivalent of preventive detention in jails used for accused persons during the hearing of their judicial cases. Sometimes internment clearly functioned this way, as when the police transferred women from a house of deposit to jail after sentencing. In this way, a woman's internment resembled a man's incarceration in jail "on deposit" while awaiting a judgment on the charges against him and during his trial. These similarities should not, however, mask the inequities. For example, when a wife initiated a case of adultery and/or divorce against her husband, and if her husband countersued, as was often the case, the judge remanded *her* to a house of deposit. If the case was one-sided, in that only the wife sued, her husband went into preventive detention, but he was usually forgiven quickly by his wife, since the offended spouse could always drop the case (under article 125 of the penal code). If sentenced, he was released after paying bail (as long as the sentence was less than two years) or absolved by the courts. Husbands did not spend as long in detention as most wives did in internment. Wives were not allowed out on bail because of the danger of moral contagion, or degeneration, that was somehow seen as leaking out to "honest" women through their flesh. Women could be deposited—in effect, incarcerated—even though not accused of any crime, which made depositing actually much worse than anything a man was subject to. Internment was touted as preferable to jail, because more comforts were available, but this did not mitigate the jail-like nature of the houses when a woman was placed there for little more than irascibility.[43] Judges defensively asserted that houses of deposit were not jails, like the judge in the Solari/Bisso case discussed later in this chapter (but the protagonist and her brother did not agree with him). Internment and incarceration in a house of deposit before conviction carried an added layer of shame that preventive detention for men did not carry. In addition, once enclosed in a house, a woman's stay, though it might be only a matter of days, more commonly stretched out for several months or even a year. Moreover, even though a court ordered a woman's release, it might be some time before her lawyer could obtain it. The legal procedure that set limits on a husband's authority to deposit his wife against her will and in a place opposed by her existed only in theory.[44]

Criminal cases clearly reflect the intentional inequity of the system. A "deposited" wife was, after all, an investment by her husband in his honor, much as money invested in a bank earned interest. Correctionals benefited husbands as "sanctuaries," where men's "lacerated" honor might be protected from further harm.[45] Some men expressed regret at their estrangement from their deposited wives for reasons of affection, for want of childcare, or because they needed their wives' help in family businesses. The advantages, though, seemed to outweigh any disadvantages, because it meant the opportunity to punish and perhaps improve their wives' behavior, especially when the depository was a public and socially approved institution. Husbands could avoid domestic scandals this way and restore their honor. Actual resolution of cases did not seem as important as the public humiliation of difficult wives. Abandonment of cases by husbands thus occurred frequently, and wives languished in houses of deposit for months, waiting for their husbands to pursue their cases against them or forgive them. A woman arrested and deposited in the Spiritual House in June 1872 was not released until July 1873, after the court decided that her husband had abandoned the case against her.[46] Sometimes incarceration greatly undermined a wife's ability to control her own financial affairs. When an *estanciero* returned from a two-month trip to Europe in 1867 and learned that his wife had taken up with one of their peons and that she wanted to live with him, the husband asked a civil judge to send his wife to the Spiritual House. The wife and peon denied the charges, but the wife was put on deposit. She was the primary owner of their *estancia*. Unable to defend her property from her husband, she requested the court to issue a restraining order to keep her husband from transferring her assets. She had reason to worry, since he had already sold more than eight hundred sheep and pocketed the money. Her lawyer requested that the buyers be told the identity of the real owner and that an inventory of the property be conducted.[47]

The Institutions

The three most frequently used depositories, the Spiritual House, the Good Shepherd, and the Women's Hospital, shared the ethic of a religious and/or work regimen run by nuns; a relationship with a civil charitable organization, the Beneficent Society, and the police and courts; and an extralegal and moralistic surveillance of their inmates. The institutions differed in their mission, in that the purpose of the Spiritual House and the Good Shepherd was to moralize and regenerate, while the purpose of the Women's Hospital was medical care without an overt moralizing goal. The institutions also differed in the age of their inmates, in that the Good Shepherd was the institution most commonly used by the Defense of Minors Office for placement of minors. The Spiritual House also had two clienteles: a core of religious women, women who had taken up residence there voluntarily, and young female students; and women detainees, prisoners who had been ordered to live there by outside agencies or by male authorities. While there was a difference between detainees and prisoners, the detainees, although not yet convicted, lived much like women who had been. Because of its distinct mission of caregiving, it might be assumed that the Women's Hospital would have been the public institution of choice for women facing depositing. Judging from the complaints of a hospital inspector in the late 1870s, however, detainees who were not too ill to work performed the hospital's domestic chores. Because of lack of space, detainees slept in the patients' rooms under the beds. Crowded together on mattresses under the beds, badly covered in winter on the damp floors and suffocating from heat in the summer, they "used up" the air needed by patients and at the same time were contaminated by this "noxious air" of infectious disease. These were inhumane and immoral conditions, the hospital inspector protested, which hurt the "robust constitution of detainees [even] more than an illness."[48]

Statistical data gathered from the cases consulted, which are unfortunately sketchy, suggest a greater use of the Good Shepherd. Approximately twenty-four women were sent to the Good Shepherd between 1882 and 1904 for irascibility, bad character, and adultery or suspected adultery, and seven women to the Spiritual House between 1867 and 1886 for similar reasons. When these women were ill, they were shuttled in and out of the Women's Hospital from the Good Shepherd and the Spiritual House. The Hospital was also a destination point for women who were assigned to work there as their form of incarceration. The Good Shepherd also housed all the women accused of abortion or infanticide, a total of sixty-eight between 1862 and 1905 for Buenos Aires and Córdoba combined. Elite and professional women were to be found in all three institutions.

Even if these houses of deposit/detention had not started out with the intention of harboring a heterogeneous clientele, by the late nineteenth century they included a broad sample of the population. While prison reformers talked about the need to separate different types of criminals in jails, the period witnessed a trend toward commingling. Detainees and prisoners were mixed together. Minor offenders deposited for "irascible behavior" and "misconduct" were mixed together with major offenders deposited for "maternal crimes" and prostitution. Houses were also not class-specific, and even the Good Shepherd and the Women's Hospital, whose goal was to serve the lower classes, had a broad mix of internees. Well-to-do women from business and ranching families; middle-class professionals, merchants, and artisans; and lower-class laundresses, servants, and seamstresses shared internment together.[49] It was not unusual for fathers and husbands of the *gente decente* class to put their daughters and wives in places such as the Good Shepherd, where they lived alongside lower-class women and criminals. Occasionally, concerned citizens complained about this mixing, such as a journalist in 1892, but the practice continued.[50] For example, Josefina Durbec, sent to the Good Shepherd at the request of her husband in 1902 for the crime of adultery, taught in a secondary school. Carmen Bernabé, also sent to the Good Shepherd by her husband in 1902, directed a *colegio*.[51] The mixing of different levels of delinquents and different socioeconomic classes possibly occurred because of overcrowding. Just as likely, though, separation may not have been desired by the depositors. Threats of association with contagious immoral elements in houses of deposit, damning to a woman's reputation, surely must have been a superb deterrent for any wife contemplating making an offensive remark or committing a crime.

Cases of Isolation

In all the cases of depositing, the ease with which men manipulated the police and courts stands out. Husbands, familiar with their rights, referred in the 1870s to treating their wives with the "necessary severity" allowed them by law for "licentious behavior"; to using police and judge to change their wives' deposit from private homes to public and shaming institutions like the Spiritual House; and to being "obliged" to use the "faculties that the law provided" to punish their wives' "perversity" and "holy impudence" with prison, in response to their wives' pursuit of cases in court against them.[52]

Men also enlisted the aid of state agencies and public institutions to justify depositing as a way to protect women from their (men's) anger, in essence helping men engage in their own self-control. When disagreements between Pascual and Eusebia reached an intolerable level in 1870 after twenty years of marriage, Eusebia went to the ecclesiastical judge, who worked out a six months' separation for the couple. As was his marital right, Pascual had Eusebia confined in deposit, along with their children, in a rented room, certain that he would be able to keep an eye on her this way. Depositing her also gave him the opportunity to curb his anger, he explained, and thus protect his wife from any harm he might want to inflict on her and save himself from committing a possible crime against her that might send him to jail. Eusebia, too, was advised to practice self-control while on deposit—learning to accommodate her husband's wishes, acquiesce to his authority, and respect his position as head of the family—which would aid her husband in assuaging his anger. Courts saw this as an exemplary use of the system of depositing. Pascual's behavior might have seemed exemplary. Moreover, he could have had her placed in a religious house, and without her children, but chose instead to preserve her honor and position as a mother and rent an apartment for her.[53] Pascual's kindness ran out when he came to suspect Eusebia of engaging in an illicit relationship while on deposit, however, thus undermining his attempt to curb his passion, as will be seen in chapter 6.

Because the law gave respect to the system of depositing, women sometimes ended up having to resort to self-deposit in order to prove their innocence. Convinced that self-depositing could help their legal case, some

women went voluntarily to a house of deposit. This was similar to the strategies imposed on infanticidal women by the law to prove their honor, covered
in the next chapter. Voluntarily going to an institution was a legal strategy
used by wives to demonstrate their goodwill and integrity to the court, to help
them in their lawsuits. For example, Gervasia, then living in Salta, was surprised when her husband in Buenos Aires accused her in court of adultery.[54]
He was "doubtless angry," she said, "because of my request to the *curia* [eccle-
siastical court] for divorce and subsistence payments." She was surprised
because neither in the *curia* nor at the civil court did her husband attempt to
defend his six-year-long adulterous relationship, which was incestuous into
the bargain. By this time, Gervasia had also committed adultery. Gervasia was
angry about her husband's countersuit, but she nevertheless chose to enter the
Spiritual House on deposit. She suggested that her husband probably countersued because he did not believe that she could defend herself, and that if
he took her by surprise, she would give in. That was when she decided to put
herself in the Spiritual House in order to be judged innocent of any charge of
infidelity that her husband could make against her. The judge instructed the
Spiritual House to keep Gervasia as a *presa*, or prisoner, and told her to name
a defense lawyer or take the *defensor de pobres*. This was in February 1872. But
by May, Gervasia was asking to be released from the Spiritual House so that
she could "exercise [her] rights." She was asking the judge to exempt her from
the charge of adultery; however, she had already admitted to it, so she could
not be released from the Spiritual House. Yet she needed her freedom in
order to defend herself and justify her exemption. But the husband insisted
that Gervasia be convicted, pay the costs of the case, and be deprived of their
joint property, the *sociedad conjugal*. In November, both the defense lawyer
and the prosecutor told the judge that they had resolved to end the case and
asked him to release Gervasia. Gervasia was not released though until March
1873. Her choice to go to the Spiritual House backfired.

In contrast, Luisa Bisso put up a spirited protest against her husband's
choice of her place of deposit. She had sued her husband Juan Solari for adultery and divorce in 1871 and then spent two years contesting his choice of
deposit for her before her case could even get under way.[55] Luisa had been
married to Juan for twenty years, and they had seven children. Between the
two of them, they had a long list of accusations against each other. Luisa was
suing Juan for divorce on the basis of slander, ill-treatment, concubinage, and
bigamy. Juan was countersuing for divorce on the grounds of adultery and
incest, charging Luisa with having an illicit relationship with their son-in-law;
refusing to accept reconciliation; insulting him in a public place; and, throw-

ing him out of the conjugal house, which had forced him ignominiously to seek lodging from his neighbors. Even though Luisa was the first to sue, she was ordered sent to the Spiritual House. Luisa appealed. Although the law was stacked in Juan's favor, his wife more or less successfully fought him for two years over the place of her deposit. Juan wanted the Spiritual House; Luisa wanted her brother's house. Finally, the judge decided in Juan's favor, but he expressed his anger with both of them for maligning the system of depositing. "Deposit," he wrote, "is not a penalty linked to the supposed or true criminality of the wife; neither is it an exclusive right of the husband." Nor should it be considered the same as jail. In the Solari/Bisso case, as in others, no basis for the husband's accusation was found by the court and the case was dismissed.

The lack of a legal conviction of Luisa, however, might have been made up for by the fact that Juan had succeeded in having her incarcerated. Luisa protested because she knew that deposit in the Spiritual House would damage her reputation in the eyes of her family, business associates, and the community—by the indictment of her morals and by her enforced incarceration. Luisa protested that her "deposit prejudiced [her] reputation," and her son-in-law added that she had been carried off to the Spiritual House "like a convict." There were three "takes" on depositing represented by the protagonists in this case. For Juan, winning the place of deposit was a matter of honor and confirmation of his marital rights. In a public institution, his wife would be more shamed and her conduct would be under constant scrutiny and her movements curtailed. For the son-in-law, who had supported Luisa, depositing in the Spiritual House, though it might have once had the purpose of guaranteeing the personal security of a woman, was a violation of Luisa's freedom. As he told the judge, it was scandalous and publicly dishonoring to send honorable women to places where prostitutes were taken, and wholly unprogressive. Moreover, it was undermining for motherhood, because Luisa's young daughters were deprived of her guidance and thus more inclined to go astray. For Luisa, depositing meant damaged honor and reputation, exposure to corruption, instability, and physical discomfort, and family breakdown. The practice of disposing of people at will, she argued, was inegalitarian and abusive.

FEMINISM

With the women's movement under way in Argentina, and with the influence of an urban culture that attracted figures from abroad, wives began to act like Luisa and to press for the right to dispose of their own persons and to be more involved in the direction of the family business. Much of the public and the popular press, however, opposed women's independence and its threat to the home and marriage. The judicial profession sometimes agreed. In one of the main legal journals, the *Revista Jurídica*, articles appeared that criticized women's suffrage as not only frivolous but also a serious disruption to the family. A woman should "dazzle with the brilliance of her honor, dignity, and modesty, not with her education," the editor wrote in an article opposing feminism. Only the home would save her, and to be attracted to it, she needed to put all her effort toward making it an "Eden." If she wasted herself in meetings, lived on the street and in the salon, mixing with "society," she would be like a "Lola Montez to Argentina, as useless as a Messalina" (women who were both notorious for their licentious behavior and for damaging important statesmen's reputations).[56] Meetings where women discussed politics, women's rights, and social issues were considered part of this "wasted" time. There was a strong sentiment that this would lead to the "inversion of the natural relations between the sexes," and that it would eventually mean the "masculinization of women and even lead to hermaphrodism or the identification of the sexes." The French feminists Luisa Michel, described as ugly and unfeminine, and Jane Dieulafoy, who dressed in a man's suit, were presented as typical of the trend and proof of Lombrosian theories.[57]

An Argentine litigant, Graciana Urrutigarray, was criticized for being one of these women. In 1882, she brought a complaint to the ecclesiastical judge accusing her husband of entering a prostitute's house. He had reportedly been seen by witnesses, including his own son, and stolen money from Graciana to set up credit for his concubine at a local store. Wounded and angered by this accusation, Graciana's husband Juan raised the ante by charging in *criminal* court that his wife's accusations were false and malicious, and that she had damaged his dignity and honor. Because Juan's son testified against him, Juan claimed that his wife had "incited [his] own blood against [him] and wrenched from [him] the affection of [his] children and the respect that [he] deserve[d] from them." According to Juan's testimony, his wife had rudely insulted him, hit him in front of the children, clawed his throat and ears, struck him with a silver candlestick, and threatened him with economic ruin and death. His physical wounds were so bad, he claimed, that he had had to stay in bed for more than a month, meaning that, as defined by law, the injuries were serious. Three family friends had tried to negotiate the couple's differences so that the family could "maintain a life of decorum." Unyielding, however, Graciana had reportedly continued her verbal and physical abuse of her husband in their presence. Moreover, she went ahead in her case and asked the judge for a divorce on the basis of her husband's extreme cruelty and adultery.[58]

The ecclesiastical judge granted the couple a provisional separation of three months, and Juan began the search for an alternative house for his wife and children. But Graciana did not find any of the houses that Juan suggested suitable, so she continued living in the comfort of her own home, but separated physically, *de cuerpo*, from Juan. Juan did not turn around and charge Graciana with adultery, as often happened, in which case he could have had her deposited in a correctional. Even without charging her with adultery, though, he could have had her deposited in an institution, even a correctional, or a private home. Maybe he chose not to because of his family's status, although family status did not enter into other cases. Or perhaps Graciana would have protested too much. In any case, whether she was grateful for being saved from formal depositing is not recorded.

Graciana's supposed conduct during the provisional separation would have confirmed Lombrosian analyses of women. During this time, Juan charged, Graciana disturbed his repose and interrupted his work and business in his study and outside his home. When Juan asked her to do an errand for his business, she threw bricks at him. It is interesting that he even thought that this was a logical expectation of his wife under the circumstances. When he approached the sickbed of one of their children, where Graciana was caring for the child, she lashed out at him in fury and chased him to the patio hitting him with a stick and crushing his hat.

Juan's tone of indignation throughout this testimony was motivated by two things: first, his wife's physical ferocity, and second, her strident and offensive feminism, which, he argued, was to blame for the physical nature of her attacks. At lunch one day—with everyone at the table, Juan emphasized—Graciana had enthusiastically praised a speech by Luisa Michel that she had just read about in the newspaper. "These are the ideas that I like," she announced to the whole family. "These are the doctrines that I want to see triumph before I die. Man is a pygmy; woman is a giant." The children were "stunned" by this clear challenge to marital authority. From then on, in Graciana's words, it was a "war to the death" with her husband. Juan failed to persuade either the *curia* or the criminal court to move against Graciana, however, and the case was dismissed in June 1883. There is no evidence that Graciana pursued the case either.

Even with a growing women's movement toward the turn of the century, the depositing of wives for common offenses continued unabated. In 1892, a husband asked a civil judge to put his wife in the Good Shepherd because he could no longer endure her bad temper and violent character, her scorn of his authority, and her contradicting him.[59] They were middle-aged small businesspeople from France and had been married less than a year. The wife's offense was that she had refused to move with her spouse when he had changed residence, thus violating the article of the civil code obligating wives to live with their husbands. The husband told the judge that his wife needed to be "sent away" so that she could avoid exposure to family members who were giving her "suggestions and bad advice" that led her to want "to assert her will over his to dispose of her own person and of his business as it takes her fancy." He did not want a divorce and he did not want to assert his authority over her with "violence" by making use of the police to force her to move with him. The peaceful alternative was to send her to a convent, where she could be "cured" of her deviant behavior. He suggested that the length of her internment should be "enough to absorb the advice and good teaching of the sisters, to reform her character and teach her to respect the principle of authority."

Popular magazines provided some entertaining twists to the debate on marital authority. A 1907 cartoon series called "Equality of the Sexes" invited readers to imagine the world of the future, when a wife would order her husband to clean the dining room while she went to the stock exchange, and since they were equal, it would be as if *she* were doing the cleaning. There is a nice inference to flesh in the wife's explanation that because of their equality, it was as if she were doing the work rather than her husband. In another series called "Liberty," also from 1907, dinner gets cold while people debate feminism, and the result is indigestion. Feminists' references to "slavery" were mocked, as was their supposed rejection of beauty as a way to attract a man; it was as if women had to be "ugly, educated, and smell of the essence of rat." And then there were the "Yankee" women who were trying to "discover the microbe of love, to destroy it as bacteria," maintaining that feminism would cure the evils of society. In a 1905 cartoon captioned "Niñas modernas," a little girl explains to her mother that she has separated her dolls "so that the others don't fill their heads with their ideas of feminism." Articles also reflect the fact that society was not keen on the fashion of women adopting men's clothing. Even a tolerant man (at least as he described himself), who had been completely tranquil in spite of the growing development of feminism—with women wanting to be doctors and anarchists and learning Kant's *The Critique of Pure Reason* by heart—was horrified when he received a fashion catalog and could not tell the men from the women. Critics of feminism, worried about its repeated triumphs, referred to the movement's "growing and constant invasion, absorbing half of humanity." Described as "insatiable, Napoleonic, voracious, respecting nothing, and stopped by nothing," feminists were blamed for empty homes, the end of sweet sentiments, and advertisements for oil of acorns, laxatives, liver oil, and corn removers, which were apparently being used as abortifacients. Men needed to put their foot down and tell their wives that the *patria* needed men and women, and not sissies and tomboys. Even when some critics acknowledged that the inequality of the sexes was an important aspect of the social question, they never doubted that it was better to be a woman, "loved, protected, enveloped in sweetness, than to turn into a man."[60]

CONCLUSION

While women were gaining a greater place in public life, this has to be put in the context of new medical and legal constraints. Now proven biologically inferior and criminologically held more likely to be guilty, women were isolated in institutions for common offenses against male authority. The use of houses of deposit, the mixing of women of different socioeconomic classes, varying levels of culpability, and different degrees of "nervous disease" seems especially strange in a society that stressed the importance of class distinctions and the dangers of contagion. Models of behavior differed greatly for upper- and lower-class women, and lower-class models could hardly have been seen under normal circumstances as a good influence for women of social rank. Especially in light of the contagion theory, the indiscriminate mixing of women in houses of internment would seem counterproductive and worrying, because it violated the boundaries of the very moral system that the houses were trying to preserve.

Even though women had been gaining more recognition as individuals and contributors to the new nation, they still remained the objects of a great deal of prejudice. Furthermore, with the support of science, women's situation became more frustrating. For example, while women had gained the right to request a divorce, they were discouraged from doing so. All along, there had been opposition to the law that gave wives this right, and pressure had been put on wives not to proceed against husbands in the interest of decorum and the greater public good. The most offensive act that a wife could commit, after adultery, was to bring charges of adultery against her husband in a court of law or sue for divorce. When this happened, husbands commonly responded by charging their wives with adultery, or sometimes mistreatment, and initiating their own cases of adultery or divorce. Because a husband held marital authority, he then had the upper hand. His honor would be restored and might even be enhanced with the assertion of his rights. More pragmatically, if he won the case, he might avoid having to pay for his wife's support. Instead of using their legal right to sue their husbands in a public court, a lawyer explained in 1871, women should use their "natural" female attributes to express their complaints. Using their "moral superiority and gentle weapons such as pleadings and tears" was seen as more decorous for women than open opposition. If a woman endured verbal and physical abuse with patience while on earth, she could gain a place in heaven, the ecclesiastical and secular authorities explained.[61] This was considered to be for women's own good. For example, Escriche wrote in the mid 1870s that it was considered contrary to good custom to authorize a wife to enter into a legal quarrel with a husband who had spurned her for a concubine. By complaining publicly about her husband's infidelity and disputing over the "satisfaction of the senses" with his mistress, a wife lowered herself to the latter's level.[62] In an 1871 case, Paula was pressured by the two defense lawyers to drop her case against her husband for adultery. Two of the reasons given were legal principles, namely, that she had continued to live with her husband after she knew about his mistress, and that she had denied her husband access to the conjugal home. The defense lawyers also gave a third reason, however, which was that Paula was wrong to have made the case public in the first place, because it damaged her honor. They suggested to Paula that she should have left her husband's relationship with his mistress "hidden in the sanctuary of private life." What Paula had done was to highlight society's immorality.[63]

As Drago wrote in 1882, "modern legislations [had] judged that lawsuits require[d] much reflection and could bring serious consequences, so to leave them to the mere arbitration of the wife was a mistake." Thus, moral superiority and femininity were double-edged swords. While it was true that material criminal acts had to be prosecuted, the intent of much of judicial practice was to avoid unnecessary damage to personal honor. As the national constitution of 1857 held, an Argentine citizen was guaranteed the right to "life, liberty, and honor."[64]

2 Social Responsibility and Free Will

A second way in which the state found itself attempting to negotiate the vagaries of women in its striving for liberalism was in the area of reproduction. Besides relying on the family as an integrating element, the state benefited from the view that women not only had a special source of knowledge about reproduction, but that they also had an increased responsibility to treat it scientifically. However, female flesh biologically also put women on the margins of innocence, because of the natural aberrations of maternal organs, depriving women of free will. This subjected them, and midwives who helped them, to suspicion and surveillance.

Maternity was much more than a familial pleasure or a biological strategy to maintain the population; it was woman's "highest mission." Jurists, criminologists, public health experts, lawyers, and religious practitioners described motherhood in similar terms as the only natural position and passion for women. Women who rejected motherhood were denigrated as "denatured" and "monstrous," like prostitutes and born criminals, who also lacked maternal sentiment. Maternal crimes led to prostitution, just like adultery. Maternal love, though, infused society as the "most lasting, intense, and disinterested of all the human affections."[1]

The biological idiosyncrasies of maternal and newborn flesh presented politicians and professionals with the predicament of what to do with the half of the population that, because of its makeup, the lack of certainty about when life began, and so on, was only marginally innocent. By the late nineteenth century, medical scientists believed they knew a great deal more than previously about the vagaries of the maternal organs and their relationship to women's illnesses. They knew that while motherhood was an unqualified good, it could be undermined by the maternal organs themselves, which meant that attempts to judge maternal crimes in a democratic and reasoned manner were stymied by the "irrationality" of these organs. For example, disturbances in the uterus that could propel a woman to commit infanticide undermined the state's population policies and its reliance on maternal and family stability for state planning. Court doctors were attuned to the dictates of modern medicine, that is, that the physical and mental states observed in pregnancy and birth could strongly affect behavior, and turn it criminal. Thus it was very difficult to apply scientific reason to the maternal organs.

The instability of the reproductive system led to the issue of free will, which played a crucial role in assessing guilt and innocence in infanticide cases. Giving birth was one in a series of medical conditions that could affect a person's free will. Since giving birth could adversely affect a woman's morality, the question arose of whether she was really responsible for her acts. Little consensus about this existed. The positivist school of criminology opposed the whole concept of free will and maintained that the idea that people had free will was scientifically unsustainable. For others, however, free will was encompassed in the very notion of being a human being rather than a beast; it was degrading to think otherwise, and loss of free will was too much to bear, coming on top of Charles Darwin's "association of mankind and monkeys." To still others, free will was of no concern; "healthy or sick, responsible or not . . . delinquents [such as infanticidal mothers] should be separated out from the rest of society." Although all these theories were influential in criminal judges' decisions, the more widely accepted view was that giving birth influenced a woman's intellectual faculties tremendously; that if dishonor was involved, it exacerbated the situation; and that if a woman committed a crime such as infanticide, her responsibility decreased, since in such cases, her will was not free. As the defense attorney described it in an 1875 case, "At the moment of birth, she only fears; she has no will. There is no crime; just faint-heartedness."[2]

CHOICE VERSUS NATURE

Women were mothers, not by choice, but by nature, which increased their responsibility for what happened at birth, and thus for the demographic growth of the country. Since the maternal organs formed women's essence, all women as woman necessarily knew about maternity by nature or from common female lore. To deny that knowledge, a lawyer argued in 1903, demonstrated a lack of control of self.[3] Maternity was unique in this way; men had no equivalent kind of knowledge. Amerindian suspects had a reduced knowledge of it, and judges made the condition of being "indigenous"—Lombroso's contemporary savages—an extenuating circumstance in maternal crimes. Lack of civilization reduced a woman's maternal knowledge, judges argued in cases from 1898 and 1899.[4] Maternal knowledge included recognizing the difference between interrupted menstruation and pregnancy; bowel cramps and imminent birth; life and death in an infant; a fetus and a child carried to term; and the proper care of newborns and negligence. To judge by the numerous treatises written on these topics, however, doctors and lawyers themselves were not at all certain about these differences. The Spanish jurist Joaquín Escriche noted in the mid 1870s that "what used to be certain in the early nineteenth century about life and death was certain no longer," and that these uncertainties made it difficult to judge "maternal crimes."[5]

Free will was involved in this knowledge that women had by nature. Again, this was a kind of free will different from men's. Women and men had distinctly different kinds of control over their flesh. Since women were viewed as maternal "by nature" rather than "by choice," when they committed infanticide, it had to be that free will had been absent, and thus they could not be held responsible for their behavior. If a woman's nature was somehow defective and she did not know how to preserve her baby's life, it indicated that she did not have free will. It was a legal principle that delinquents could not be punished if they lacked free will. Infanticide seemed to many people by definition to indicate an absence of free will, because of the belief in the naturalness of maternal love.

Infanticide most often happened either because women feared being dishonored or because they suffered from mental and physical disturbances, or both. Jeremy Bentham had argued in the late eighteenth century that the crime of infanticide caused feelings of commiseration for the mother, so to sentence her was a barbarous torture.[6] Far from being anti-maternal, lawyers using Bentham's principle contended, these women had deep maternal instincts, which in normal circumstances would have never allowed them to kill their own children. Even the seemingly absurd assertion that infanticide was "not hatred but love," proposed by a lawyer in 1873, was invoked to protect women from harsher penalties.[7] Again using Bentham, a lawyer in 1897 argued that infanticidal mothers were to be pitied, because they had been deprived of their ability to exercise their natural maternal will.

Mental disturbances caused by disorders of the genital organs could result in irritability, outbursts, and crime. When the symptoms of mental alienation appeared during menstruation, doctors advised examining the sexual organs to avoid future crimes. There were many conditions listed that could cause dementia or insanity, such as epilepsy, love, use of tobacco snuff, and masturbation, and a change in the uterus called "uterine furor" was one of these.[8] It produced cerebral alterations, which in turn produced excitations of the nervous system. In the reproductive process, women might experience "maniacal outbursts, a perversion of their reason, and a change in their morality and affections." Sometimes, the change was merely one of temperament, and a woman might become "contemptuous and insulting." At other times, the "violence" done by the uterus could impel women to commit atrocious crimes. While such alterations alone could not fully explain an act such as infanticide, they might well be the preliminaries of a disturbance in the brain produced by the nervous excitation of birth. As one lawyer put it in 1850, this was a period when "animal birth smothered the dictates of reason." Not only was a woman's reason affected, but also her maternal sensitivity. When it could be proved that a woman had committed infanticide while in the "madness" of a postpartum state, she usually received the minimum sentence or was acquitted.[9]

Infanticide

With some slight variations, nearly all western European and American legal codes in the second half of the nineteenth century defined two characteristics of infanticide that distinguished it from homicide. The child had to be new-born, and the crime had to have been committed by the mother to hide her dishonor. In Argentina, the law was that the child could not be more than three days old, and that the child's maternal grandmother could also be tried under the infanticide law, in the belief that she shared in her daughter's dishonor.[10] In Argentina, infanticide carried a sentence of three to six years' imprisonment, while homicide could entail fifteen to twenty. Twelve of twenty women convicted of infanticide in Buenos Aires between 1871 and 1905 received sentences in the three-to-six year range, with nine women receiving the suggested average sentence of four and a half years in prison. Three women received sentences of less than three years; five, sentences of more than six years; and five were acquitted.[11] Thirteen of the twenty-six women convicted of infanticide in Córdoba between 1850 and 1901 received sentences ranging between three and six years. The key to infanticide's lesser sentence was the dishonor clause, which took precedence over the demise of the victim. There was an important medical context, too, in the definition of the crime. The child had to have been born alive, at full term, and viable; the accused had to have recently given birth; the time of birth had to accord with the state of the cadaver; and any lesions and fractures had to be due to intentional violence and not occasioned by the birth itself.

The necessary medical examinations to determine these conditions were difficult to perform, though, because of the problems involved with autopsies of newborns. Sometimes cadavers were too putrefied to examine or too mutilated, having been stuffed down toilets, up drain pipes, in sewers, animal pens, and trash bins. Even when the lungs could be examined, they might not reveal any proof. The fetus might have breathed before birth and died afterward, and there were cases reported of "moaning" fetuses. Such evidence could increase the likelihood of an accusation against a woman of infanticide, as could any artificial respiration that she might give her child. Long births produced violent contractions that could push the head of the child against the mother's pelvic bones, compress the umbilical cord and placenta, and cause a stroke in the child or inflict contusions and fractures. The child could also be strangled by the umbilical cord. All of this tended to cast suspicion on the mother. Death could also come about from omission of care for the child once it was born; from not tying off the umbilical cord; and from natural asphyxiation by inhaling expelled birth material. Most women who had just given birth alone were in no condition to give this kind of care. Accidents could also produce the child's death: it could suffer a fracture from a fall, especially in a surprise birth, or it could suffer a dislocation of the cervical vertebrae. Since many births, especially clandestine ones, took place in the water closet, a fall to the floor or into the toilet was common. Sometimes, separation of the head from the body occurred in a difficult birth or due to an unskilled assistant.

Certain wounds, though, were considered secure indicators of criminal acts. These included cranial fractures, unless it could be proved the child had fallen; lesions made with cutting instruments; punctures made with piercing instruments, such as a needle inserted into the brain through the nose, ears, temples, spinal cord, heart, anus, or vagina; asphyxiation caused by matter such as straw inserted into oral and nasal cavities; and suffocation caused by submersion, usually in a toilet.

Modern breakthroughs in medicine brought with them an increase in medical curiosity and investigative tools that were often the source of objection among the accused. Investigative tools used to determine whether a woman had given birth included physical and chemical examinations, witnesses' testimonies, and searches of the woman's home and neighborhood. When Higinia, a married, 33-year-old Argentine storekeeper in Córdoba, was denounced by a neighbor's servant in 1879, the police combed her house for underwear indicative of a recent birth.[12] They found bloodstains in her room and two brassieres soaked with a sticky white fluid. The police called on her to confess, but she refused, and her servant explained the incriminating blood by testifying that Higinia had had a hemorrhage for nine days, which she had been treating with warm oil and chamomile. When she heard that a newborn had been found in a reed bed strangled with a piece of clothing, Higinia's reaction was, "Jesus, how awful!" Apparently, the denunciation of Higinia, coupled with the bloodstains, was enough for continued suspicion of her, and the *protomedicato* (an office established in colonial times that was still being used in the provinces) was asked to perform a medical examination of Higinia. An enlarged uterus, the excretion of a liquid, the existence of milk in the breasts, and the milky secretion were the convincing evidence. An important medical point was whether the presence of milk was a sure sign of having given birth. Higinia's explanation was that she had had milk since the birth of her last child, two years before, and that after the child had died, she had taken a small dog and made it nurse at her breast for a year after, pressing on her breasts to extract the milk, because she felt that they were "getting hard, and the nipples were stinging." Whether or not using a dog in this way was a usual practice among women, Higinia still had not wanted anyone to know that she was doing it, or perhaps this was just an excuse. "No one knows that I have used this little dog like this, because I didn't tell anyone and I managed that no one saw me, even my servant, and no one knew that I had so much milk and that it had remained for so long. Since my first child until today, my milk hasn't stopped."

Additional negative evidence was provided by the team of doctors who were entrusted with the chemical examination of the stains on Higinia's clothes, pillow, sheets, sheepskin, and brassieres, and of secretions from her breast and uterus. These doctors did not stop with the chemical examination, however; they performed an entire second physical examination of Higinia. The second examination became an issue because the second team of doctors was more certain than the *protomédico* that she was guilty. Higinia protested the legality of the examination. In challenging the second medical examination, Higinia objected to the doctors' "shameful investigations" of her body and said that the examination had exceeded the limits of the law. Moreover, said the defense lawyer, quoting the Spanish doctor Pedro Mata, it had been established that, after ten days, or at the most fifteen days, a medical examination could not shed any light on whether or not a birth had occurred. The examination done on this woman, he said, had taken place fourteen days afterward, which was very close to the reliable limit. Higinia also objected to the fact that the results of the chemical examination had not been reported until the end of August and did not give the date on which the doctors had actually done the chemical tests, saying:

> These doctors doubtless wanted to make anatomical studies on a live body; so, against their mandate, they intrigued to repeat the indecent investigations of the

protomédico, because he was a layman. The first examination only confirmed the milk, and concluded that it could not explain my illness. The second examination contradicts the milk part, and considers the only sure data to be the state of the uterus and its opening, in spite of the fact that the French doctor Matthieu Joseph Bonaventure Orfila denies that birth is the only cause of these changes.

The judge focused on the second medical exam and also took into account witnesses' testimonies that Higinia had been seen groaning, convulsed, and gritting her teeth; that bloodstains had been found; and that the child's body had been discovered near her house. The issue was how she should be tried—for infanticide or homicide. The prosecutor asked for the death penalty, since she could not be tried under the infanticide law, because she had not killed out of dishonor. The reason for this was that she had no modesty to protect, nor honesty to want respect for, because she had had children before. The prosecutor explained that this was a "terrible, but necessary sentence." No autopsy had been done on the child, however, so it was uncertain whether it had been born alive, and the judge absolved Higinia.

The Demands of the Law

For a woman to be tried under the infanticide law, she had, in a sense, to testify against herself, admitting that she had felt shame. Honor and shame were used partly because science could not tell judges what they needed to know. Shame about being an illegitimate mother was viewed as a good sentiment, even when it led to murder. Witnesses, lawyers, and judges complimented accused women for showing an understanding of their shame—for knowing that otherwise "dishonor would enfold [a woman] forever, prohibiting [her] from enjoying the honored and tranquil life of the family," either her employer's or her own. Legal practice thus condoned a woman's rejection of motherhood in the present to allow for a more honorable and successful maternity in the future under the right conditions. An explanation in court that a woman had killed her child out of shame, an honorable sentiment, did not elicit disbelief or scorn, if it could be proved. Of course, honor went with shame, and a woman also had to prove that she had had honor to lose. Finally, shame and honor went with flesh. Since knowledge about flesh—that is, whether a child had been born alive, and so on—was so uncertain even for well-trained doctors, honor moved to the fore in determinations of guilt or innocence. Modern penal legislation, Escriche wrote in the mid 1870s, had adopted other arenas of knowledge, such as that surrounding honor, to compensate for the uncertainties of scientific knowledge about when life and death began, although he admitted that honor might be just as ambiguous as biological factors.[13]

The indicators of a new mother's honor, of her nondelinquency, included dealing with flesh in the correct way: concealment of pregnancy by wearing loose outer clothing and tight corsets; by claiming that weight gains and hemorrhages after birth were due to irregular menstruation or "rage"; by secretly preparing clothes for the baby ahead of time and getting help with the birth; and by cutting the umbilical cord.[14] The law thus demanded that the woman had to be collecting baby clothes, arranging for a midwife, and so on, at the same time that she was trying to simulate not being pregnant. If a woman did not seek help and gave birth alone, she could be accused of refusing to take an interest in her future child, and by implication, of not wanting it to survive. A midwife's fee was high for servants, and going to one took planning and created gossip. After birth, the new mother was held responsible for cutting and tying off her child's umbilical cord, even though she was alone and often ill. Tearing off the cord or leaving it untied was a common cause of newborns' bleeding to death. Even while striving to avoid disclosure of their pregnancy, servant women were expected to put on a public display of maternal feelings in order to have proof in court of them, which undermined any attempt at secrecy and was expensive and time-consuming. If found out, women stood to lose their jobs and might be sent to a correctional or returned to the Defense of Minors Office.

When shame could not be established, women were charged with homicide. In 1871, Juana Larramendia, a woman in Buenos Aires who had suffocated her newborn son, received a sentence of fifteen years' imprisonment, the harshest in this collection of cases, because the judge determined that she had a "false sentiment of honor" and had "violated the strongest human sentiments in the name of passion and [out of] bad motives."[15] She had reportedly weighed the cost of breast-feeding against the life of her child.

Toward the turn of the century, Ramona, a servant who confessed in 1897 that she had committed two infanticides because she feared her employers would punish her for getting pregnant, was accused of homicide rather than infanticide because she had not claimed dishonor in her defense.[16] Ramona's lawyer tried to make up for her error by arguing that she had previously been rebuked and as a consequence, "had conceived a sentiment of dignity" in which she found it too dishonoring to claim dishonor. All her actions, he stressed, showed that she did, in fact, have a sense of dishonor. If Ramona had not felt dishonored, she would have admitted her pregnancy and the birth and kept the child in her bed.

Ramona's lawyer failed, however, to establish that his client had felt a sense of shame. After almost a year of trial, the judge in her case prefaced his final decision with these words:

> It is a tough job for a magistrate when he has to accept in cases like the present one that there are human beings capable of causing death to the child [born] of their body out of the simple fear of being punished, and who repeat their crime with the same plan two years later. It is enough to read the confession that Ramona makes . . . to be convinced that the infanticide law . . . is not relevant to this case. As two of our most distinguished commentators maintain, it is necessary that "hiding dishonor" be present for the blame to be attributed to it. The [social] class, life, and customs of a mother have to convince the judge that her intention was the same one that inspired the infanticide law. It has to be proved or be able to be rationally presumed that dishonor existed. But Ramona did not confess it; it has not been proven in the proceedings; and it cannot be assumed given the particular circumstances of the class of person she is from. Since the death penalty has been abolished for women, we have to commit her to a penitentiary for an indeterminate time.

Using the same argument of class, the defense lawyer responded that people of Ramona's class were ignorant of the "weapons" that the law itself gave her for her own defense. The lawyer's description of how the court should deal with such people is physiologically poignant. With people like Ramona, he said, one has to "penetrate their brain, surprise their thought, and take the words out of their mouths that favor them and that they don't show. They have the *feeling* of shame, of honor, but they lack the [intellectual] *notion* of it." Finally, he said, to believe that Ramona had killed her children for fear of being punished was to believe that she was either an "irresponsible imbecile" or a "prostitute." In the terms of positivist criminology, it was to think that Ramona was either mentally deranged and thus lacked free will, or that she was a born criminal who had lacked moral sentiments since early in life or who was a victim of atavism and degeneration. Continuing to analyze Ramona's case in terms of the Lombrosian school, the lawyer argued that if the court applied the maximum penalty to his client, there would be no appropriate sentence for prostitutes. The defense was rejected, however, and Ramona received the original sentence.

Advantage of Brutality

Lack of firm scientific evidence ironically led judges to consider the level of violence used to dispatch a newborn. In a reversal of civilization's demand for personal self-control, it seemed that the less control a woman had over her will, the more sympathy she received in court. The more brutal the infanticide, the more compassion for the author, perhaps because of the belief in the strong links between a mother and her child. For example, in 1875 a woman in Córdoba who had mutilated the genitals of her newborn received a sentence of three years, and in 1880 another woman from Córdoba who had hanged her child was acquitted.[17]

In 1899, a European immigrant woman also received a benign sentence based on the brutality of her crime and her sense of honor. Teresa De Michelli, a single Italian maidservant, aged twenty-five, had first tried to suffocate her newborn daughter, then had tried to strangle her, and had finally severed the infant's head.[18] Teresa had been residing in Buenos Aires for eight months before she was arrested. She had come to Argentina already pregnant, leaving the biological father of the child in Italy. Teresa had a brother in Buenos Aires, but her lack of Spanish and her illiteracy put her at a disadvantage. The court concluded that she had limited intelligence and stuttered, though this could have been a result of the language difference and the postpartum trauma. She was the servant of an Italo-Argentine family that was evidently of modest means, as they only had two rooms and Teresa slept in the dining room next to her employers' bedroom. In these crowded conditions, Teresa's three trips to the latrine during the night had not escaped the family's notice. When they commented that her clothes were bloodstained, she explained it as a "discharge due to an outburst of rage," and the household went back to bed. The following day, Teresa began her work at 5 A.M. as usual. At 6 A.M., another resident of the *conventillo* (tenement house) noted while washing himself that the drainage hole of the sink in the patio was clogged; he lifted the grating and tried to clear the blockage with a stick, and then saw that it was a baby's foot. He called another tenant, who screamed when a foot came out with the water, and he then notified the building manager, who phoned the police. Teresa's employers had known that she was pregnant, they testified, but had not heard her give birth. The Italian grandmother had seen the blood in the latrine, but had assumed that it was from a tenant's hemorrhoids. Since Teresa had been the only pregnant woman in the house, however, the police charged her.

Reporting on Teresa's mental state, the court doctors noted that she was calm and indifferent, and that she gave tearful, vague, unsure, and at times foolish answers to their questions. She had no physical signs of degeneration or psychological pathological problems, and she had not exhibited any intellectual disturbances at her place of employment. Her reflexes, pulse, temperature, and digestion were good. She showed no symptoms of puerperal fever, no delirium, irritability, insomnia, or extreme anxiety. The negative testimony by her employers that she was headstrong and deceitful, and the confirmation of this by the doctors, who noted her "marked intention to adulterate the truth, to simulate a state of unconsciousness, which is easy to do, in order to change the course of questioning," did not damage her case, as it often did in other cases. The doctors concluded that she was suffering from moral shock and depression, which they decided underscored the fact that her honor had been the convincing reason for her ferocious act. Teresa's defense lawyer asked for acquittal on the basis of the medical report and argued that there had been complicity on the part of the neighbors, but she received the average sentence of four and a half years' imprisonment in a penitentiary.

In a 1903 case in which a cook dispatched her newborn in a particularly brutal way, the court showed a similarly high level of compassion.[19] When Felipa Arce's employer, a colonel in Cosquin in Córdoba, moved to Buenos Aires, he brought her along. Feeling pains, Felipa, a single 27-year-old native of Córdoba, started toward the *escusado* (water closet). But the birth caught her in the kitchen. Out of respect for her employers, she testified, and without the time necessary to go to a hospital, the first thing that occurred to her was to get rid of the baby. She squeezed her daughter hard with her hands and beheaded it with one of the kitchen knives, having first tied a dishcloth around the baby's neck so that it would not cry out. When she was certain that the child was dead, Felipa wrapped it in a sackcloth and hid it in a box. Then she succumbed to a hemorrhage, which she claimed was just a hard menstruation, and had to be taken to the hospital. The other servants found the cadaver under the coal box off the kitchen and the knife that had been left under running water in the sink. Up until the last, Felipa had been so intent on hiding her condition that in the morning, she had gone to the market as usual. She slept on the top floor of her employer's house in a room with the other servants, but they claimed they had had no knowledge of her pregnancy, though they had noted that Felipa seemed disproportionately fat. Notwithstanding the gruesomeness of this crime, and although he called Felipa a perverse mother who had forgotten the sentiments of nature and brutally killed a helpless baby, the prosecutor asked only for four and a half years' imprisonment, the average sentence in cases of infanticide. The first defense attorney and judge agreed, but the second defense attorney, Nicolás Casarino, who took on many infanticide cases, pleaded for an even lesser sentence because both of the violence of the birth and Felipa's reputation as an honest woman. Although she had previously had an illegitimate child in Córdoba, this was not publicly known in Buenos Aires, and she was trying to maintain her honorable character. A sentence of four and a half years was, however, imposed.

In the above cases, the sentences were the same or less than those handed

down to women whose newborns had died in much less clear-cut and delib-
erate ways, such as through drowning in a latrine, a fall to the floor, or smoth-
ering in bed, any of which could have also been judged accidental, whereas
a beheading almost never could be. The judges deduced from the savageness
of the murders that the women had an extraordinary sense of being dishonored. It was as if the more effort a woman took to bring about the death of her
child, the more it meant that she was committed to saving her honor. In a
way, this was almost a kind of reverse self-control, in that the less control these
women apparently had over their wills, the more self-control and free will it
indicated. The legal consistency between the mid nineteenth and early twentieth centuries in infanticide cases is that women who killed their infants in
"normal" ways and could demonstrate shame were tried under the infanticide
law; women who killed their infants in "normal" ways but could not demonstrate shame were tried under the homicide law; and women who killed their
infants in brutal ways were tried for infanticide and in addition were given
average or sometimes mitigated sentences.

SERVANTS

Most of the women who were caught and accused of infanticide between 1871
and 1905 in Buenos Aires were servants. Twenty-two of the twenty-five reported cases in Buenos Aires involved maidservants, the majority of whom were
unmarried and between fifteen and twenty-five years old.[20] Given the circumstances of servants' childhoods and the vulnerability of their position as
servants, these figures are not surprising. First, servants were often wards of the
state. The female servant class in Buenos Aires was to a great extent supervised
by the Defense of Minors Office and the Beneficent Society, whose joint goal
was to protect and place minors, though this did not mean that the two agencies interacted harmoniously. The Defense of Minors Office's job was to
respond to complaints of child abuse by parents, relatives, and guardians; to
oversee orphans, abandoned children, and delinquent minors; and to inspect
jails and the establishments of beneficence and charity where minors were
housed and monitor the progress of children that the Minors' office had
placed in private homes. The Beneficent Society, Argentina's main charitable
organization, was run by women from some of the most influential families in
the republic and managed a number of institutions.

In effect, the job of both organizations might be described as that of a combination housing and employment agency for the domestic workforce. In the
wording of the contracts between agency and guardian/employer, these

organizations delivered minors, who were usually about seven when they went to private families, to the "service and care" of private individuals, who contracted to clothe, feed, and care for the children in sickness, instruct them in morality, and provide them with some education. For example, in an 1888 contract between the president of the Beneficent Society and a private individual, the society agreed to hand over a girl from the Casa de Expósitos (Foundling Home), or *cuna*, as it was popularly known, under the following conditions. He had to agree to care for her as an "affectionate" father, to educate her morally and religiously, and to feed and clothe her. Once she reached the age of eighteen, he had to pay her a wage, the amount to be fixed in agreement with the Defense of Minors Office. If the man died or did not fulfill his contractual obligations, the Defense of Minors Office reclaimed the child. The girl had the right either to accept or reject this contract as soon as she was of age. The man ratified these conditions before the Defense of Minors Office, under whose jurisdiction he remained.[21] Although contracts obliged guardians/employers to provide caring families for minors, the reality was that the complaints by angry contractees to the Defense of Minors Office read like employers' disciplinary reports. For example, a 1905 letter from such a guardian/employer explained that she had taken a *chica* from the Foundling Home in 1899 when the girl was nine, but now that she had turned fifteen, the employer found it very difficult to "dominate her as she wanted." She had thus put the girl in a workshop run by a religious order, to learn a job and to avoid trouble. Finding the workshop deficient, however, the Defense of Minors Office had reallocated the girl, apparently without notifying her guardian/employer. "I'm deprived of my *chica*, who serves me; she's learning for her own good; the judge who watches over minors did not give me any warning. They have sent my girl to her relative's house. They didn't tell the relative that she was mine. I want the Foundling Home to take her back, so that I know she's well cared for."[22]

Cases of servants who suffered physical injury from their employers, who were minimally fed and clothed, and so on, were not rare. For example, in 1906, a twelve-year-old girl was found in the Foundling Home whose guardian/employer had wounded her in the head with a kitchen knife, paid her with whatever was at hand, dressed her in rags, and made her sleep on the floor.

Sometimes child servants struck back. A fourteen-year-old Amerindian girl from the Chaco confessed in 1890 to having laced her employers' dinner with rat poison because they insulted and hit her. She referred to her position in the family as that of a *presa* (prisoner), saying, "I hated them and wanted revenge." The medical doctors concurred that the motive for her crime had been vengeance,

> a sentiment that does not take control of a cultivated intelligence, nor the reflection that imprints [itself] on age. She did not try to resist her [desire for] vengeance; she submitted various persons [to it] who had to take the same food and suffer the action of the toxic agent. Her first instincts are savage, inspired by what she saw and heard among her *semejantes* [fellow creatures]. These first impressions were important to her and hard to forget. She could not distinguish between good and bad. She might not know that poison kills. Who could ever imagine that an Indian of under fifteen, with the rude and ignorant character of her race itself, could come to be so wickedly perverse as to try to kill an entire family?

It is not entirely clear, but it would appear that this girl was acquitted.[23]

If the Defense of Minors Office's placement of minors in private homes as servants was rife with abuse, so were the institutions of the Beneficent Society, as we saw in chapter 1. Turning to a different institution, the Foundling Home was criticized for clinging to the outmoded practice of the *torno*, a turntable used to deliver infants to the Home in such a way as to protect the identities of illegitimate mothers, which could be misused by parents who crammed older children into the narrow space. It was finally suspended in 1901. Inspectors also criticized the Foundling Home for allowing the same mother to have several children there simultaneously; for permitting parents to deposit children in the institution during their younger years and reclaim them when they were old enough to work; and for letting parents leave children there for long periods while they themselves returned to Europe. When parents came to reclaim their child and could not pay the money "owed" to the society for the child's maintenance, the society kept the child as a "pledge." Employers who were upset with their child servants could easily return them to the Foundling Home, or turn them over to one of the society's *asilos*, namely, the Good Shepherd, for correction. Or sometimes employers just consigned their servants to other guardians/employers without the knowledge of the authorities.[24]

Accusations that the rights of minors were being abused divided the Defense of Minors and the Beneficent Society, who both thought they were doing a good job. In a case from the 1870s, a lawyer argued that the Beneficent Society had denied his young female client her right to name her own guardian. She had been deposited by her parents in the Foundling Home and transferred to a private individual by the society. Once she had turned fourteen, the law stated that she had the right to choose a *curador*, that is, a guardian for children who were over the age of fourteen and under twenty-five, and minors under the jurisdiction of the Defense of Minors had been used to exercising this right. However, the Beneficent Society wanted to deny the girl this right. "The society's pretensions are truly incredible," said the lawyer, who stressed that the institution was an "anachronism" totally out of sync with modern times. The society had been created in colonial times by an absolute monarchy, as part of the principle of noblesse oblige. In defending itself, the society had even invoked old colonial royal *cédulas* (decrees). In the democratic Argentina of the late nineteenth century, the lawyer argued, such distinctions and privileges were rejected by good sense and condemned by civilization. "Justice is one and the same for everyone, and all are equal before the law." The Beneficent Society's attempts to impose guardians on minors and to take back children at its pleasure had a "subversive" tendency. The society claimed that it was avoiding abuses, but the most important abuse was its own "arbitrary and violent" appropriation of individuals' rights. The society was no more enlightened than the philanthropists of the slave era, the lawyer argued, in that both maintained that their charges could not survive without their "owners."[25]

The Defense of Minors Office was pleased that this case had been brought to court, since the issue had often created tension between it and the Beneficent Society. Up to then, the society had been "guided without doubt by good motives," the lawyer argued, but it had recently fallen into error in trying to maintain its independence of the Defense of Minors Office, which was legally authorized to inspect all orphans and it could not be restricted in doing so by the society. The royal decrees that the society invoked did not square with the new liberal institutions of Spanish America. The society was a corporation whose main task was to provide subsistence for orphans, especially during infancy, whereas the role of the Defense of Minors Office was "wider and more elevated." In the end, the judge ruled that an institution of charity should not be turned into a prison for unfortunates who were kept there until they reached their majority. Minors, even though they were foundlings, could not be denied the rights given to all minors by law.[26]

Abuse of the rights of minors at the Good Shepherd was another area of concern for the Defense of Minors Office. Not only were wives sent to the Good Shepherd for irascible behavior or adultery, or because they had sued for divorce, girls were also sent there by their parents or guardians/employers for minor offenses, as were minors who had been convicted of infanticide or prostitution. Most of the inmates were there for disciplinary reasons, but girls from good families were sometimes sent there while their parents were away from home for long periods.

Correspondence about the Good Shepherd between the Defense of Minors Office and the Beneficent Society between 1887 and 1895 reflects the growing tension between a national ministry under a liberal democratic government and an elite society of matrons whose establishment dated back to colonial times. Democratic government and a colonial institution fought it out over minors' bodies. The Defense of Minors Office charged that children were being deposited and released from the Good Shepherd without the office's knowledge, and that the office's intervention in the Good Shepherd was "obligatory" and "advisable." The society responded by saying that these were minors who were not under the jurisdiction of the Defense of Minors Office, that is, they were children who had been deposited by their parents or tutors. The society charged that the Defense of Minors Office had been discourteous and threatening, but that "this [did] not frighten [them]." Nevertheless, there was the danger that the Good Shepherd might lose its government subvention, which was perhaps why it chose to publish this correspondence in the newspaper *La Tribuna*.[27]

The most important abuse was that the Beneficent Society was keeping minors in the Good Shepherd beyond the legal maximum of one month established by article 278 of the civil code. During an inspection in 1887, the Defense of Minors Office found between 120 and 140 children who had been interned for four years. In defiance of the Beneficent Society and in defense of the civil code, the Defense of Minors Office began removing these girls and sending them back to their families or depositors. The society, on the other hand, defended its long deposit period by citing the objectives of the Good Shepherd, arguing that article 278 did not apply, because the Good Shepherd was not a jail, but rather a house of "preventive charity and moral correction," designed to rid minors of immorality and instill religion and the work ethic into them, which took from two to four years.[28]

The Beneficent Society was confident of the moral regimen at the Good Shepherd and took pride in its star "pupils." When an event occurred in 1882 that tarnished that reputation, it became clear that the society had detractors who did not hesitate to gloat. The newspaper *La Pampa* almost gleefully reported the moral downfall of one of the Good Shepherd's "glittering" protégés in 1882. The girl had been raised well in a branch of General Lagos's family. Probably from the time this girl was about seven, she had been working as a domestic servant for the Lagoses. In 1880, she had been placed in the Good Shepherd, apparently as punishment for something she had done, since the Lagos family planned to take her back, although it could have been that the Lagoses were traveling. The girl stayed there for two years, and according to the staff of the Good Shepherd, she became a model of morality. When Señora de Lagos offered to release the girl and "give" her to the Reybaud family as a servant, the Reybauds were pleased to have such a virtuous addition to their family, even though they objected to being charged for the girl's upkeep for the two years she had been in the Good Shepherd, a total of 3,000 pesos. A reformed servant did not come cheaply! After being with the Reybauds in Montevideo a few months, the girl began to "bulge irregularly." Señora de Reybaud determined that the girl was pregnant and was shaken to think that this might have happened under her own roof, but she was relieved to find out from the girl that the sacristan at the Good Shepherd was responsible, and that he was accused of having had similar relations with the other girls at the institution.[29]

The Vulnerability of Servants

The reality of a servant's life made it difficult to do what was considered the right thing by her child, that is, turn it over to the Foundling Home. First of all, servants were concerned about offending their employers and losing their jobs, so they were very reluctant to make known their pregnancy. Municipal regulations concerning servants only served to reinforce this fear. An 1888 ordinance that sought to regularize domestic service and place it under the control of the municipal government resulted in new controls over servants and some inconvenience, though slight, for their employers. The regulation called for issuing a *libreta* costing fifty centavos to every domestic servant. All servants had to carry this booklet, which contained a certificate of the servant's conduct provided by her patrons, the dates of the servant's hiring and departure, the reason for leaving the service of the employer, and a record of the servant's vices and criminal acts. The requirement that patrons do this or be punished with a fine or prison created a "guild of spies, informers, and secret police." Critics labeled the regulation a violation of the home, in that employers were supposed to hire only people who had an identification booklet, that is, whom the municipality had determined to be suitable employees. Furthermore, it was alleged, this was bound to hurt immigration. To the detriment of servants, the regulation violated the penal code, in that it was a "serious injury" to impute a vice or lack of morality to anyone. It meant "slavery," in that a servant who did not want to continue working for his or her employer could be fined or imprisoned. Moreover, it commanded servants to respect and obey their employers, to be diligent, to watch over their patrons' interests, and so on—matters for treatises on good manners, said a critic in 1888, but not for law. In sum, it was arbitrary and repugnant to civilization to make people carry and exhibit proof of their morality, vices, or crimes.[30] The *libreta* was not, however, unlike other identification systems already in use or being developed, whose goal was to identify the innocent segment of the population and those who had been arrested but had paid their dues to society for their delinquent acts.

Second, in addition to fearing for their jobs, servants had almost no privacy. In wealthier families that had more than one servant, the servants usually had their beds and trunks on the top floor, sharing a single room. In families of more moderate means, a single servant often shared a child's room or slept in the dining room. It was not easy for a servant to leave the house on her own; or if she was sent to market, for example, for her to find a secluded place to give birth or the time to take her child to the Foundling Home. This was why newborns turned up exposed in plazas or other places. Thus, in urban areas, especially, the water closet was one of the few places where a servant could legitimately be alone. It was a good place for a secret birth and concealment of the newborn and gave women a good defense and a reason to assert that they had been surprised by birth while using the toilet and had accidentally lost their child. In trying to determine a woman's guilt or innocence, judges heard extensive testimony about women's toilet habits. The water closet was usually located at the back of the house or off a patio, and it seems to have been widely in use throughout middle-class and elite neighborhoods of Buenos Aires. Refuse was flushed with water down drainage pipes with the aid of poles. The poles, pipes, the toilet itself, and bloodstains on the floor were introduced as evidence. Although the water closet was a likely place to give birth even when the woman did not intend any harm to her child, moralists made contemptuous associations between these women and the toilet. Commenting on the frequent discovery of newborns in water closets, a nineteenth-century European jurist in 1886 postulated an "intimate link between the corruption of a woman who kills her child and the place where the child is thrown." The woman's soul, he remonstrated, is "black and dirty like the latrine, a putrid heap that taints, makes one nauseous, and horrifies."[31]

MEDICINE IN SERVICE TO THE STATE

Although the municipal government realized the importance of good birthing practices and actually encouraged the immigration of better-trained European midwives to Argentina, medical practitioners and the courts viewed midwives with suspicion. The fact that they had become better trained by the turn of the century did not matter as much as that they had the ability to collude with pregnant women and subvert the reproductive process. Midwives performed many services that aided a servant in keeping a birth secret, disposing of a newborn, and so on, but a late-nineteenth-century crackdown on midwives made this more difficult. The courts judged midwives harshly for two reasons: their ignorance of scientific knowledge when they were uneducated and misuse of it when they were certified; and the fact that they had a misplaced sense of responsibility, that is, they were anxious to help women escape from illegitimate pregnancies.

There were good reasons for the need for more professional midwives. Midwives' notions of obstetrics, the Argentine obstetrician J. C. Llames Massini wrote in 1915, were not only "rudimentary and dominated by false beliefs about the forces of nature and fate" but based on an "amalgam of tradition and fraud." He attributed Argentine midwives' obstetrical lore to the traditional practices of Amerindians living along the La Plata River (the Querandíes and Charruas), as well as to Spanish traditional practices and superstitions of Arab origin. From this mix came "strange amulets and curious tricks, which, applied together with methods that were more or less ridiculous," sometimes worked, but also caused numerous deaths.[32]

These beliefs, Llames Massini stressed in 1915, were not just a rural phenomenon. They were to be found, and were in fact on the increase, even in Buenos Aires. Llames Massini recalled treating a woman in 1905, for example, who had retained the placenta after a normal birth and gone to a certified midwife for help in expelling it. The midwife's method consisted of splitting a live black hen in half and applying it directly, bloody side down, to the patient's stomach. This had occurred only a few kilometers from central Buenos Aires, where doctors were trying to train women to be "discreet, moral, and learned midwives" to be planted like "good seeds" throughout Argentina, "suffocating and banishing forever the bad yerbas, the bad habits from long ago," Llames Massini wrote. In another situation, this time in a humble rancho in the countryside, Llames Massini found his patient squatting in the corner of the room grunting valiantly, with three men's hats on her head, which the midwife had recommended that she wear in order to hurry the birth. The midwife had instructed that they had to be the hats of three relatives or acquaintances named Juan. In another case of delayed birth, the midwife put the expectant mother in a vat of milk in the belief that the child would not be able to resist its proximity and odor. Still another way that birth was accelerated was to apply ointment to the woman's bottom to tempt the expulsion of the meconium, that is, the first excrement of a newborn, which announced that the child was about to be born.[33]

While some of these practices would have done no harm, others, and mid-wives' reported ignorance of hygiene, could cause real problems. One of the prejudices still in vogue in the early twentieth century was the advice to preg-nant women not to touch water for several days after giving birth, in order to prevent the formation of abscesses on their hands and other complications. This would have been less harmful if the midwife herself had subscribed to modern ideas of disinfection, but there were still midwives who either did not know about hygiene or who scorned it. At an *estancia* just eighty kilometers from Buenos Aires, a local midwife reportedly could not understand why a woman of her profession would wear any but her dirtiest clothes when assist-ing women giving birth.[34]

Attempts to modernize midwifery had begun in earnest in 1882, when the head of the Council of National Hygiene, Pedro Pardo, an obstetrics special-ist and forensic doctor, succeeded in getting new regulations passed that upgraded the admission standards of the school of obstetrics. Entering stu-dents had to be vaccinated for smallpox, be free of any physical impediments, have completed the fourth grade, and be at least eighteen years old. They had to present a certificate of good conduct from their parish priest, the local judge (*juez de paz*), or two honorable persons. The fact that new admissions immediately dropped shows that these measures were a drastic change. In 1883, only two admissions occurred, and in 1884, only three, whereas in 1875 there had been fourteen. Moreover, to admit even this handful of students, Pardo had had to make exceptions in his new admissions' standards, allowing in students who could not write. Enrollment increased in the following years, however, and in 1890, it was up to fifty-six.[35]

It was not just flesh that midwives came into contact with and could con-taminate; it was also the thing that gave flesh value, that is, morality. A mid-wife's intimate contact with families, advice, and knowledge of family secrets presented a possible danger to households. To improve the profession of mid-wifery and counteract society's perception that midwives contributed to moral contagion in Buenos Aires, Llames Massini added an extra year of training in ethical and obstetrical morality to his program. His concern was that if moral-ity had not truly taken root, it would be lost with the "harshness of profes-sional life," in which midwives were tempted to perform abortions to help their clients and profit financially. Llames Massini acknowledged that some midwives tried to right the wrongs done to women by helping them to abort. Other midwives established houses purportedly to assist births, but that peo-ple knew were really places of abortion and infanticide, camouflaging their criminal activities in newspaper advertisements using phrases such as "reserved midwife"; "instant cure"; "painless and without hemorrhage." Llames Massini intended the moral training he proposed, not just for midwives who committed criminal acts, but also for those midwives who, influenced by science, rationality, and materialism, "reacted to the vicissitudes and sufferings of [their] environment with hard hearts and positivism."[36]

With increasing immigration and professional training in Buenos Aires, the number of certified midwives increased. Whereas there had been only one certified midwife, a Frenchwoman, in Buenos Aires in 1830, there were 65 Argentine midwives in the city and 223 foreign ones by 1898.[37] Many uncertified midwives operated in the city as well. Llames Massini alleged that many of these midwives, certified or otherwise, "wandered from their duty" and engaged in immoral or illegal practices in order to make their livings. This was how abuses developed, from midwives' invasions of specialties that they had not studied and from the whole series of illicit procedures they employed for lucrative ends. For example, there were reportedly ten or twelve *parteras* who did most of the "recruiting" for the Foundling Home. They offered a "package deal" to their clients, which included caring for the pregnant woman before, during, and after birth; taking the child to the Foundling Home and giving false information to the Reception Office; getting the mother a job as a wet nurse (*ama*); and giving a promise to return to the Foundling Home to redeem the child if and when the mother chose to do so.[38]

By the turn of the century, a group of midwives concerned about the discrediting of their profession established the National Obstetrics Association with the goal of improving the public's opinion of midwives. The association had eighteen founding members in 1901, and by the end of that year, membership had increased to sixty-five. The editors of the association's journal, the *Revista Obstétrica*, founded in 1902, tried to combat the public's scorn for the profession; its view that midwives were socially inferior, and lacking conscience and science; and its belief that midwives daily performed the crime of abortion.[39] This was a first step to protect the guild from the accusations of people such as Dr. Pardo.

Along with promoting a higher level of applicant for the guild of midwifery, and longer and better scientific training with more clinical experience, came more frequent charges of malpractice. The charge of malpractice was leveled at doctors and male healers as well. But the comparable surviving cases of actual accusations of malpractice for men are in the field of pharmacy and do not parallel cases against midwives well, because the cases lack the moral aspect.

An interesting aspect to the professionalization of midwives is that, although often the target of malpractice suits, they also criticized doctors for malpractice.

Two cases show that a more educated guild of midwives reproached doctors for the doctors' alleged lack of medical knowledge. In the early stages of trying to build a midwifery practice in Córdoba in 1873, a Swiss woman new to Argentina, with diplomas from Switzerland and Uruguay, and a recertification from Argentina, was accused of provoking an abortion. She had been asked by the attending doctor to intervene in the case but had countermanded his prescription; an abortion had occurred, and she was accused. Her words expressed her disbelief and outrage: "I'm new here. I'm trying to build my reputation. Is it credible that I would deliberately do an abortion on someone I didn't even know; that I would commit an atrocious crime and sacrifice an innocent being; all without any motive and against all my convictions and my future in this place? And why would I do this to a patient whom a doctor was already attending?"[40]

The doctor had diagnosed metrorrhagia, or hemorrhage of the womb. The woman thought that she might be three months pregnant, and the doctor had performed "every examination permitted by science," but could not confirm this. She just did not fit the model of a pregnant woman that was sanctioned by obstetricians, he said. Indeed, obstetrical treatises emphasized the difficulty of knowing whether a woman was pregnant, and generally doctors could not be sure of pregnancy until the fourth or fifth month. Not wanting to examine his patient because of her "delicate" state, the doctor decided that she had a congestion of blood, placed her with her pelvis elevated above her head, and called the midwife, for reasons of "modesty," to apply eight leeches to the woman's pubis on the places he had indicated with ink.

In walked the midwife, and with her experience, she said, judged immediately that the patient was pregnant, with the fetus completely detached and outside the uterus, and with abortion thus imminent. Leeches would have been totally wrong for a woman about to lose a great deal of blood in an abortion, so she recommended that the leeches be returned to the pharmacy. Instead, she did what "any woman would have done, with or without a certificate in midwifery"; she gave the patient irrigations to facilitate the emission of the coagulated blood. "This blood doesn't serve life," she explained. If it were not removed, it would decay. With the second irrigation, the fetus came out dead. The hemorrhage, which the doctor had thought he could combat with leeches, had been, in the midwife's words, "nothing more than a sick and bloody secretion from the uterus." The midwife explained that she had merely "favored the action of nature" and that in no way could an irrigation have produced an abortion if the fetus had not already been outside the womb, which was confirmed by both science and common sense.

The midwife charged the doctor with several errors. First, she said, the doctor had erred in not giving her a written prescription. This was required in order "to avoid all the abuses, errors, and caprices of patients and healers, and in order to inspire faith in the officials of medicine and phlebotomists so as to avoid throwing suspicion on them." No one was obliged to perform an operation, she maintained, if he or she had only been told verbally that the doctor ordered it. For example, suppose that a maniac told a phlebotomist that a doctor had ordered that ten leeches be put on her eye or fifty on her temple, or some other foolishness, was it then obligatory for the phlebotomist to do it? The midwife would not have hesitated to comply with a doctor's written prescription, she explained, since she would thus have been absolved of responsibility, but with just a verbal order, it would have "bothered her conscience and been contrary to her profession." Second, was it not legal for a phlebotomist, obstetrician, or a pharmacist to suspend a prescription or a treatment prescribed by a doctor, unless it was an urgent case, until the doctor could confirm it? Third, for the doctor to have indicated the places for the leeches directly on the body of his patient was "unnecessary, inappropriate, and a serious offense to the laws of modesty." "According to medical morality," she said, "he should be professionally discredited. He should have just designated the anatomical areas to me." Finally, she charged, what lay behind the doctor's accusations was his "wounded vanity in a branch of science" with which he was unfamiliar. He knew that he had erred and because she had had the "misfortune to recognize his error and avoid its consequences," he had decided to file charges against her. His reaction was a far cry from the gratitude shown by the painter Rafael to an ignorant farmer, she said, who had pointed out Rafael's error in the positioning of an ear of wheat in one of his paintings. The midwife had done the same with the doctor, but he had not risen to the generosity of Rafael. Not only this, the doctor's vanity apparently allowed him no sense of humor. He had been "childishly angry and hateful," she said, when she had remarked that "women [knew] things that doctors [did] not." What a state the world was in if this universally accepted in-joke among women could become "twisted into something criminal."

The judge in the case released the midwife from jail, put her in house confinement for a year, and then absolved her, saying that she had been "purged of disobedience" with time served and the payment of costs. This sentence was later upheld.

Criminal Abortion

Undoubtedly, many women with unwanted pregnancies successfully induced abortions, rather than resorting to infanticide, and continued their lives with society none the wiser. When discovered, abortion, like infanticide, carried a maximum sentence of six years' imprisonment. I have found only six abortion cases in Buenos Aires; however, two of them were extremely long.

According to medical practitioners in the last quarter of the nineteenth century, three types of provoked abortion existed. First, abortion could be brought on with footbaths or warm sitz baths, bleedings of the feet, excessive fatigue and nausea, and exterior violence. There were also a variety of natural causes of abortion, some of which could be induced. Among these were thunder, intense emotion, dieting, stimulating delicacies, abuse of liquor, the rocking of carriages, tight clothing, stretching, immoderate laughter, and the abuse of coitus.[41]

Second, abortion could be brought on with substances, such as strong purgatives, that increased blood circulation and induced contractions. Other substances used included Spanish fly; stimulants such as tea and coffee; herbs such as rue and savin; and the often-used fungus called ergot of rye (*cornezuelo del centeno*). Mineral substances were also used, such as mercury and opium, the most reliable, and also arsenic, chromium acid of potassium, sulfate of copper, and sulfate of iron. Sometimes, the only effect of these substances, however, was to produce a toxic action, without necessarily affecting the fetus. Doctors used these substances to bring on menstruation, which, a lawyer argued, was nothing "except pregnancy and monthly birth, in that the same medications that [could] produce an abortion [could] make suspended menstruation return."

Since abortive substances were generally unreliable, "mechanical" means of abortion were given primary place by the major obstetrics experts like Ambroise Auguste Tardieu, Joseph Briand, Ernest Chaudé, and Marie Guillaume Alphonse Devergié in France and the Briton J. Bruce Thompson. Mechanical means included maneuvers that worked on the womb and directly attacked the fetus or its membranes, killing the fetus by premature expulsion. A finger introduced into the vagina was especially effective when the uterus had descended and the neck was soft and open so that the finger could reach the membranes and tear or detach them. The same could be done with probes of different types, such as stylets for probing wounds and knitting needles. A probe inserted through the neck of the uterus and then slid between the egg and the uterine wall could provoke an abortion in a few hours. Working as a foreign septic body, it produced uterine contractions, dilation of the neck of the uterus, and expulsion of the fetus. A probe required practice and skill and was not infallible, but it had the advantage of being relatively safe and it did not leave signs of intervention.[42] However, an inexperienced hand could cause a lesion and once the uterus became inflamed and the woman entered a puerperal state, her condition was often fatal. Forensic doctors lamented modern gynecology's discovery of the probe, "the abortive par excellence," because it allowed midwives to actually "own" the agent of their "immoral commerce," in contrast to herbs and other substances that had to be located and gathered outside their homes. To facilitate the introduction of probes, the neck of the womb was dilated using a prepared sponge, laminaria (seaweed), gentian root, or any substance capable of dilating through irrigation with liquids. A good midwife, Dr. Pardo said, preferred the sponge, which gradually dilated the neck of the uterus. Liquids were also injected that only percussed the neck of the uterus or penetrated the uterine cavity. Sometimes, women did not immediately feel the effect of these instruments. At other times, they experienced intense pain and the discharge of the amniotic liquid.[43]

One of the most often quoted experts in maternal crimes, the Spanish doctor Orfila, writing in the 1830s, maintained that, using these methods, it was difficult not to produce an abortion within from thirteen and a half hours to six days. Tardieu's studies in the 1860s showed that, in cases of puncture or perforation of the membranes, the abortion could be more immediate, between five hours and eleven days, and that abortion happened more rapidly with the injection of liquids into the interior of the uterus. All these maneuvers were eminently dangerous, since the trauma produced in an organ as delicate as the uterus in gestation usually created serious complications, such as hemorrhage and inflammation.

This was what happened to a patient of the improbably named midwife María Baby called Antonia, who died in 1882, leaving her fiancé and María charged with abortion.[44] A Spanish woman concealed under a thick veil reported the death to the editors of the Spanish immigrant community's newspaper *El Correo Español*. She was telling the newspaper rather than the police, she said, because she did not want to get involved. The paper ascertained from the municipality that a body had recently been buried, and the exhumation and autopsy of the dead woman took place. With visions of scooping a sensational story, the editor introduced the case to the public in his newspaper based solely on the statement of the anonymous woman, even before the police became involved, responding, he said, to the "just curiosity" of the public and the need for justice and an exemplary punishment. Several articles were published on the day the news broke, and in the following days, extra editions of the paper appeared, carrying updates on the police investigation of the case.

The newspaper first targeted the dead woman's fiancé Federico as a possible suspect. Both were German, and they had been together for four years, but then the fiancé had begun to stall. He had said that he could not marry Antonia until his financial situation improved. Antonia had become pregnant, perhaps to hurry Federico along the road to matrimony (but we do not know this). Federico had then turned immediately to the solution of an abortion, to "reconcile her with her family and stop the gossip." So Antonia began making the rounds of midwives in Buenos Aires. First, a young English midwife told her to take footbaths to bring on her period, but "take heed," she advised "because the body gets used to this too," implying that the baths worked through their initial shock value of heat or cold. Nothing happened, however, and Antonia returned to the midwife a couple of months later, who probably gave her a more reliable abortifacient, such as quinine. When this did not work either, and Antonia was now three months' pregnant, Antonia's sister confronted Federico and demanded that he marry Antonia. But all Federico did was to resort to a more secure form of ending the pregnancy. He took Antonia to another midwife to have an abortion, but the midwife refused and assured Antonia that maternity would surely console her for her suffering and for the scorn of her family. In any event, there was always the chance, the midwife said, that after Antonia gave birth and Federico saw his child, he would marry her. Further searching on Federico's part, however, produced a midwife who was more amenable to his plan, for a fee of 2,500 pesos.

The newspaper editor also implicated Antonia's family, speculating that Antonia's sister and brother-in-law were complicit in the crime, because they had tried to buy an abortifacient at the pharmacy. Speculating that the couple had done this in order to "cleanse their honor, which Antonia had stained," the newspaper editorialized that unfortunately honor was "never recovered with a crime." The couple had also offered to raise the child as their own, after Antonia had given birth in the *campo*—which the Palermo and Belgrano areas were then considered to be—but Antonia preferred to commit suicide rather than "live with her father's preaching and moralizing."

The third target of the newspaper was the midwife María, a Frenchwoman in her mid thirties. As the case against María unfolded, and family and fiancé dropped away as suspects, the focus shifted away from the crime to the character of the supposed criminal. She was described as evil, but it was less because of the crime she had committed than because of her nature. Abortion was actually a relatively minor crime in terms of the culpability of the pregnant woman, if honor was involved. However, when midwives were suspected of being involved, the law dealt harshly with them as with the worst of female criminals. They were often considered to be ignorant, unhygienic, evil women, who deceived doctors and overstepped their bounds, who knew women's secrets, and who dealt in life and death for money. The prosecutor charged that María had neither genuine sentiment, which was a sign of the born criminal, nor scientific expertise, which she lacked in spite of the fact that she was certified. Instead of her certification earning her greater respect, it seems as if its only effect was to increase the authorities' suspicion of her. The midwife, who had previously been merely a rustic *curandera*, had come to be seen as a natural criminal. Moreover, although she had been incorporated into the criminal classification system, she did not seem to be able to take advantage of any of the growing crop of attenuating circumstances that were accorded to other delinquents.

The first forensic doctor to conduct an exam in this case, Julián M. Fernández, judged cautiously. Although he concluded that Antonia had had an abortion by mechanical means in the third month of her pregnancy, he stopped short of incriminating the midwife. He asked that Dr. Pardo, the country's leading obstetrician, do a second examination to be sure. Pardo did and reached the contradictory conclusion that the midwife was criminally responsible. He charged that María had deliberately lied to attending doctors in order to mislead them about her patient's real condition, and criticized the doctors for believing her. "The poor state of our society, we believe, imposes on doctors the duty of investigating fully when an illness of this type appears in a midwife's house, because the possibility of a clandestine, perhaps even criminal act, cannot help but come up." María's lawyer's take on Pardo, however, was that Pardo "detested" midwives and had thrown the whole weight of the National Council of Hygiene and its "disgust and hatred of the profession of midwifery" against her.

María's lawyer argued that abortion could come about in a number of ways that did not involve a midwife. In fact, Antonia herself might have performed her own mechanical abortion. For example, she could have done it "with a speculum and a mirror, using a probe or her finger, which a woman with a short vagina can do; or she might have used a sponge." If prostitutes in Paris and Buenos Aires, who were not professional midwives, could manage to place a sponge soaked with vinegar in the neck of their own uteruses as a contraceptive, the lawyer argued, Antonia could have introduced a probe, since the sponge actually presented more problems. The lawyer also argued that a good midwife like María would have used a sponge, not a probe; and that if she had used a probe, she would not have hit the uterus, because using the probe was not difficult. "It's so easy," said María's lawyer, "that the obstetricians in Paris, Madrid, and other capitals who do abortions use any old piece of metal, and generally the thumb and index finger, taking the membrane of the egg and giving it a poke."

Pardo's insistence that María had performed an illegal abortion that had resulted in the death of her patient convinced the judge, however, and he sentenced María to six years' imprisonment in a penitentiary.

Police Tactics

By the turn of the century, the Buenos Aires Police Department was providing detailed training for its officers on how to investigate the crime of abortion, in part through the publication of a course on penal law written by a police officer, M. Mujica Farías, in the *Revista de Policía* in 1899. If they suspected a crime, the police sequestered bloody clothes, objects that might have been used, suspicious medicines and liquids, instruments, substances such as ergot and savin, probes in general, any small pieces of metal, knitting needles, syringes, or apparatuses used for injections, and any dry compressed sponges. The police were instructed to question neighbors about the woman's antecedents, activities, and conduct, and to find out about her pregnancy and the childbirth; to make inquiries among pharmacists about leeches, footbaths, and purgatives (especially important for identifying any accomplices), as well as among laundresses (especially useful as regards bloody clothing); to locate the fetus; and to arrange for an examination by a police doctor. The only procedure off-limits to the police was the physical examination of the woman herself.[45]

Sometimes judges condemned these police investigations as illegal. When the police, who had received a denunciation in 1904 from an employer that her servant had had an abortion, decided that they did not have enough evidence against the participating midwife to arrest her, they chose to enlist the help of the servant in a sting operation against the midwife.[46] The crime actually involved more women than the police at first realized. Networking with the cook of an English family, the servant had been referred to an intermediary midwife, who had agreed to introduce the servant to another midwife for a fee of 5 pesos. This second midwife, who had an Argentine title from the Medical Faculty of the University of Buenos Aires, issued in 1894, agreed to do the job with a probe for a fee of 200 pesos. After the expulsion of the fetus, which would occur at the servant's home, the midwife cautioned her patient to throw the placenta in the toilet, tearing it into pieces so that it did not block the pipe. As for the fetus and the probe, the midwife said to first put them in a trunk or some other piece of furniture that could be locked with a key, and to come back in a week's time with the items wrapped in a page from the *La Prensa* newspaper, and she would dispose of the package for an additional fee of 20 pesos.

When the police caught the servant, she had not yet fulfilled this last instruction of the midwife. Having no choice except to cooperate in the sting operation, the servant returned to the midwife's house. She paid the midwife with two police-marked 10 peso notes and left the package with the fetus and probe on the dining-room table. This was a risky business, and the midwife was afraid of the curiosity of her tenants, so she warned the servant to grab a carriage and get away from her house as quickly as possible. The servant left the house and went around the corner, where she met the policemen.

The second part of the plan began with the policemen's visit to the midwife with the excuse that a doctor needed her to assist with a birth that was happening at that very moment. The police showed her the doctor's professional card with his request. Believing the policemen's story, the midwife immediately left with them, and on the way to the police station, she conversed with them about the inconveniences that doctors and midwives experienced, being on call all the time. Entering the police station and seeing the servant, the midwife knew that she had been caught and confessed everything, though she told the completely different and probably dubious story that she had tricked the servant and had inserted an inoffensive catheter, not a probe, into her vagina, and had thus not performed any abortion.

Expressing strong sentiment against what he saw as unfair police procedure, the midwife's lawyer, Juan Antonio Argerich, pointed out that the police's first illegal maneuver lay in their planting the evidence, the fetus, the *cuerpo* of the crime, in the midwife's house. Their second illegal maneuver lay in their inducing the midwife to leave her house on a false pretext. These were "mischievous acts," which the police "took pleasure in doing, playing with hiding cadavers and other ruses." The lawyer's opinion that the police should be punished for these "macabre, shameful, and tragi-comic" practices was evidently supported by the judge in that he absolved the midwife and sentenced the aborting woman to two years' imprisonment.

So ready was the public to believe in the natural criminality of midwives that if a case came to public light, it was hard for a midwife to get a fair trial. María Baby, for example, had had a good reputation going into her trial in

1882; she was professionally certified and had been practicing in Buenos Aires long enough to have established a good reputation. But after her "pre-trial" in the newspaper, her lawyer was unable to persuade the court to consider the possibility that no crime might have been committed at all. To add to the pre-trial, the police inspector who made the initial report seemed to get caught up in matching the "lyrical-dramatic" tone set by the newspaper.

Another midwife, Susana Breuil de Conderc, described by the prosecutor as a typical Lombrosian figure of delinquency, also had difficulty getting a fair trial in 1891. She was arrested in 1881 and again in 1891. The description of her as a mercenary and her house as one big operating room was supported by the reported evidence of large flasks of human fetuses all over her house, on the chairs, table, floor, and in the wardrobe. Most of these fetuses were between one and six months in age. Supposedly, she had also flushed a good number down the toilet before the arrival of the police. "The most appropriate thing to do with her," argued the prosecutor, "is to hang the San Benito [mark of infamy] around her neck. She's an abominable monster of perversity." The judge was overly anxious to convict the midwife, perhaps because in 1884, she had returned to the court about a previous case in which she had received a negative verdict and forced the judge to hold a second trial in order to clear her name.[47] The 1881 case against her had been dismissed for lack of proof, but this had not really absolved Susana, she said, or restored her reputation. She applied for the annulment and preferably the revocation of her sentence. Her "arbitrary and scandalous" imprisonment had damaged her reputation, and she requested that she be acquitted, as should happen in any "civilized" country. The most the court agreed to, however, was that she was innocent for lack of proof. In the 1891 case, Susana was eventually absolved, but not before she had spent eight years in prison.

CONCLUSION

The issues raised in the prosecution of infanticide and abortion took medical and legal professionals into deep discussions of some of the most crucial problems of contemporary society. In contrast to the generally accepted injunction not to kill, in the case of newborns, a mother's sense of shame and dishonor could mitigate even murder. It was clear that some flesh in society, such as an infant's, did not have the same value as that of others. Furthermore, a lawyer argued in 1897, rational science demanded that the law take into account the woman's "position, her interior struggles, the motives that made her commit the crime, and the culpability of her sex itself."[48] The courts heard the cases of many domestic servants and women of all classes who were unmarried, fearful of losing their jobs and/or reputations, and generally considered weak, impressionable, and driven by the irrationality of their "maternal organs." Not only did the woman's position have to be taken into account in sentencing, but also that of the fetus and child. In the classical school's view in the late eighteenth century, the evil of the sentence for the accused had to be compared to the evil of the crime. "The crime, that is, the death of a child who ceased to exist before having known existence," Bentham argued, "could only cause feelings of commiseration for the person who, out of shame and compassion, did not want the child to grow up under such sad auspices." The criminal's sentence, on the other hand, was a "barbarous and offensive torture imposed on an unfortunate mother blinded by desperation, who [had] harmed almost no one except herself."[49] But in the late-nineteenth-century world, it was the criminal herself who became the focus of the courts and criminologists, not the crime or the punishment.

3 Social Poisons and Contagion

Although elegant and charming to some, Buenos Aires was also full of dangerous contagions, or "poisons"; it was a place that played on people's "ignorance, impotence, and vanity" and spat them out when they could not attain the well-being that they desired, Carlos Olivera wrote in 1899. World capitals at the turn of the century were often criticized like this, which was also a critique of modernity. The contrast was what disturbed, because civilization was believed to be at its summit, yet contagions flourished in Buenos Aires and had brought about a degeneration.[1]

Urban growth provided new sources of contagion, not just in stationary locales such as cemeteries, but also in emanations from the flesh. Vicious contagions lurked everywhere and could potentially affect anyone, regardless of their class or residence. Any discourse concerning foreign immigration, public health programs, and the practice of criminal investigations ended up in the arena of contagion. Residents agreed that safeguards needed to be put in place to combat the diseases of the tenements and the streets, such as tuberculosis, and curb moral contagions, such as materialism, anarchism, feminism, immorality, and crime.[2] Professionals warned, however, that no one was totally safe, because public health affected everyone. Equipped with new technologies and sensitivities to the moral dangers of the era, the judicial and penal branches of government became much more thorough at the turn of the century in their search to identify contagious elements. Government efficiency came at the expense of the invasion of perceived personal rights, however, and the idea of applying identification procedures to all groups in society especially angered the public. Many professionals became involved in the process. Lawyers checking out the contagion in dance halls; police researching contagion in criminal investigations and taking fingerprints; criminologists isolating contagion by measuring heads; medical doctors investigating contagion in hospitals; and public health doctors sniffing out the sources of

contagion in cemeteries and latrines figure among the political and professional elites seen practicing their respective professions in the city in this
chapter.

PHYSICAL CONTAGION

All the urban institutions that were proliferating with the growth in population, such as tenements, cemeteries, hospitals, jails, and houses of deposit,
were highly susceptible to physical contagion. The unique concepts of mias-
ma and contagion contributed to the period's focus on flesh, through which
miasmas passed that contained the contagions. Both miasmatic and contagion theories were seen as being progressive innovations over the theory of the
spontaneous generation of transmissible diseases. The miasmatic theory,
which was dominant during the first half of the nineteenth century, held that
poisons produced by miasmas were responsible for *all* diseases. Disease prevention simply meant removing the putrefying material that caused miasmas.
In European cities, "smells commissions" were established to locate the sites
of bad odors that indicated insalubriousness. These were usually sites where
there was rotting garbage, excrement, or decaying bodies.[3]

Medical descriptions of miasmas showed them as truly sinister. In the
1870s, Dr. Llames Massini wrote in 1915, miasmas were seen as "impalpable
beings that swarmed and spontaneously generated in the air and lived in intimate association with the atmospheric dust particles, hiding in furniture and
clothing." They infected the air, making it less mobile and elastic than ordinary air, and incubated epidemics. They were "irritating gases" that escaped
from decaying organic material or from sick organisms. They were "small
beasts that penetrated the body of patients" through the very air that they
breathed. They penetrated the body, the flesh, and effectively knocked out
weak members of society.[4] Even in 1907, doctors advised perspiring people to
stay away from sick rooms, because as their bodies cooled, their pores would
absorb the miasmas of disease. Doctors also advised fasting persons to stay
away from persons with contagious diseases, since, being weak, they would be
more vulnerable to miasmas. Healthy people were also advised not to sit
between a patient's bed and a stove, because the heat of the stove attracted
infectious emanations that would be breathed in by healthy persons.[5]

Contagion and infection were recognized as related, but their relationship
was confused. In discussions about how disease spread, there was little understanding of infection. No one at this time, Llames Massini wrote, thought
about disinfecting medical practitioners' hands, patients, or medical instru-

ments. Midwives only washed their hands if they looked dirty; the same sponge was used for all patients; unguents of olive oil, almond oil, or butter were left out and were full of flies and insects. Given the high rate of mortality in childbirth in Argentina in the second half of the nineteenth century, higher than in Europe, contagion among women giving birth in Buenos Aires was a concern. However, the acceptance of disinfection practices was delayed for some years in Argentina. When regulations about disinfection were proposed for adoption in hospitals in the 1880s and 1890s, they were considered to be an exaggeration and were rejected. With the advantage of hindsight, Llames Massini observed in 1915, moreover, that these regulations seemed extremely deficient.[6]

Llames Massini attributed the Argentine reluctance to adopt disinfection practices to French influence. Almost all the professors and doctors in the medical faculty at the University of Buenos Aires belonged to the French school, Llames Massini explained, so it was not surprising that Argentina did not adopt the prophylactic innovations introduced by Ignaz Philipp Semmelweis in Viennese maternity wards, especially as he was the object of scorn and irony on the part of his contemporaries, particularly of the French. Then Louis Pasteur, who disproved the theory of spontaneous generation, advanced the germ theory of infection in 1878. In 1879, Pasteur presented the agent that caused puerperal fever, a major cause of death among women giving birth, to the Academy of Medicine of Paris. Not until 1881, however, was separation of the sick put together with knowledge about disinfection.[7] Hygienists in Europe generally embraced Pasteur's germ theory, and bacteriology was gradually adopted in the 1880s and 1890s. Doctors abandoned the miasmatic theory of infection with reluctance, though, and Pasteur himself was a member of a "smells commission" in Paris set up by the minister of agriculture in 1880. The theory invited belief because it provided a relatively easy method to win the fight against disease by getting rid of these sites.[8]

Argentine medical practices reflected this reluctance and continued to ascribe illness to miasmas. Puerperal fever, the major cause of the high death rates at the Women's Hospital in Buenos Aires, continued to be associated with miasmas, which new mothers were said to exhale. This was partly because "*puerperas* gathered in themselves a great potency of atmospheric foulness," according to the Argentine doctor Alfredo Parodi in a talk to the Asociación Médica Bonaerense in 1878, and partly because the city's maternity wards also functioned as houses of correction, according to the Argentine hygienist Emilio R. Coni.[9]

Sleuthing for Contagions

Between the 1880s and the turn of the century, the Argentine public hygienist Eduardo Wilde, a prolific author, was an especially vigilant sleuth in the
search for the sources of organic vapors that contained organisms of "infinite
subtlety that formed algoids, fungoids, spores, or cells that multiplied rapidly"
and caused disease. The gases from decomposing bodies, latrines, and sewers,
for example, promoted the absorption and spread of disease. Because of this
decomposition, Buenos Aires's streets, houses, and public buildings were
completely capable of generating epidemics, Wilde wrote. Crowded tenements exuded bad air in the city. The waste from human and animal flesh literally flowed in the streets, and decomposition in the meatpacking district, in
latrines, in sewers, and in cemeteries produced poisonous gases that interfered with normal breathing. Epidemics spread through putrefaction, especially when decaying material was kept in dark, airless places. Gases escaping
from latrines spread outward to infect houses and public buildings. All the
waste from houses, streets, and so on, added a large amount of organic material to the soil and subsoil of Buenos Aires and contaminated the water. Like
people with dissolute habits and poor diets, such as fish eaters, people in cities
produced more girl babies, verifying the nineteenth-century city's poor
hygiene, Wilde averred.[10]

All this investigation took Wilde into the most intimate areas of homes and
personal lives. Often this offended personal rights and privacy, especially
because one of the most important points of Wilde's message was that while
public hygienists and public institutions had a responsibility for providing
mechanisms to control disease and pollution, just as important was the admo-
nition that individuals themselves were responsible for controlling their own
flesh. Control included the proper disposal of the "waste" of human flesh,
including cadavers, feces, and urine.

Wilde acknowledged that the equation of human remains with liquid and
solid waste shocked people, but he insisted that the danger of cadavers was on
a par with other kinds of rubbish that had to be removed or destroyed, and
that people should become accustomed to thinking in this way about cadavers.[11] The issue for public hygienists was what to do with human bodies.
Wilde, although he opposed embalming on the seemingly subjective grounds
that mummies were repugnant to look at, justified his opposition to cremation
on grounds of health. Cremation took on average a long six hours and produced deleterious gases, he wrote; moreover, it was "sad" and made forensic
examination of the body impossible. Burial also posed problems. The custom
of burial at home or in the grounds, patios, and vaults of churches was a threat

to health because of the infectious gases that were produced by the decomposing bodies. Cadavers, which were an "element of disease," should be kept out of sight "in honor of our civilization," Wilde wrote.[12]

For these reasons, Wilde argued, cemeteries should be located outside city centers. The working-class Chacarita cemetery was thus well situated, but the elite Recoleta cemetery, located near the city center, polluted the city through both its living and dead clients. Fancy caskets, clothing, and family burial vaults retarded decomposition. An unhealthy environment surrounded visitors to Recoleta, there to see the "repugnant spectacle" of monuments to the dead. The force of gases emanating from decaying bodies combined with the humidity and cracked the walls, allowing poisonous gases to escape. Neither the rich nor the Church, Wilde wrote, should be allowed to harm public health like this, and he recommended moving all urban cemeteries out of the city, with trees, hills, and rivers in between acting as buffers separating the living from the dead.[13]

The length of the decomposition process depended on the nature of the flesh of the cadaver. Each "constituency" in a cemetery had its own term. Women, for example, decomposed more rapidly than men, because in general they had "soft flesh." Fat people also decomposed quickly, as did lymphatics. People who had died violent deaths preceded by great pain also had bodies that decomposed quickly, as did people who had had putrid diseases like typhoid fever, yellow fever, puerperal fever, measles, gangrene, and so on. The bodies of bilious, nervous, and thin people, on the other hand, took longer. Certain weather events also affected decomposition. Storms accelerated the decomposition of bodies, because the air was loaded with electricity, while certain liquids delayed decomposition, such as latrine water, which was known to delay the decomposition of victims of infanticide.[14] The inability to know how long the process of decomposition took, and thus whether noxious gases were still present, meant that the maximum precautions had to be taken to keep the living and the dead separate.

Separation was also crucial in the treatment of another form of human waste, namely, excrement. Wilde recommended a proactive approach, involving the separation of solids and liquids, and drew an analogy between the city and the human body. Cities were like people, he wrote, in that they had arteries and veins. The arterial system was really a network of tubes for the provision of water, while the blood system was the network of tubes for getting rid of waste. Cities, like bodies, were provided with more or less pure water for their physiological functions. Later, this water, full of damaging products, was thrown away and expelled by means of sewers outside the city, to mix with natural water and be used for irrigation. Then it evaporated into the air, like blood to the lungs, and fell as rain on the ground. The same happened with blood; it exited pure, refreshed from the heart, which was the driving machinery for filtering water. Blood circulated by means of the arteries to the whole organism, nourished the tissues, and afterward released through them the liquids of excretion. The blood that escaped through this metamorphosis went to the lungs to load itself up again with the vital elements. Then it entered the arteries again to be redistributed and fulfill its important functions.[15]

To reduce the potential harm from the decomposition of urine and feces, separation was necessary. When separated, Wilde explained, this material did not putrefy as quickly, so that it could be left in the house longer. Also, the liquid separated from the solid could be thrown into the sewer. Wilde posed two methods of separation of human excrement. In the first, the person himself was responsible for the separation. As unhygienic and absurd as this might sound, Wilde suggested that at the moment of the emission of urine and feces, one manually separate the two substances. Even though admitting that this method was fraught with difficulty and offended personal modesty, Wilde still recommended it, at least as an ideal. The problem was that most likely the individual's main thought at the moment of defecation was not about the advantages of manual separation to public health. Voluntary, premeditated separation by the defecator, making sure that the excrement fell in one place and the urine in another, Wilde accepted, required doing things contrary to decency and good manners, which was why in the end this method was unworkable. Although the body expelled these two substances via two distinct paths and the two materials were found in totally different compartments in the body, the proximity of the organs through which emission occurred presented difficulties in adopting the position or practicing the operation that was needed to effect the division. Nature apparently did not consider personal waste management to be as high a priority as Wilde did.[16] Abandoning the idea of separation before the material went into the receptacle, Wilde opted for separation in the receptacle itself through filtration, straining, or decanting.

Regardless of the system used in separation, Wilde wrote, all toilet receptacles were sources of infection, which was why he was critical of the "pernicious" new custom of putting them in bathrooms. The bathroom, which should be a "model of cleanliness and pleasantness," was turned into an insalubrious place when toilets were placed there, with their permanent cloud of fetid gases. Moreover, these gases entered other rooms and made the atmosphere there noxious. True, people could use disinfectants to absorb the gases; the best was charcoal, but poorer families used ashes. The mixture formed a paste, which in countries such as Holland and Belgium was sold as fertilizer by latrine-cleaning companies. Rather than increasing the number of sources of infection, that is, toilet depositories, and putting them indoors, Wilde recommended reducing them. He also recommended that the size of the depositories be reduced, or that the depositories be done away with entirely and sewers used instead. All one had to do was to look at the endemic nature of dysentery in the military and the classic common ditch latrine to make the connection between fetid gases, contagion, and disease.[17]

No subject was out of reach to public hygienists or lacked its own seriousness, even toilet etiquette. After all, what was the use of a good system of toilets if people used them incorrectly. Wilde therefore engaged in a lengthy discussion of the human physique as it related to the proper positioning of the body in the latrine. Toilet seats should be made in such a way, he wrote, that people did not have to use "uncomfortable maneuvers and indecorous acts" in order to avoid dirtying the surface nearby. There were some very comfortable models available, made of marble, porcelain, or wood, but people preferred to squat over the hole and avoid the seat. Wilde lamented that hygienists' attempts to make people use latrines the proper way were in vain. They even sometimes used them for romantic trysts, and they were careless. Especially when using public toilets in cafes, public offices, and so on, people did not make use of the seats as such, because the surface was not clean, and also because it was the "habit of the immense majority" not to use them this way, since most people defecated while squatting. Medically speaking, Wilde argued, squatting was a good practice and should not be considered "crazy," because there was less force needed, and therefore less danger of causing hemorrhoids. Concluding that it was better to accept people's habits, Wilde recommended redesigning the openings of latrines to conform to popular customs.[18]

In the new age of megacities, the flesh as waste itself—as cadaver, and as a producer of waste in the form of urine and feces—leveled the playing field for public health. Cities allowed and even encouraged the mixing of elements that ought to be kept separated. This unavoidable mixing extended all the way from the mixing of cadavers and the living, feces and urine, and clean water and dirty water to the mixing of socioeconomic classes. The inhabitants of the city center, the aristocrats, thought that they were living hygienically and imagined that they were free from contamination and bad influences because they could avoid the poorer neighborhoods and the slaughterhouse and meat-processing districts, Wilde wrote. But they forgot that even if they did not go

there, these places came to them via the atmosphere. When they opened their
windows to the night air, they let in masses of harmful gases from cemeteries
and so on. And these were gases generated by all social categories. At any
moment in cities, day or night, Wilde wrote, there were latrines in use, which,
when their valves were opened, let gases pass into the air. The waste of rich
and poor mingled in the air, water, and streets, as if the outlying neighborhoods wanted to take revenge for being scorned by the elite, "hurling into the
windows of rich houses bad odors and disease." The central neighborhoods—
aristocratic, rich, luxurious, and cleaner than other areas—could not be
healthy unless public health became a priority. The outskirts needed a pru-
dent program of public hygiene that would build gardens, guarantee clean
streets, and construct decent housing. For their own well-being, the elite had
to take care of the living conditions of the poor, because the health of the city
was the result of many factors and not a product of only one section, street, or
neighborhood.[19]

Medical columns in popular magazines in 1906 contained warnings about
unhygienic practices such as kissing religious statues in churches and using
the telephone. On the other hand, it was clear that the public enjoyed laugh-
ing at hygienists' exaggerated expectations that people could be persuaded to
police their personal habits and mocked their confidence in new theories. A
1906 cartoon series called "The Model Street" featured various artistic but
ridiculous designs for sidewalk spittoons and even proposed a spittoon for
dogs. Affecting alarm, the author suggested absorbing "homicidal dust" by tar-
ring sidewalks, renovating the atmosphere with oxygen balloons, providing
antiseptic depositories along the streets for handwashing and for disinfecting
money, and moving water closets underground.[20]

MORAL CONTAGION

Named and described in the early eighteenth century, moral contagion posited a three-step process of, first, the escape of vapors through the pores of the
skin; then the mingling of these vapors in the air; and, finally, people's inhala-
tion of one another's vapors. The physical and the moral complemented each
other. A condition such as "nervous contagion," for example, was regularly
listed in typologies of contagious diseases such as typhoid fever, yellow fever,
and plague, and could explain how contagious convulsions occurred in
cemeteries, or how abnormal nervous conditions were transmitted that caused
crime.[21] In 1887, for example, Dr. Lucas Ayarragaray described tuberculosis as
the "material expression of the decadence of the psychic being." Mental con-

tagion combined with the physical contagions found in filthy streets, inadequate sewers, infectious *conventillos,* and cemeteries to produce tuberculosis, syphilis, madness, and puerperal fever. Public health experts also argued in favor of including both physical and moral health components in their reports.[22]

In the nineteenth century, the conceptualization of social phenomena as mental or moral contagions grew. The concept was especially developed in France, and Argentines borrowed and adapted heavily from the French.[23] Two major nineteenth-century French formulations of moral contagion, by Prosper Lucas in his thesis of 1833 and by Eugène Bouchut in 1857, were frequently cited in Argentine literature and criminal cases. The basis of moral contagion, according to both Lucas and Bouchut, was what Lucas called "example" and Bouchut called "imitation." Heightened nervous vibrations in one individual could set up a corresponding pattern in other individuals in proximity. Labor strikes, anarchist demonstrations, and so on were interpreted as outbreaks of moral contagion. Some individuals had a natural immunity to contagious mental and nervous diseases, but many people succumbed, which allowed the introduction of new anxieties into society.[24]

Buenos Aires's size, congestion, and cosmopolitan population disposed vulnerable people to disease, who in turn provided convenient avenues for the penetration of moral contagion into Buenos Aires. As public health officials refined their definition of contagion, they found that the phenomenon had permeated much of society. Evidence of moral contagion was found in alcoholism and suicide; in undesirable behavior and the ideas of immigrants and anarchists; and in the "unnatural" women, feminists, infanticidal mothers, and midwives discussed in chapters 1 and 2. As with physical contagion, it was impossible to avoid moral contagion, and rich and poor alike succumbed to contagions circulating in the streets and public buildings. Public institutions such as the Women's Hospital, the Foundling Home, the Spiritual House, the Good Shepherd, and jails and penitentiaries were rife with moral contagion. The jails were filled with "gangrenous members of society who should be *extirpated* forever," the Argentine criminologist Eusebio Gómez warned in 1906. Prison merely functioned as a "hothouse" for their poisonous germs, which "overflow[ed] like a sewer" into society. Supporters of capital punishment rather than long penitentiary sentences pointed to the danger of contagion as one reason. Private homes were also subject to moral contagion — from outsiders such as maids and midwives, who might introduce ignorance and bad habits into the home; from ideas in circulation such as skepticism and materialism; from newspapers; and from literature that excited the passions. Children who had absorbed these "infectious germs" had to go through a moral disinfection process before being brought together with healthy children.[25]

Degenerates, prostitutes, repeat offenders, sexual deviants, and even celibates—all those perceived as living a *mala vida*—were seen as significant sources of moral contagion, and elimination of such pathological behavior, which morally infected society, was an important aspect of fighting crime. The idea that mental contagions were multiplying, forming concentric circles around the population, led to vigorous and drastic attempts to improve the mental health of cities. With contagions present in society, José Ingeneiros wrote in 1902, people with degenerative "terrain," regardless of whether it was innate or acquired, were predisposed to absorb these contagions, these abnormal ideas and behavior. Moral contagion's influence on crime was such, Dr. Luis María Drago suggested in 1921, that the advance of progress was contradictorily being accompanied by concentric movements creating entire families of assassins and other miscreants. Such epidemics were bound to nullify the strength of the nation. This tendency depended on social elements, rather than on the anthropological factor of inheritance promoted by the Lombrosian School as responsible for crime. Still, the introduction of the theory of atavism as an explanation for criminality made contagion even more of a concern. Contagion had to be controlled because it promoted degenerative characteristics in the population that would be passed on to future generations. An alcoholic today might produce an epileptic or criminal child tomorrow.[26]

Morality in the Flesh

In July 1890, moral contagion totally undid the prosperity of two important Argentine families, one from good Argentine ranch-owning stock and traditional values, and the other from Italy, accused of materialism and loose morals.[27] The case went to court soon after a deeply unsettling revolution had occurred in Argentina. Unfettered economic expansion had led first to financial and then to social and political disaster, culminating in July 1890 in a revolution against the government of President Miguel Juárez Celman (1886–90). Argentines had been living free of major military conflict for only about a decade; and the Rosas era and the civil and foreign wars that followed it would have still been vivid memories for them. It was no surprise that the July revolution added anxieties to those already assembled. For people facing financial ruin as a result of the crisis, it was a frightening time. The inability in 1889 of Baring Brothers Bank of London, which had been funding Argentine development with British money, to secure new loans, triggered an interruption of British investment. Export earnings fell, land lost half its value, public employees were discharged, general unemployment grew, and wages fell.

The economic crisis hit people like the protagonists in this criminal case hard. Both families were important *estancia* owners at Lobos in the province of Buenos Aires. Lucio Cascallares Paz's family was an old and respected one, which included a judge, a military officer, and local officials. María Bidone's family were immigrants from Italy who owned real estate and a business in Buenos Aires. This case did nothing to improve Argentina's souring love affair with European immigrants, who were increasingly suspected of importing socialism and anarchism. It also fed into concern with other social problems—the moral contagions of materialism, new money, dissimulation, and abortion.

This story played out in court along two conflicting lines. First, it was a story of new money and of a young woman corrupting old money, native values, and a sound family. Second, it was the story of a young man taking advantage of this woman. The story line that is more relevant here is the first one, because it was given credibility in the court case. Briefly, the landowner Lucio Cascallares Paz, aged twenty-six, broke off his engagement to the Italo-Argentine María Bidone, aged sixteen. When María became pregnant, Lucio responded by arranging an abortion for her, not marriage. Since he had twice avoided signing a nuptial agreement, one might suppose that he had never intended to marry María, and that her pregnancy posed a real threat to his plans. María's father tried to blackmail Lucio, and when this failed, he accused Lucio and the attending midwife of abortion. The case reached scandalous proportions. Both Lucio and the midwife were eventually absolved, but not before he had spent three years in prison and she had spent eight.

In 1885, Bidone had opened a restaurant/dancehall called the Belvedere in the Recoleta area of Buenos Aires, near the Naval School, to the men of which it especially catered—a business that would not have been seen as decent by established elite families. As a female and as a nervous person, María was susceptible to the corruption of the place and easily affected by its moral contagion. Moreover, Bidone had traveled to Brazil for several months on business at a crucial time in his daughter's life, leaving her alone with a young female relative, who did not keep watch over her and allowed her to get involved with Lucio. It even seemed as if Bidone himself had actually set his daughter up to seduce Lucio, allowing her to stay with him at his ranch in Lobos for a long period of time to recover from her mother's death. This combination of a supposedly corrupt father and questionable surroundings transmitted a set of evil miasmas to the daughter. As to the midwife, she was, by nature of her profession, a source of moral contagion and culpable.

In 1888, the Bidone family moved to the Belvedere, where, Lucio's lawyer argued, María had "absorbed the vapors, the deleterious miasmas, emitted by the 'low life' that hung out there." A court diagram of the living quarters at the restaurant revealed how easy it had been for María to have illicit trysts with the restaurant's waiters and customers, as well as her betrothed. A witness testified that one day her father had surprised her shut in the latrine with a waiter. A midwife who had examined her said that María's vagina was as large as that of a woman who had been married for ten years.

Into this miasmatic scene walked Lucio, presented by his lawyer as straight from the innocence of the pampas, "oblivious of the malice that civilized centers create[d]." He was in Buenos Aires administering his "worthy" rural interests when he met María, from a family with less worthy business interests. Lucio's "simple soul" was fascinated by María, and he thought only of marriage and a family. In a poetic letter to María, Lucio declared his intention to marry her. She responded with frank, spicy words of "blind, mad, delirious" love; she wanted to enjoy him "like a mosquito." She apologized for her lack of Spanish, but her message scarcely needed a translator. The opposing lawyer compared her letters to the writings of Émile Zola, citing one in which she told Lucio to "give her affections to the bird [*al uchelo*]," that is, Lucio's penis. Instead of being content to snare a lesser man, Lucio's lawyer argued, María had gone after a man with an illustrious surname and fortune, seduced him, and tricked him into taking responsibility for an abortion. The judge himself was so convinced of María's perversity that he argued that her story's simplicity and naturalness indicated that it must have been an invention or a script that she had learned in order to mislead the court, and that she was only simulating innocence and purity.

María's father was also accused of dissimulation. Bidone had launched his accusation against Lucio, the latter's lawyer argued, with "cynicism and a show of false honor." Fake honor, fake modesty, cynicism about revered values, the simulation of sentiment—all this was bad and a sign of the changing times in Argentina in an age that had been ushered in with an alluvial immigration of materialists and utilitarians. Apparently, Bidone had not opposed Lucio and María's relationship at the Belvedere, or later on at a house on Montevideo Street. And then when Lucio balked twice at signing the preliminary civil papers so that they could be married, Bidone began to press in other ways. He chose a residence for the future couple and told Lucio to put his own name plate on the door, which Lucio did, although, feeling uncomfortable about this, he later took it down. Bidone indicated to Lucio that the doors of the Bidone home were always open to him, even if María was there alone. Thus, the links between the two families had been established, only to be broken by Lucio once María's pregnancy became known. Lucio had enjoyed his conquest, however, Bidone charged; the "letch" and "libertine" had exhibited his triumph at a public bar in the form of a bloody piece of clothing with María's initials on it. In a desperate last attempt to absolve himself from guilt, Lucio disclosed to María that he was a hermaphrodite and therefore could not have impregnated her. Not succeeding in getting his daughter married to the important Cascallares Paz family, Bidone demanded an indemnification payment of 30,000 pesos from Lucio. When Lucio refused to pay, Bidone dropped his demand first to 20,000 pesos and then to 10,000. Lucio's act of seduction had diminished Bidone's "capital," his *honrada* (honorable) family, and the future of his children.

Bidone attempted to establish equal honor for his family to compete with Lucio's family honor by placing his daughter in the correctional of the Good Shepherd, which he described as a place in which María would be physically isolated in order to stop the gossip, to frighten or coerce her into confessing, thus supporting his case against Lucio, retrieving his honor, and punishing her.[28] Supposedly, he sent her there because she had fought with her new stepmother. His claim that María had chosen to remain in the Good Shepherd until her case was decided, so that she could leave with her honor restored, was a standard explanation of the purpose of such institutions. A newspaper article on the case speculated that after leaving the correctional, María would in fact become a nun. Her stay at the Good Shepherd lasted seven months. Bidone was criticized for putting his daughter there together with hardened criminals. The correctional was a breeding ground for nervous diseases, and even madness, which science had shown was contagious. Seven months in such a poisonous atmosphere, observers said, "asphyxiate[d] noble sentiments and [taught] lessons of perversion."[29] Bidone wanted her there, however, so that she would have the "chance to appreciate the immensity of her misfortune." When she continued to be kept there, even though she had confessed, she smuggled out a note to a friend begging him to get her out, saying that she would die of "martyrdom."

When the judge, Eduardo French, absolved both Lucio and the midwife, Bidone appealed. The new lawyer, Jorge Argerich, presented an interesting commentary on immigrant and native society. Buenos Aires was a place where only a few people shone because of their intrinsic merits, he argued, and many because they naturally gravitated toward money. An even greater number of people united the two factors, however, because of the accidents of cosmopolitanism and immigration. Even though María was very far from being a "star of first magnitude" in the middle of the "variegated heaven" of *porteño* (Buenos Aires) society, she had doubtless been educated according to strict principles of moral virtue. That is, Argerich explained, sarcastically passing judgment on the entire society, "with principles that are compatible with our Latin decadence," and with her damaging social and moral environment. Perhaps she had made her first mistake too early, but that was just human frailty. The lineage question, which was supposedly a reason for Lucio breaking his commitment to María, was a "very relative concept in a mobile society like Argentina, where only personal abilities were important and where men of ancient families who did not have them were left behind." Besides, it had been suggested that the Bidones were actually wealthier than Lucio. Lineage, however, did count for something. Argerich argued that although "deceit was hateful and repulsive in all forms," it was worse when practiced by people of "illustrious lineage."[30]

FOREIGN CONTAGION

The torrent of immigration to Argentina, especially from Latin countries, was seen as an important source of contagion. In proportions relatively greater and more rapid than in the case of the United States, Argentina had come to be a "crossroads of nations." At times in the late nineteenth century, as much as 60 percent of the population of Buenos Aires was foreign-born, a population, it was noted with alarm, that remained unidentified in any systematic way. Buenos Aires had become the home, temporary or permanent, of Italians, Spanish, French, Germans, British, "Turks," Russians, and various Latin Americans, among others. Professionals and politicians worried in the late 1890s about the "brusque incorporation of great masses of [people] who emigrate[d] from all latitudes" to Argentina.[31] This marked a change from earlier in the century, when the Argentine statesmen Juan Bautista Alberdi and Domingo Faustino Sarmiento had vigorously promoted European immigration. By the late nineteenth century, however, observers were attributing rising crime rates to immigrants and accusing them of introducing the less desirable characteristics of the Latin races into the population, failing to adapt to Argentine customs, and irretrievably altering Argentine identity.

According to late-nineteenth-century criminologists, the immigrant and foreign population in the world's capital cities was more delinquent and thus bred more contagions than the local population. Partially, it was urbanization itself that increased the likelihood of the immigrant becoming a delinquent. A delinquent immigrating to a city, Cornelio Moyano Gacitúa argued in 1899, was like a sick person who goes to an unhealthy place, that is, his sickness increased.[32] Although most immigrants belonged to the vigorous element of the population, many were like evil "germs" (*germenes viciosos*) trying to "take root in a fertile land in order to poison the surrounding atmosphere." The Argentine judicial system was to blame, too, jurists charged, because it was too lenient. The foreign criminal took advantage of this and planned to commit his crime on Argentine soil, confident of impunity or a light sentence. Professionals and politicians lamented the "degenerates and criminals"—the "dregs"—that Europe exported to Argentina, bringing disorder and crime with them, Dr. Juan Ramón Fernández wrote in 1898. Anarchosocialists, who were criticized for contaminating the minds of the youth and workers of Buenos Aires, were included in this group. The city's crime statistics, including the large number of repeat offenders, indicated to many observers that Buenos Aires was a unique center of delinquency, fed by "Europe, which sends Argentina armies of professional criminals," Ernesto Quesada and Fernández wrote at the turn of the century. Immigrants' feverish efforts to get rich quickly also contributed to criminality. The foreign immigrant was like a "new organism," consumed by ambition and the ferocious pursuit of progress.[33] Too preoccupied with enriching themselves to adapt to their new country, immigrants became alienated. Race, which is discussed at greater length in chapter 5, was also a contributing factor. According to Italian criminologists of the early twentieth century, such as Cesare Lombroso, Giuseppe Sergi, and Angelo Zuccarelli, the Latin "race" was biologically and hereditarily more apt to commit bloody crimes because of its organic and moral decadence. Buenos Aires's institutions necessarily reflected this large foreign population. Italians and Spaniards made up the majority of the immigration. The children in the Foundling Home at the turn of the century, for example, were 45 percent Italian, 18 percent Spanish, 19 percent miscellaneous foreign, and 18 percent Argentine—that is, over 80 percent foreign.[34] Latin populations, of course, dominated in Argentina, especially Italians and Spaniards. As often as the Italians were denigrated, they were also often held up as preferable to Spanish immigrants. Comparing the two was like comparing a "free worker to a servile one," the Argentine jurist Roberto J. Bunge declared in 1900. Italian immigrants, he wrote, adapted more quickly, were hardworking, sober in the extreme, and almost avaricious. On the other hand, they lived miserably in Argentina, saving money for a future back in Italy. They had no aspirations, did not know how to progress up the social ladder, and were ignorant of the advantages of comfort. To avoid problems with the more questionable Italian groups, such as the Neapolitans, Calabrians, and Sicilians, who were more susceptible to the "poisoning life" of Buenos Aires, he recommended that they be removed from the city and relocated in provinces such as Misiones, Tucumán, and Salta, which would provide them with an environment similar to Italy.[35] Even though the ascription of greater criminal tendencies to the Latin races was no means wholly accepted, the thesis was generally diffused throughout the Western world. Clearly, observers believed that the large number of foreigners threatened the stability of Buenos Aires.

Immigrants, who were prone to physical contagion because they were in transit, were highly effective vectors of disease. They often arrived in Buenos Aires carrying germs or, being weak from hard travel, were especially susceptible to germs circulating in the city. The fact that immigrants were often rootless and uncommitted to Argentina, Fernández argued in 1899, also made them a threat to the moral health of the nation by "absorbing" Argentine ethnicity and spreading dangerous political ideas.[36]

AN INTERNATIONAL MURDER

A famous murder case in 1894 involving two Frenchmen (referred to with Spanish first names in the records) displayed another type of moral contagion, cold-blooded self-interest. Raúl Tremblié slit the throat of his fellow countryman Francisco Farbos, cut up the body, bagged the parts separately, deposited the sacks in different parts of Buenos Aires, making clever use of the many construction sites in the growing city, and disappeared.[37] This bloody, coldly calculated crime, committed by a Latin motivated by greed, seemed to justify extremist proposals at the turn of the century by criminologists such as the Italian Giuseppe Sergi for the castration or elimination of criminals. Tremblié had been operating a contraband trade in copper money, bringing Argentine coins over to France, for several years prior to 1894. Since French gold was strong in Argentina, and all of South America, Tremblié was able to buy 300 gold francs' worth of Argentine currency for only 100 gold francs. He simply exchanged the French gold in Buenos Aires for the Argentine copper coins, which he then took to France in false-bottomed trunks and sold to counterfeiters. In the early 1890s, while sitting at a café in Burdeos, Tremblié had related the story of his lucrative trade to Farbos, apparently thus enticing Farbos to suggest that the two of them form a partnership, to which Tremblié agreed. In 1894, Farbos arrived in Buenos Aires carrying 8,000 francs, went to meet Tremblié in his room on Calle Cangallo, and was not seen again alive, or in one piece.[38]

The trunk of Farbos's body turned up first, in a sack at the work site of a market going up in Calle Montevideo. Some passersby had been attracted to investigate because of the size of the bundle and its fetid smell. The blood was minimal, since the body had been packed with salt and sawdust, cushions, and rags. A policeman walking his beat in a section of the Avenida de Mayo found the next installment of the body, the arms and legs. Still a construction site, the avenue, which was to be inaugurated in July, had few sidewalks or buildings because the gas company was still laying pipes. Finally, a month later, the long-awaited head of the body appeared on May 16 on some vacant land at the port near South Dock on the River Plate. It had been found by children looking for birds' nests in the marshes in what is today called an "ecological reserve."[39]

The police found themselves with an unidentified body and an obvious murder and no suspect. But with diligent investigative work, they managed to identify the body, came to suspect Tremblié, and gathered enough evidence against him to telegraph the French police to arrest him when he disembarked at Dunkirk. To facilitate Tremblié's trial, the French judges requested that the principal witnesses and professionals, such as the judge and the doctors who had performed the autopsy and chemical analysis, be brought over to France from Buenos Aires to testify in the case, at a cost to the French of between 3,000 and 4,000 francs.[40] In the end, Tremblié received the death penalty, but he was later pardoned by the president of France. The one good thing to come out of this horrendous case were the French court's compliments to Argentine police and judicial work. Since Europeans usually focused on the deficiencies of South American science and civilization, this was quite a coup.

The police work in the Tremblié case attracted attention because of the massiveness of the investigation and because the police had really started with nothing, not even all the parts of the corpus delicti. Upon discovery of the trunk of Farbos's body, the investigating judge, Servando Gallegos, ordered a systematic questioning of the relevant sectors of the city's population. Because the weight of the sack with the torso would have required the use of a cart, Gallegos included three hundred cart drivers in the questioning. He also included the owners and occupants of hotels, brothels, cafés, and restaurants. In addition, the French lawyer and *Figaro* journalist Albert Bataille, who was openly complimentary about the job done by the Buenos Aires police, reported that the Argentine judge had ordered a general house-to-house registration of some 60,000 city inhabitants, carried out by 3,000 policemen, who had also searched all the drains and latrines in the city while conducting their registration. This was quite a feat, as Bataille pointed out, since Buenos Aires extended over an area more than twice the size of Paris.[41] The Argentine government also offered a reward of 25,000 gold pesos for recovery of the head.

The high commitment of police resources did not end there. At the autopsy office, the trunk and limbs of the body were washed; unusual features were noted, like the smallness of the feet; and the parts were weighed. When the head was found, it was taken to the anthropometric office, where it was washed by a police doctor, Agustín J. Drago, and photographed. Drago added something new, however, to his usual procedure. He commissioned a sculptor to make a plaster cast of the head and then had it painted. This model was put on display at the anthropometric office, along with other evidence from the crime scene, such as two monogrammed handkerchiefs, in what he called a small "museum of the crime." The model of the head would presumably have been easier to view than the actual head, which all the inhabitants of Argentina, reportedly, were also invited by a police order to examine. Photographs and descriptions of the head and of the items found in the sacks were published all over Buenos Aires. More than a thousand people came forward with information for the police about the body's identity. The members of special groups like prostitutes, pimps, hairdressers, and barbers were required to file by the head to see if anyone could identify it. In the end, a fellow Frenchman recognized Farbos's photograph in a newspaper and confirmed his identification at the police department's exhibit.[42]

THE MODERN CONCEPT OF IDENTIFICATION

Modern identification theory and techniques that observed the flesh with intensity, measured and photographed it, and tested it with heat and cold met strong professional and popular resistance. Measurements of body flesh used in the Farbos/Tremblié case constituted a new approach to crime solving, though they were far from being universally accepted. Argentine scientists had been in on the debate over the Bertillon system of identification based on anthropometric measurements since its first use in France in 1882. In 1886, Samuel Gache, a skeptical Argentinian delegate, took on the French criminologist Alphonse Bertillon at a congress in Rome, where the latter had demonstrated his osteometry instruments and exhibited photos of delinquents whom he had measured. After Bertillon's talk, Gache asked Bertillon to take his (Gache's) measurements, assuring the nice maestro that I [Gache] was a recalcitrant recidivist of moral crimes. He smiled at my pretensions, but agreed. I hoped that he would at least declare me a psychopath, but he told me that I was healthy in body and mind. So I consoled myself by thinking that half of humanity suffers from my illness—of moral crime—and that my crimes do not figure among those punished by the penal codes of modern societies, since they are more perversions of conscience. Fifty percent of men are psychopaths, or suffer from neurosis.[43]

Gache's mockery of Bertillon's system was motivated, a fellow conference participant explained, by his suspicion of positivism. This was unfounded though, according to the participant, because *bertillonage* was strictly a mechanical system and had nothing to do with positivism. The same participant objected to Gache's challenges to Bertillon, saying that Bertillon was not so foolish as to immediately declare someone a criminal on the basis of his physiology. Rather, a great deal of information went into such a judgment.[44] Once again, there was little agreement in the search for a reliable universal system of identification of criminals, except for the fact that such a system was desperately needed. The flesh could fool.

In accordance with this newest method of identification, however, the Buenos Aires police department created an anthropometric office for the city in 1889. This was the first office to be established in all of Latin America, and even predated this innovation in much of the "civilized" world. Only France, England, and the United States had a few years earlier established such offices.[45] The anthropometric office of Buenos Aires, using Bertillon's system, performed well in the Farbos/Tremblié case, measuring, weighing, modeling, and photographing the victim. The office had been established at the initiative of Alberto Capdevila, the chief of police, and Dr. Agustín Drago, who became the office's first director, to address the problem of the city's growing population and increasing crime rate and recidivism. Drago had been commissioned by the police department to study Bertillon's system of anthropometry when he visited Paris in 1887, in preparation for establishing the system in Buenos Aires. Anthropometry went far beyond the registers of people under suspicion, on trial, or convicted as criminals, the other means used by police and magistrates to combat crime.[46]

While Capdevila and Drago were enthusiastic about the office, many people were skeptical. First, the office had been created by a police "order of the day," which started it out on a weak footing in the view of one of the period's chief magistrates, Ernesto Quesada, writing in 1897. A law, an executive decree, or a ministerial resolution, he argued, would have given the office a firmer base, although ideally it should have been placed solely under the judiciary. Second, the police order that created the anthropometric office was itself unclear about when and to whom its methods could be applied. The issue was whether the anthropometric office was an internal part of the police administration, an independent department, or an auxiliary office of the courts under judicial jurisdiction. According to the order, police precincts were obligated to send the day's detainees and prisoners to the office for measuring and photographing. At the same time, however, the office suppos- edly could not proceed to identify these people without a judge's authoriza- tion; that is, although the office was under police jurisdiction, the judges and courts also had partial jurisdiction over it. The order further blurred the pic- ture when it permitted the application of anthropometric techniques only on conviction. Plus, the records could be destroyed if requested by the criminal and approved by the judge. In cases of acquittal, even if the acquittal was merely for lack of proof, records were destroyed. To clear up the confusion and establish its right to jurisdiction, the Buenos Aires police department requested the court of appeals in September 1889 to obligate judges to coop- erate with the office's full program of measuring detainees and prisoners. This is where the third issue erupted, because the court held that *bertillonage* involved the mistreatment of people under prosecution. Measuring and pho- tographing people were intrusive acts, the court argued, and were similar to calumny and slander in that they damaged a person's reputation. Thus, judges should not be required to authorize anthropometric techniques. The office's effectiveness was clearly problematic from its inception.[47]

The undermining of the office at this high level, along with steady chal- lenges and noncompliance, led to a reduction in the office's importance, even among certain elements of the police department itself. The police department was, however, critical of itself in this regard. In articles in the *Revista de Policía*, the department's journal, in 1900, the police berated their own department for allowing the office to fall behind as a leader in the appli- cation of anthropometric techniques, when it had once been a model labora- tory in the Americas. By police order, the office was restricted to the identifi- cation of those criminals involved in crimes against property; in serious crimes against persons if the accused was not a recidivist and as long as the victim had not suffered injury; and in cases of the counterfeiting of money. For any other detainees, the chief of police had to authorize the use of iden- tification. The refusal to apply *bertillonage* to *all* delinquents was inefficient and led to charges that the office was arbitrary.

Because the very concept of identification lacked general acceptance, detainees and even prisoners were successful in their refusals to be measured, which made the office an "almost useless wheel of penal justice," and unable to fight recidivism, Quesada wrote in 1901. Inability to identify recidivists prohibited judges from applying the "aggravation of penalties" section of the penal code. Even recidivists successfully protested identification, as two famous cases in 1900 illustrated. Moreover, when records *were* kept by the police and the anthropometric office, they contradicted each other so frequently about people's antecedents, age, nationality, and so on, that courts considered them unreliable.[48] Although people had resisted identification in other countries too, there it had been a "passing thing," Quesada explained, whereas in Argentina, it still persisted, even after ten years. Bertillon, when faced with this problem, had maintained that once identification became obligatory, delinquents submitted to it "with pleasure," being convinced that it was their last time. Quesada speculated that this remark was merely typical of Bertillon's "exaggerated optimism" and did not foresee this happening in Argentina, where he saw more resistance to identification techniques.[49]

Even when identification was done, the records were regularly destroyed, not only of accused persons who were later absolved, but also of criminals who had completed their sentences, thus completely undermining the identification of recidivists. A judge in 1897, for example, ordered the destruction of identifying information of an indicted person and a "notorious recidivist" after the man had fulfilled his sentence. In 1900, a judge granted a man convicted of homicide the "favor" (*gracia*) of being exempted from anthropometric measurement. "Among nations that have adopted *bertillonage*, the Argentine courts are the only ones that have given in to demands that anthropometric information be destroyed and that do not recognize this police function," Police Chief F. Beazley complained in 1897.[50] This contrasted sharply with the authorization that Sergi had received in Italy to establish a biographical bulletin or personal card (*ficha*) on each student in all *colegios* and normal schools that recorded the results of medical examinations, including anthropometrical measurements, Quesada noted in 1901. Argentines were trying to do this as well in Buenos Aires, at the Colegio Nacional, but were encountering resistance.[51]

Still, by 1903, the anthropometric office in Buenos Aires had accumulated 18,000 index cards of criminal identification, although undoubtedly many did not contain full anthropometric information. Of these, 10,000 to 12,000 were estimated to be repeat offenders, meaning that police had identified at least 10,000 criminals. If the unknowns were estimated at another 5,000 to 10,000, then it meant that Buenos Aires had a criminal population of between 15,000 and 20,000. The city's total population at this time was 800,000. Eliminating women, children and the elderly, the police arrived at a population base of 200,000, which meant that for every fifteen law-abiding adults, there was one professional criminal.[52]

Challenges to identification techniques had a lot to do with people's views of flesh. Measuring and identifying flesh implied an offense to honor, not a scientific "advance." All the arguments in favor—that these advances secured a person's innocence; that measurements were just a perfection or extension of other information, such as name, age, and height; that "identification" by anthropometric means was simply a person's police "civil state" and was the same as his inscription in other kinds of registers, like registers of birth and marriage—did not convince the public, or even all officials. The challenges to anthropometry were part of the changing philosophy of identification at this time. An important condition of new modes of identification of the late nineteenth century was that they should be nonstigmatizing. The use of special clothing, brands, mutilations, and tattoos was now seen as intolerably defamatory. Although prisons experimented with less offensive marks than branding in the early twentieth century, such as the implantation of a bit of glycerin under the skin of prisoners, most penologists were attempting to find other ways of identification that were less prejudicial. Underlying these attempts was the public's sensitization to the concept of "honor," explained by a lawyer in 1904 as "the highest symbol of the human personality," or "identity." Someone who made the "personality," that is, the "identity," of a person "disappear" was guilty, not only of an outrage, but also of a crime against the person. It was a stain that could never be erased. Argentine law safeguarded honor as the highest symbol of the human personality. Being sensitive to the issues of honor and dishonor, Luis Reyna Almandos wrote in 1900, the public objected to anthropometric measurements and other such "advances" in identification as stigmatizing and prejudicial.[53] Taking measurements, for example, necessitated that the subject disrobe, which was offensive to the modesty of women, and, because of honor, was also objectionable to men. Photographs of criminals, which were posted in police stations, also fell into this category. The reference to honor is implicit, for example, in a public prosecutor's argument in 1896 that the police expression "sending a suspect to be photographed" was considered in the legal sense to be a "serious injury, which sounded like the crack of a whip to the reputation of an innocent person."[54]

The general public undoubtedly appreciated the humor of a spoof in a popular magazine in 1906 that proposed a psychometer that could identify a potentially good politician. Smaller than a clinical thermometer, the psychometer's reading could be taken without a person's knowledge. All the investigator had to do was to touch the cerebellum of the political aspirant with the apparatus. Another cartoon making fun of the measuring frenzy of anthropometrists featured a small boy who failed to learn anything in school because he was constantly being measured. Serious articles appeared too, such as one in 1907 that described Bertillon's Museum of Anthropometry and its monstrous deformities.[55]

THE MORAL TRUTH OF FINGERPRINTS
AND THE UNIVERSAL NUMBER

In the city of La Plata, fifty miles south of Buenos Aires, Juan Vucetich, a Croatian immigrant, had been developing an alternative system to anthropometry and a way around people's resistance to measuring flesh. For Vucetich, the reason for the resistance stemmed from the limitations of the system itself. Anthropometry had a high percentage of error and was offensive, especially to women. Moreover, it required expensive equipment, trained personnel, extensive time to take the measurements, and time afterward to search the files to make the correct identification. It also could not be used on anyone who was not yet fully grown. Human error had also to be taken into account, as Vucetich found when he visited Drago's laboratory in the early 1890s and found Drago—who had even studied with Bertillon in France—measuring the left foot of a subject without removing the man's socks and shoes![56]

Most important, from the point of view of penal justice, *bertillonage* could not actually confirm identity; it could only describe and classify. Since measurements were only approximate, they could only eliminate suspects, that is, they could only show the *non*identity of a person. After several years of unsatisfactory experience with anthropometry in La Plata, Vucetich concluded in the early 1890s that the system was "annoying . . . and full of complications" and argued that Bertillon himself had recognized this. In fact, Bertillon had had to introduce a "table of tolerance" to compensate for the inexactness of what he called a person's "verbal portrait," which had converted his system, critics charged, into a "disordered mixture" of science and spiritism.[57] Ordered by the chief of police to establish an anthropometric office in 1891, Vucetich complied, but he never liked the Bertillon system and never applied it successfully. In a letter to Quesada in October 1900, Vucetich wrote: "I can assure you that never, between 1891 and 1895, during which time we used anthropometry, in spite of our efforts, could we determine with certainty the identity of even one subject using these means." Continuing his campaign against anthropometry, Vucetich wrote to Dr. R. A. Reiss at the University of Lausanne in 1906 that daily practice had shown that anthropometry was highly overrated.[58]

Given the limitations of anthropometry, what would have greatly aided in criminal investigations like that involving Farbos and Tremblié was the fingerprinting system that Vucetich had been promoting since the early 1890s as a means of exact and positive identification. Fingerprints were more accurate, inoffensive, and less expensive than anthropometric measurements. In addition, they had the advantage of being permanent and were there even before birth and after death. They did not change over time, and even if the fingertips were burned or mutilated, they would usually grow back with the same print. Fingerprints were also of infinite variety and thus could be totally individual. They were usually left at the scene of a crime and could be used to identify possible suspects. Vucetich's contribution to the history of fingerprinting, already developed by Francis Galton and others, was his classification system. In contrast to Galton's three-type classification, Vucetich created a new system, which he simplified in 1896 and named the "Argentine dactyloscopic system," formed with four fundamental types of papillary lines—the arch; the loop with internal inclination; the loop with external inclination; and the whorl. Each of these had five subtypes, and the patterns were further subdivided by counting the ridges. He further developed an apparatus, the *dactilómono*, that represented a dactyloscopic card with the ten digital impressions, within whose ten gyrating hidden discs were the "four types," which instantly showed all the possible dactyloscopic combinations, a total of 1,048,576.[59]

Having emigrated from Croatia to La Plata in 1884, Vucetich soon became employed in the city's police department, and he had become head of its statistical bureau by 1889. La Plata provided him with an interesting scientific and literary community. The Argentine naturalist and anthropologist Francisco P. Moreno had established a Museum of Natural History in the city in 1877, reportedly the first scientific institution in Argentina.[60] Florencio Sánchez, who was to become one of Argentina's most famous dramatists, worked as a clerk in Vucetich's office. Sánchez, as it turned out, was as much of a propagandist for dactyloscopy as Vucetich, and he reportedly practiced his French language skills in order to better debate with Europeans who defended *bertillonage*.

Introduced to Galton's work on fingerprinting by a journal article given to him by his police chief in 1890, Vucetich subjected the conclusions to his own experiments, taking prints of the arrestees who were brought to his office and examining the prints of cadavers at the morgue and of Egyptian mummies at the local museum. Having worked out his own classification system by July 1891, he registered it on September 1 of that year.[61] Vucetich put his system officially into use in La Plata in 1891, using it along with Bertillon's anthropometric system, in spite of his doubts about anthropometry, because he was required to use it by the police department. He found it hard to fight the favoritism shown French science in Argentina, and *bertillonage* was, after all, widely accepted in much of the world. His solution of the infanticide case against Francisca Rojas in 1892, using fingerprints left at the scene of the crime, represented a real breakthrough for dactyloscopy. This was the first time a murder case had been solved using fingerprints. The road to acceptance was rocky, but in 1895, the La Plata police officially adopted dactyloscopy as a complement to *bertillonage*, and in 1896 they abandoned anthropometry altogether and adopted dactyloscopy, renamed from Vucetich's rather cumbersome original name, *icnofalangometría*. The focus of icnofalangometry had been on finger-sign measurement, whereas dactyloscopy emphasized the science of looking at fingerprints. The La Plata police department's move marked another major breakthrough, in that it was the first time in the world that a police force had decided to use *only* fingerprinting for making identifications.[62]

In the plans of Vucetich and his supporter Reyna Almandos, fingerprints were to become the basis for nothing less than, to use a modern term, a new world order mechanism based on each individual's right to identification. This was a totally different way of looking at flesh: flesh was not to be dishonored by measuring but to be honored by universal identification. It was a global plan and was quite innovative in its conception, on the order of book projects that purported to hold all of humankind's knowledge about a certain subject. Believing that selective and sporadic identification was what the public objected to, Vucetich proposed to combat their resistance by instituting nothing less than a *universal* system of identification, one applied without distinctions. Unlike branding, for example, fingerprinting left no permanent mark, and unlike measuring, the taking of prints was done inoffensively. Vucetich's grandiose plan to establish three international laboratories of identification that would function on the La Plata model was introduced and debated at a Latin American scientific congress held in Montevideo, Uruguay, in 1901. Vucetich had, of course, been using dactyloscopy for at least ten years, but for other conference participants, this system was still just a laboratory method. For them, Vucetich's plan landed "like a bomb." *Bertillonage*, after all, still dominated in police departments around the world, and the Bertillon "bloc" at the conference tried to ensure that Vucetich's plan was voted down, although the congress in the end voted Vucetich's system a "useful complement for the identification of persons and very good for the identification of cadavers." Then in 1902 came a real coup when the Paris police began teaching Vucetich's dactyloscopy to its agents, and even Bertillon adopted Vucetich's dactyloscopic identity card as a complement to his own system in 1903, although he did not cite Vucetich as its creator. Vucetich's book *Dactiloscopía comparada*, published in 1904, received worldwide attention. In 1905, at a Rio de Janeiro congress, an International Police Convention was approved between the police of La Plata, Buenos Aires, Rio de Janeiro, Montevideo, and Santiago de Chile that established not only an identity card based on dactyloscopy for delinquents but also, for the first time, an identity card for "honest" citizens based on Vucetich's model, which he had been issuing in La Plata since 1899. The convention also approved the plan to create the three proposed international laboratories. Two major figures in French criminal science, Alexandre Lacassagne and Edmond Locard, paid tribute to Vucetich, Lacassagne by renaming the system "Vucetichism," and Locard, by declaring it a "perfect" system.[63] The Buenos Aires police department officially adopted fingerprinting in 1905, and the 1906 Code of Penal Procedures incorporated fingerprinting into several of its articles: for detainees and the condemned; to verify a person's antecedents; and to identify cadavers. In 1909, the provincial government gave Vucetich the title of *perito identificador*, "expert identifier," meaning that only he could testify in court regarding fingerprints. Vucetich's system began to be implemented for immigrants in 1912 when the Immigration Directorate established an immigrant identification register. Fingerprinting also began to be used as an identification system in paying illiterate municipal employees, as well as for identifying police agents, prostitutes, the residents of neighborhoods, voters, domestics, mendicants, bank employees, and conscripts. But the idea of identifying an entire population was still viewed with suspicion in Argentina. In 1916, the provincial legislature of Buenos Aires sanctioned a law creating a general register of identification, which would have been the first regional register in the world based on dactyloscopic identification. Nine months later, however, the plan was declared unconstitutional by the national intervenor for the police, and all the personal data that had been collected were destroyed. Vucetich, who likened this to the destruction of the library of Alexandria, was not deterred, though, from pursuing, along with Reyna Almandos, the broader applications of fingerprinting to potential delinquents.

To Vucetich, the flesh of the ends of the fingers contained a kind of "moral truth." Fingerprints held something sublime, which was emitted through flesh. Just as Gabriel Tarde had argued that in the *moral* world, each person had his own interior mark, his inalterable trait, his own essence that was permanent from birth to death, a "first element" that had "stored powers," Vucetich identified special marks in a person's *physical* world. Thus, although Vucetich did not align himself with Lombroso and Bertillon, he too was looking for the physical key that would unlock the inner person. Fingerprints, Vucetich argued, were the "perfect expression of the physical ego" and contained "more distinctive traits than the face and perhaps more distinctive traits than the whole exterior body." Like a moral code that controls through prevention, Vucetich's system was in a sense a preventive system, with a panoptical vision. If a person knew, Vucetich argued, that he could be tracked throughout the world by means of his fingerprints—this bit of his essence left behind by the flesh of his fingertips—it was possible that he would "try not to commit transgressions and would respect the law of others." The implications for the promotion of "civilization" in the world were important, especially to the Argentine elite who had been working through the dichotomy of "civilization and barbarism" since midcentury. Not only would social relations improve within nations with national programs of fingerprinting, but international identification systems would contribute to harmony between nations.[64]

By creating a symbol for each person that would prove his or her identity, or "self," Vucetich argued, an individual could be assured of having a well-defined personality, what Vucetich called a "legal or juridical personality." Identification was a guarantee for the "honest" individual against confusion of name and antecedents with "dishonest" people.[65] It was protection against "dissimulation," a major concern especially in the context of "honor." Concerns about dissimulation and honor may have actually aided the campaign to encourage people to accept identification as their "right" and as a means of their protection. Thus, personality/identity would include in this system the "history of civil individuality," that is, the origin and civil evolution of each person—their births, marriages, deaths, judicial sentencing, divorces, nullifications of marriage, descriptions, including scars and defects, and changes of name. Vucetich envisioned that each person's identification card would contain the number and series of the act of registration and place and date of issuance; personal data, including visible individual marks or deformities; the print of the right thumb; a photograph of the right profile; signature; and signature of the director or head of the Civil Register. Of course, the general register would also include more specialized lists of people who were only marginally "innocent," that is, potential criminals, prostitutes, the insane, and delinquents.

Reyna Almandos, writing in the 1930s, carried the idea of identification as a natural right further, arguing that this right was even a new juridical concept. The global aspect of his plan shows that global policing is not a new idea. Evidence that this reflected a changing view can be found in the 1932 edition of the *Encyclopedia of the Social Sciences*, which explains the switch from the idea that identification was only for criminals to the view that it had become an increasingly important means of safeguarding civil rights. The question was what sign to use. It had to be something that was precise, permanent, not confusable, and peculiar to each human being; and something that would serve as a link between the individual and the exterior world. Brands and other marks were unsatisfactory. Photographs too were inadequate, because it was possible to end up with substantially different pictures of the same person. Anthropometry did not achieve sufficient differentiation and had other limitations. Birthmarks and other natural signs on the body were too nebulous to be used. Names did not constitute a link, because they were not "in the body" of man. Nor were signatures, and although they were considered to be the closest thing to the perfect identifying sign, according to Reyna Almandos, signatures were still not a true system of identification. Fingerprints, though, could absolutely identify a person, but they had a problem in that they could not be used to maintain a register of individuals, because the formula pertained to the group as well as to the individual and because the dactyloscopic number had too many digits.[66]

Reyna Almandos's contribution, then, was to use Vucetich's dactyloscopic system as the basis for, in his words, a "personal number," which could be used to build a national and even international "book of personality." It was a mathematical expression, just like fingerprints. To indicate the universal symbol of identity, he chose the symbol Y, which he took from the word *yu*, meaning "law or judicial tie" in the language of the Brahmans, Reyna Almandos said.[67] A possible number for John Doe then would be "Y1,597,000." This number was exclusive, successive, untransferable, perpetual, individual, and social. It even had a moral character as a register of a person's rights, actions, and property, and because in Reyna Almandos's scheme, personality/identity was the same as honor. Identity was an individual's property, just as honor was. It belonged to his or her flesh. The personal number corresponded to one individual only and was based on the dactyloscopic system. "Each number," Reyna Almandos explained, "would be the individual himself; it would be the 'civil person' of every man." Consistent with the panoptical vision of the world, people's numbers would always be there to reveal their identity and rights, but also to hold them accountable for their actions.[68]

The personal number was to be the basis of a new social organization within the state—a national register that would be a summary of the nation, a civil biography of the nation's flesh. At the same time, it would be a coordinated conjunction of all individual biographies within the juridical concept of personality. The resulting "national book of personality" would owe its existence to two factors: one, the dactyloscopic formula, and two, the personal number. Only with this combination, Reyna Almandos argued, could a society organize the colossal files of individuals. The national book of personality for Argentina, for example, would have 24,000 volumes of 500 pages each, equaling the country's total population, at that time, of twelve million inhabitants. Although Reyna Almandos recognized that this was a grandiose project, he maintained that it was quite in line with other colossal projects, such as the eighteenth-century Chinese collection of classical authors. Its considerable cost would be well worth it, he said, because, among other things, it would act as a permanent national census, which would save Argentina money and time.[69]

In an interview in 1924, shortly before his death, Vucetich commented that the role of fingerprinting had finally been expanded to the "vast field of social progress." It was a means of organizing the "permanent defense of life and affairs, individual rights, and the collective well-being," and had become a "factor of social evolution." His desire had been to perfect man, improve society, and he felt he had found the "infallible instrument of prophylaxis of the moral life of man," thus serving justice and social order.[70]

Reyna Almandos expanded these ideas, also emphasizing the "civilizing" advantage of his identification system. In his essay "The Personal Number and the National Book of Personality," published in a bizarre fashion first in Spanish in a Brazilian journal in 1934 and then in English in a Spanish-language journal in 1936, he included the following dedication: "To the promoters of civilization in Brazil, Chile and Mexico: my respects." In this article, he argued that the personal number was a "civilizing undertaking" that would "guarantee the defense of Order and Law." Grandiose as it might seem, he also argued that the personal number would stabilize international relations, bring about a universal order and justice, perfect relationships, eliminate warfare, and strengthen the family.[71]

There is a final uniqueness to Reyna Almandos's enthusiasm. Believing that "remembering or carrying one's number should become, in the process of time, a habit of healthy foresight," he recommended tattooing the personal number on people's bodies.[72] The fact that he could move from a condemnation of branding bodies, to a condemnation of measuring bodies, to support of an identification system that purported to avoid dishonoring the flesh, and finally back to advocating branding bodies with a tattoo seems explainable only by fear of criminal contagion and belief in modern science. A return to a potentially dishonoring act in this period that was sensitive to dishonor seems dubious. Yet it was advocated in the name of "civilization." This is part of the background, perhaps, for what was to come later in the 1930s, when the "end" of social progress, justice, and social order warranted any "means." Reyna Almandos had gone full circle, from rejecting visible signs known to all, such as brands and special clothing; to visible signs known to experts, such as head measurements and fingerprints; to assigning this complex of traits a number that would appear in a register and be known only to experts; to making it known to the public by tattooing it on the body. The difference was, of course, that this tattooing was for the person's own use and well-being, as well as for society's protection against crime. It almost seems to predate the current proposals to encode a person's complete genetic sequence on a computer chip and implant this in the iris or the navel.

CONCLUSION

Contagion, both physical and moral, was not only important for Argentina internally. Through its massive immigration, the republic was linked to the global migration of contagions, which had a "leveling" effect. Within Argentina, lawyers, doctors, and public health professionals worried about the numerous contagious infections that were purported to coexist in crowded barrios with little physical resistance. There were the physical and moral contagions of tuberculosis, dyspepsia, bad digestion, neurasthenia, alcoholism, and madness. But the danger was also global. With the "leveling" in the nineteenth century, that is, the whittling down of "social, intellectual, and geographical barriers," contagions could spread more easily and become epidemics. Ideas of contagion threatened the boundaries of the individual as an autonomous being and undermined his or her security, because contagion made a person vulnerable to the new, modern mass society. Contagion no more had the effect in this era than in our own time of uniting humanity in a common campaign to eliminate it; rather, it was a divisive factor, which was especially useful in encouraging the self-management of society. For the good of the whole, people had a responsibility to avoid sights, desires, displays of emotion, and thoughts that might literally corrupt the flesh. Cadavers, Wilde wrote, elicited excess emotion that was harmful to the living, and they should be removed from human sight. More sinister was his advice to workers. Workers should act in a way consistent with their class and not pursue education in excess of their positions for reasons of physical and moral health. First, education increased a worker's sense of identity and egoism and engendered aspirations that were incompatible with what he needed more, namely, the aptitudes of submission and resignation. Second, impossible aspirations threw the body into a constant state of disquiet that was injurious to good health. Workers should be taught that the simple life was the happiest; that the existence of hierarchies was the condition of social organization and order; that attacks on capitalists were inexcusable and hurt workers themselves; and that the relationship between workers and industrialists did not depend on voluntary conventions, but rather on formal economic laws, which could not be changed.[73]

4 Modern Diseases in the National Identity

An important project of Argentina's liberal democratic state was to create a "new race," an Argentine race, in some ways, a new flesh, to dilute negative traits with positive ones. Degenerative characteristics arising from "race," defined as both national origin and phenotype, were seen as predisposing the population to debilitating medical conditions such as hysteria, epilepsy, and neurasthenia. Susceptible "degenerative" individuals were believed to serve as hosts in whom phenomena such as racial weaknesses and diseases took root and spread through the process of reproduction and the environment. A person who was predisposed to degeneration might be susceptible, not only to hysteria, for example, but also to committing criminal acts. And unlike honor and passion, which were seen as noble, there was nothing noble about degenerative diseases. Contagion with organic and behavioral degeneration threatened both living Argentinians and their unborn descendants. Politicians and professionals saw degenerative characteristics, not only as integral physical states of individuals, but as causes of Argentina's underdevelopment, political instability, and lack of respect among the civilized nations, and as symptoms of modernity's less desirable features.

DEGENERATION IN MODERN TIMES

Degeneration theory had become widely accepted by European alienists in the second half of the nineteenth century. The Frenchmen Benedict-Auguste Morel, who formulated the theory in the 1850s, and Valentin Magnan, who modified it in the 1880s, were frequently cited in forensic medical texts. Morel focused on the increase in mental disease in the post-Napoleonic crisis period, attributing the increase and the incurability of mental disease to degeneration in both the healthy and the sick population.[1] To answer the question of how a family could degenerate, Morel developed a six-part etiological schema. First, alcohol intoxication, an insufficient or bad diet, a marshy environment, epidemics, and violations of the law of hygiene could result in degeneration. Second, degeneration could be caused by the social environ-ment, that is, by bad housing and work conditions and the resulting poverty, alcoholism, and venereal diseases. Third, a previous morbid disease in a per-son's history in which lesions of the nervous system had occurred, such as epilepsy, hysteria, or hypochondria, could lead to degeneration. Fourth, degeneration could be caused by "moral" disease, that is, by vices such as masturbation and other sexual aberrations. Fifth, congenital diseases or dis-eases acquired in infancy, such as atrophies, hydrocephalia, ossification of the cranial sutures, convulsions, tuberculosis, blindness, congenital muteness, and so on could cause degeneration. Sixth, degeneration could be caused by hereditary influences that it was "useless to try to fight," which was why there was a poor success rate with many psychiatric treatments. Morel, who pro-posed the idea that degenerate conditions caused criminality, held that med-ical doctors had the job of proactively preventing them.[2]

The most important modifications of Morel's theory were made by Magnan, the chief of a psychiatric hospital in Paris. In an 1885 book, Magnan developed his theory of degeneration based on a person's predisposition to the condition; the presence of stigmas, moral and physical, indicating degenera-tion; some sort of disequilibrium and lack of harmony between the different organic functions; and episodic syndromes, such as obsessions, impulsions, and delirium. He applied what he took to be the lessons of Charles Darwin's *On the Origin of Species by Means of Natural Selection*, published in 1859, to degeneration theory. Darwin's work had been unknown to Morel when the latter published his treatises in 1857 and 1860. Magnan's contribution was to argue that degeneration was a true pathological state. This situation, which made the degenerate person physically and psychologically less able to engage in the struggle for life, was translated into permanent stigmas. The eventual end of degeneration was the "annihilation of the species."[3]

Degeneration theory became an important diagnostic tool for forensic medical doctors in part for the same reason that Lombrosian criminal anthro-pology had become useful. According to both models, criminals carried iden-tifiable physical stigmata and constitutional deformities that betrayed their organic decadence. As an explanation for criminal behavior, criminologists used both Lombrosian atavism and degeneration, but there were differences between the two. Morel had favored atavism in viewing degeneration as exclusively inherited, by a process of the simple transmission of abnormal characteristics. The theory of atavism attributed criminal characteristics to a delinquent's "primitive" ancestor. Later in the century, however, others added to Morel's theory and began to include deleterious conditions acting on the body, especially during the fetal period, as a cause, along with poverty, alco-holism, "imitation" (that is, contagion), and mental exhaustion. Any of these conditions could inhibit a person's ability to adapt.[4]

Clearly, the nearly irreversibly downward spiral spelled a fatal end for those afflicted by degeneracy. Some observers suggested that with degeneracy cre-ating growing numbers of criminals, the end of progress in civilization might have been reached.[5] The idea that, through contagion and degeneration, the progress of civilization was being accompanied by "concentric movements that created entire families of assassins and other delinquents" that would self-destruct was laid out well in the example of the Juke family in New York State, who were made famous by Richard L. Dugdale in the 1870s. Beginning with the alcoholic Max, the Juke family fell into a progressive degeneration, which, over the next generations, produced two hundred thieves and assassins, two hundred and eighty-eight invalids, and ninety prostitutes. Thus, alcoholism, a lesser disease state, evolved into more serious diseases and criminal behavior in subsequent generations of the Juke family.[6]

The French psychiatrist Charles Féré and the criminologist Gabriel Tarde argued in the late nineteenth century that degeneracy did not necessarily have to be inherited. Signs of it such as "neuropathic manifestations, insani-ty, and scrofulism," which were often noted in criminals, could not possibly be attributed to atavism, they contended. Their point was well taken. It was logical that the conditions of insanity and so on were not likely to be compat-ible with normal reproduction. Moreover, Féré and Tarde argued, other char-acteristics noted in criminals, such as "lowness, cruelty, cynicism, cowardli-ness, laziness, and bad faith," could not have come from ancestors, since these traits were incompatible with existence and self-preservation. People could become degenerates on their own, owing to environmental factors, then, without inheritance playing a role.[7]

In Argentina, the criminologist Luis María Drago also supported a more balanced view based on both environmental and biological factors to explain the republic's criminal world. Challenging Lombrosian theory, Drago argued in 1888 that the so-called unique features of "born criminals" identified by the Lombrosian School were not signs of atavism but rather either acquired or the result of congenital degeneration. Moreover, far from denoting only crimi-nals, these features could belong to people who were "stable, normal, and achievers of great civilizations, such as the Inca." To Drago, the criminal was a product of biology derived from, or actualized by, familial and social cir-cumstances. Drago's explanatory model for delinquency began with a degen-erative change in the "nutritive functions of the brain-modular centers," which was actually an "adaptation of organs to new functions." Starting with the argument that the more an organ was exercised, the more it adapted, Drago concluded that a one-time delinquent who exercised an organ with a degenerative condition could thus easily develop into a habitual delinquent. Although one could not know for sure when degeneration began or whether it was inherited or social, Drago maintained, degeneration could be understood as "an organism's adaptation to the conditions that nature imposed on it, or to the progress and imperfections of collective life."[8] He saw this adaptation in the Argentine gaucho's supposed conversion into a delinquent, which created a new, though still abnormal, equilibrium. The fictional characters Martín Fierro and Juan Moreira, both of whom enjoyed lawful familial lives until they were forced to adapt to circumstances that turned them into criminals, were a good example. They mirrored the events that were taking place on the pampas of Argentina, of gauchos adapting to the arrival of immigrant farmers who turned open grazing land into farms and forced up the price of land.

The Argentine psychiatrist Francisco de Veyga held a similar view that atavistic explanations were too narrow. First, Veyga argued in 1905, degeneration was just a morbid agent that attacked the body and could be cured. In any case, it did not make sense that morbid inheritance worsened with each new generation. Normal inheritance, in fact, usually won out over morbid inheritance. Second, alongside degeneration was the phenomenon of regeneration, which was the tendency to survive. Survival happened because life perpetuated itself.[9] Veyga's optimism might well have stemmed from the developing concept of a new race in formation in the temperate zone of South America, which was contrasted with the "less desirable" races. Race was the social and environmental condition that at bottom was the culprit to many people.

RACE

Degeneration theory often drew on "race" as an explanation for biological and social aberrations that could lead to uncivilized, unprogressive, and delinquent behavior. Race, as a degenerative characteristic, thus became a crucial element in understanding the possibilities and limitations of individuals, societies, and nations.[10] The concept of "race" had a number of meanings at the turn of the century. It meant superior or inferior races; nationality, as in "the Italian race"; and, finally, the biological core of a population that might succumb to degeneration and disappear or, conversely, be worth preserving. Not only was race an important element of personal and national character, it was

also an important part of new medical and criminological theories that analyzed social problems as inherited and acquired pathologies, and that studied
methods by which to preserve the population from the ravages of degenerative traits. In Argentina, race also became an explanation for the supposed
deeper root of the republic's problems. The commitment to racial hierarchy
and racial purity, far from being the belief of a fringe minority, was considered
progressive and was accepted by many different sectors of the population,
both in Argentina and abroad. Argentine criminal cases frequently, though
not systematically, listed a person's race, for the white population, as well as
for those of color.

New ideas of race changed everything, including Argentine development
policy. The mid-nineteenth-century focus on improving education as a necessary precursor to development, suggested by the Argentine statesman
Domingo F. Sarmiento, for example, was considered by the turn of the century to be somewhat irrelevant and was being replaced by a focus on something more innate. The new focus was on elements inherent in the nature of
the Argentine race as the causes of degeneration and crime.[11] No longer could
inferior education be considered the only obstacle to development. Rather,
an ethnic and racial *modo de ser*, or way of being, was held to be what inhib-
ited Argentine development. Like individuals, population groups had different abilities, including political ones, the Argentine jurist Miguel Romero
maintained in 1901. Some nations led in religion, others in art, and so on.
Thus, it was accurate to say that "psychological atavism was also the law of
nations." If nations were composed of atavistic people, then those nations
would be degenerate. In the case of Argentina, it had been the Celtic spirit
implanted in the Spanish organism centuries earlier that had begun the
degenerative process. History showed that all the defects that kept Argentine
politics chaotic were "flourishing sprouts of the Celtic Spanish tree, transplanted to the fertile soil of South America," Romero argued. Argentina's
attempt at national political organization had failed because of anarchy, the
passion of local caudillos, lack of respect for order and national government,
and tyranny, all of which stemmed from the population's "blood and inheritance." In sum, he argued, the influence of race in the political development
of nations was a widely accepted fact of experience. If a people had long submitted to a given political order, they developed habits and modes of action
that affected their political progress. The political instincts of Argentines had
their origin in a prehistoric age. Only a few people refused to recognize the
influence of race on politics. Thus, the roots of the abnormality of Argentine
politics went deep into the population's past.[12]

The problem that the Argentine population faced for the future was whether it would transform its nature. If the inheritance of race exercised a great influence over the political development of nations, as Romero believed, then the cure for Argentina's problems would be "to reverse the impulses of that instinct by incorporating new elements through immigration and the naturalization of foreigners." This would correct the ethnic defects of the national character. It was crucial to correct these defects, because "decadent" nations were a danger to world peace. Progress, and the stronger nations, would roll right over weaker nations; for Latin America, this meant both European powers and the United States, with its Monroe Doctrine (1823).[13]

In the early twentieth century, the scientific investigation of race in Argentina moved beyond the Spanish population with its Celtic roots into the realm of the "races of color." The well-known Argentine psychiatrist and sociologist José Ingenieros wrote in 1905, for example, that while not all the white races were equal, they were certainly all superior to the colored races. Moreover, because of natural selection and the survival of the fittest, races of color would always fail when they came up against the white races. Enslavement of Africans had been totally appropriate and was merely the political and legal sanctioning of a purely biological reality. They had the "attitudes, gestures, language, preferences, aptitudes, and sentiments of domesticated animals," he wrote, and lived and ate poorly. They had "no religious ideas, which were an index of culture among men of inferior mentality," and they were certainly incapable of replacing religious ideas with any secular notions. The system of slavery protected "these unfortunates" in the same way that civil law protected incapacitated persons, the mentally ill, and animals. For Africans, slavery was a "relative felicity."[14]

One ought nevertheless to treat Africans ("scraps of human flesh") with compassion—at least as well as the "animals at the London Zoological Garden, and not the way a Mississippi court had just done in condemning a Negro to ten years' forced labor for marrying a white woman." While it was all very well to sympathize with the African slaves, Ingenieros wrote, it was important to look at their responsibility in the formation of the American people and character. The Africans who had been imported to the American colonies were an "opprobrious scum" (*oprobiosa escoria*) of the human species. The addition of Africans to the Argentine population had been like "leavening that had actuated all the worst characteristics" in a population already suffering from the degenerative traits of the republic's Amerindians.[15]

Since the law could not change Africans' biological and social inferiority, Ingenieros argued, it should limit itself to interpreting these inferior phenomena and adapt itself to the biological and social reality. Africans' inferiority meant that they neither were nor could ever politically and juridically be the equals of the white race. The "rights of man" were only applicable to those peoples who had reached a certain stage of biological evolution, and it was not enough to belong to the human species to understand those laws and use them. Thus Africans were not "persons" in the juridical sense. Basically, wrote Ingenieros, it was "anti-scientific to do anything in behalf of Negroes and absurd to stretch out their existence as a people indefinitely, which was what miscegenation did." All one had to do was to look at Africans' craniums in anthropology treatises and museums to see that the skeleton confirmed the exterior traits that indicated their "animal mentality." Even sympathetic writers such as Max Nordau maintained that Africans' inferiority was "incontestable." In Ingenieros's opinion, "to lament the disappearance of inadaptable races to white civilization was equal to renouncing the benefits of natural selection. To be sentimental was to ignore the facts. To maintain that the issue of race existed only in the hearts of the white races was absurd."[16]

The first thing in creating a new race was to determine whether where the Latin race stood vis-à-vis supposed Anglo-Saxon superiority was owing to race or innate. If it was innate, then Latins were doomed to decadence. Argentina's temperate climate, though, saved it. Some people argued that it was not race that produced the state of a people, but the environment, and that races were constantly improving. If Napoleon had remained on the island of Corsica, isolated from the world, Ingenieros argued, he would never have risen to importance; he would simply have resembled Eduardo Gutiérrez's (1851–89) fictional gaucho outlaw hero Juan Moreira, limited by his rancho and his petty life. Ingenieros and others hoped that the temperate climate of southern South America would favor the acclimatization of the white races. After all, the two large immigrations, almost totally Latin, over the previous four centuries had pretty much replaced the indigenous races. The history of Argentina had really simply been an episode, Ingenieros wrote in 1905, in the "struggle of races and part of the expansion of these white races." And perhaps now, in the twentieth century, the republic was destined to become the nexus for the radiation of a "future neo-Latin race" that was forming in the Southern Cone. Ingenieros pointed to the progressive economic and conceptual consolidation of Uruguay, southern Brazil, central Argentina, and central Chile and these countries' pacifist solidarity and cooperation against foreign imperialism. The only defense that South America had, he said in a speech at an international scientific congress in Montevideo in 1901, was to develop a great nucleus of the white race, capable of balancing extracontinental influence.[17]

From the early nineteenth century on, Argentinian politicians and professionals had consciously aimed at creating a new character, mentality, and race in the country—a *raza argentina*. Optimists hoped that the mix of Amerindians, Creoles, and new European immigrants would produce a population that differed from traditional Spanish society but was nonetheless a branch of the privileged Caucasian race, which was "better endowed than the other races, with an extensive cranium and intellectual and perceptive faculties." Because this population was still in the process of formation, Argentina had no reason to be ashamed about the embryonic state of its civilization. In contrast to the anthropometric characteristics denoting degeneration and criminality focused on in the late nineteenth century, which took generations to evolve, the new race would be distinguished by shared customs and ideals, which, it was hoped, would develop relatively quickly and coalesce into an integrated population. This nascent race would have a sense of its own uniqueness, neither American indigenous nor European colonial, formed by a shared experience of adaptation to Argentina and of involvement in the formation of a new nation. The new nation might not have many ancient "memories and ruins," but it had the hope of being the "workshop of a new civilization" for a large number of people. All who felt and thought "Argentine" talked about the future; no one said the word "yesterday."[18]

It was hoped that this new Argentine race would be able to overcome the stigma of ethnic inferiority being propagated in much of Europe about South America. While it was not always known which foreign countries would be sending the most emigrants, and the exact nature of the future Argentine population was thus difficult to predict, the one sure characteristic that the new race would have was that it would not contain elements of the indigenous race. The only role that the Amerindians would have was as "historical background" for the new race, Ingenieros argued in 1904. In their spare time, members of the new Argentine race would read the "legends of the extinguished indigenous races; the histories of the mestizo colonial race; the gaucho poems *Martín Fierro* and *Santos Vega*; or [Gutiérrez's] novelas *Juan Moreira* and *Pastor Luna*." The problem, according to Ingenieros, was that the "Indian" was "not assimilable to white civilization," because he could neither "resist our diseases" nor "assimilate to our culture." Moreover, he did not have enough "organic resistance" to compete with whites. People like the Mexican revolutionary Pancho Villa hurt their country and conspired against civilization by protecting Amerindians, Ingenieros argued. The new nations needed to form a *white* population; without that, there would be no nationality; a large Amerindian population "held" by a small group of whites did not make a nationality.[19]

The catalyst for the Europeanization of character, mentality, and ethnicity was the republic's temperate climate, which allowed the white races to thrive, Ingenieros explained. Within a relatively short space of time, Argentina could be politically and economically transformed by a race that would respect justice and peace, both at home and abroad. Finally, after a hundred years of independence, Argentina would have a population of "Euro-Argentines," people who would be familiar with "bathrooms and reading, symbols of civilization."[20] Preferably, this new race would include many Anglo-Saxons, and when it became clear that a majority of immigrants were coming from southern Europe, Argentine politicians and professionals voiced concern.

Also going on at the turn of the century, however, were experiments that proved that Argentina was going to have a hard time of it creating a successful new race. In an experiment conducted in the late 1890s, Víctor Mercante sought to illustrate the dangers of racial mixing and contagion in Argentina and the degeneration of southern European immigrants in the republic, which many feared. Starting from the assumption that immigrant countries were problem-laden, he developed a study of two hundred cases from the Normal School in Buenos Aires, revealed in 1899, to show that this was the result of the mix of environments and customs that informed the children of immigrants. These environments and customs went back thousands of years, and the act of immigration opened deep fissures in their ways of seeing and thinking. When the ancestral lines and adaptation were not concurrent, children became unstable, because they had within them two spirits fighting against each other. The one created and the other destroyed. There was no other explanation for the weak will of Argentine youth, Mercante wrote. It was the natural consequence of the mixture that had erased the most recent traces of selection. The ethnic makeup of Argentines was thus the country's greatest problem.[21]

The aim of Mercante's study was to prove that, in classifying individuals, an abnormal voice in a child was as significant a sign of atavism or degeneracy as anomalies of the cranium, large jaws, narrow forehead, and facial asymmetry. It purported to show that there was a profound difference between the children of European parents and children of whom either one or both parents were Amerindian. The children whose parents were European were said to have a voice quality substantially superior to that of Amerindian children, confirming that the generally accepted hierarchy of races correctly placed the European race at the top. European superiority was allegedly shown in the fuller development of the European children's vocal cords and their greater flexibility, potency, and clarity. Indigenous children were considered to have "unpleasant voices, like animals' voices that were hoarse and strident." These children's voices, it was claimed, never embraced a range greater than four notes. When their voices were low, they lacked clarity; when they were high-pitched, they were thin and poor. Their voices came from the throat, rather than from the chest, and were always forced and not sonorous. Their vocal chords lacked elasticity and their lungs lacked development. Children's voices that were weak, thin, with a short range, out of tune, and coarse were seen by Mercante as similar to degenerates' voices. Thus, anatomically considered, these children were seen as manifesting the anomalous traits that the Lombrosian School called "atavistic regression." On Mercante's scale classifying voices from zero to ten, anything less than four was evidence of atavism or degeneration.[22]

Many Argentine politicians and professionals believed, like Ingenieros and Mercante, that Amerindians were inferior to Europeans, but Mercante went further. He had discovered, he said, that the voices of the children of descendants of Europeans who had adapted to Argentina had actually degenerated. The inferior voices of these children who had originally been European could only be due, Mercante wrote, to the process of their adaptation of a century or more to a new country and climate. The voices of these children, although they were in tune and had range, were thin and without potency. It was very disturbing to find that the descendants of European immigrants, who were supposed to be transforming the ethnic composition and values of the Argentine population, actually deteriorated when they adapted to life in the republic. Mercante questioned whether this regression was atavistic or degenerative—whether it implied a reversion to bad traits in people who had lived in Argentina or meant that when immigrants adapted, they degenerated.[23]

As a part of his study, Mercante separated his two hundred subjects into "normal" and "abnormal." Characteristics that he found in the twenty-eight "abnormal" children—the stigmata of the anthropological criminology school—included long, narrow craniums, large teeth, small eyes, jug-handle ears, an imbecilic look, and narrow foreheads. The children ranged in age between ages six and twelve. In the twelve cases where Mercante included the nationality of these children's parents, four were Argentine, three were a mix of Argentine and Spanish, four were indigenous, and one was Italian. As to personality, Mercante found that these abnormal children lied, quarreled, physically attacked their classmates, did not cry or feel anything when scolded, and faked emotion when necessary. When he classified the children's voices, Mercante found a total of twenty-four children with this kind of voice indicating atavism or degeneration. Dividing this group of twenty-four children with inferior voices into abnormal and normal, he found sixteen abnormal and eight normal children. Thus, Mercante figured, in a hypothetical group of one hundred abnormal children, 57.2 percent would have inferior voices and 42.8 percent would have natural voices. Mercante thus reached two disturbing conclusions: not only could one not count on Amerindians improving, but the descendants of immigrants might be expected to deteriorate after a few generations.[24]

In studies published in 1902, Mercante again sought to prove the inferiority and lack of adaptation of Latin immigrants in Argentina. In Mercante's forensic examination of a sixteen-year-old male delinquent, for example, the boy's southern Italian origin, gypsy background, and "African or Asian (Arab) race" were used to explain his criminal tendencies, "since people accepted that hatred and anger were typical of southern Italians." The boy's upbringing in a warm climate also helped explain his weakened nervous system, which had impeded his inhibitory centers, preventing him from controlling his passions.[25]

The boy had immigrated to Argentina when he was aged two and a half, had been taken back to Italy at the age of five, and had returned to Buenos Aires when he was eight. He was described as having a number of good traits. He worked, in a hat factory, a carpenter's shop, and a bar. He drank only moderately at meals and went to bed early, except when a cousin read to him from the newspaper or gave him arithmetic lessons. And he said his prayers and went to mass on Sunday. Apparently, however, with so much time spent working and because he was unable to attend school, the boy did not get to know the social environment of Buenos Aires. He preferred Italy and only played with children of his own "race." This seemed to explain why he had attracted the hostility of a group of neighborhood boys. When he was doing an errand at eight o'clock one night, twelve to fifteen boys attacked him. "He was a foreigner who fell like a dog of Constantinople in alien mud." They were waiting for him and surrounded him, "all possessing the contagion of the same evil." They called him a "pimp of the police" and beat him up, which was what "common boys did to foreigners." Mercante explained this was a hereditary bad habit that probably came from gaucho customs. The boy fought back and injured some of his adversaries. The fact that the incident had happened during the summer was also used to explain the violence.[26]

Although the boy's family allegedly did not have any signs of insanity, epilepsy, or alcoholism, the boy himself was reported to have some atavistic characteristics that were "inappropriate to someone his age or to someone who was living in modern civilization." The medical diagnosis was that he had premature physical development and some atavistic stigmata. Physically, he had round, open eyes; arched eyebrows; an uncommonly developed lower jaw; a premature appearance of down on his upper lip; an upturned mouth and nose; long, curving arms that were robust but not very "refined"; and a tic in his shoulder similar to an epileptic tic. He also had a nervous temperament, which was not that of an "irascible or exalted person." It was acceptable to be nervous because one was "irascible" or "exalted," but this boy's nervousness was not appropriate to civilization. The doctors' conclusion was that the boy's character was due almost exclusively to the "anthropological factor of race." He had not adapted to Buenos Aires and lacked a "regular and harmonious development of all his aptitudes." His reasoning was that of a fourteen-year-old, but he lacked sufficient penetration to appreciate complex cases. He wanted to learn a job and do useful things. He had no vices and no organic features that indicated degenerative or psychic weakness, "except," Mercante stressed, "for race." "His sentiments [were] the ones common to his race. He hate[d] change, which further alienate[d] him from society and provoke[d] him, without apparent cause or motive, to habitual spite, with small doses of hatred and anger, so characteristic in people from southern Italy."[27] His violent reaction to his attackers, Mercante seemed to be saying, was accounted for by his race, rather than by the fact that he had been attacked.

HYSTERIA

Hysteria, like race, came to be thought of in the late nineteenth century as an important sign of degeneracy. Flesh held many secrets, and one of the most important was the nervous energy that drove it. Nervous energy was important, but showing an excess of it was harmful. Rather, it should be conserved and expended judiciously. Hysteria, which was often cited in court cases as a factor contributing to criminal acts, and could also be an extenuating circumstance, was the object of study by Ingenieros in 1904. The word's etymology, from the Greek *hystera*, meaning uterus, or womb, shows that a causal link was perceived early on between sensations and movements in the uterus and fits of hysteria. Hysteria was considered organic and was portrayed as an "animal" located in the stomach of a woman that sought to realize its reproductive functions. Galen and others attributed hysteria to the stagnation or decomposition of sperm and blood in the womb, with the distribution of a malignant vapor through all the regions of the organism, or simply as a reaction of the uterus on all the other organs of the body.[28] The peregrinating animal eventually evolved into a migrating organ, the uterus, which until the seventeenth century was conceived as rising up from the abdomen to the chest and throat, causing a lump to form in the throat, which resulted in heart palpitations and feelings of suffocation. If the womb reached the head, the woman went into convulsions and lost consciousness. The ancients had attributed wandering wombs primarily to unmarried women and widows, that is, women who had presumably been abstaining from sex, which caused the womb to dry up, lose weight, and go wandering in search of moisture. Wombs, it was thought, could be lured back to their proper position with aromatics or could be pushed back down to their proper location with foul-smelling salts like ammonia.[29]

In the first half of the nineteenth century's revival of the theory that hysteria originated in the uterus, the symptoms remained similar to those postulated earlier, that is, a numbness in the pharynx and other body parts, a blockage of the throat, and changes in character. When doctors were brought in on criminal cases, as in a case from 1903, they continued to examine deviant women's uteruses, tubes, ovaries, and menstruation. Remedies for convulsive disorders related to hysteria included asafetida, a strong-smelling gum resin; valerian, a plant with bitter roots; and leeches applied to the cervix.[30] Home medical manuals explained that virgins and young widows who suffered from a nervous temperament and menstruation problems were more likely to have hysteria. Hysteria was also typical of women with weak constitutions, weakened still more by "disordered passions, laziness, a hatred for work, tribulations, long illnesses, poverty, injustices, and weak reason." In popular manuals, the symptoms of hysteria included "a disquieted spirit with sighs and excessive crying; stomach pains, difficult digestion, and lack of appetite; heart palpitations; lethargy; a burning sensation in hypochondriacs; a contraction of the stomach that seemed like a big pill that rose up to the throat and threatened suffocation; and delirium and short attacks similar to *locura* that left no memory [of them]." If hysteria did not go away by itself or was not cured with the help of vomitives and purgatives, it could end in dementia or death. Even though hysteria was accepted as a genuine disease in the later nineteenth century, hysterics, both female and male, were often described pejoratively as individuals "of feeble purpose, limited reason, wanton humours, irregular or depraved appetites, and . . . indefinite and inconsistent complaints," who were "foolish, often fat and lazy, and always selfish."[31]

In the mid to late nineteenth century, scientists such as J.-M. Charcot, Paul Richer, Désiré Bourneville, and Paul Regnard were undertaking new analyses of hysteria at the Salpetrière hospital in Paris. Some doctors attributed it to a bitter and bilious principle disseminated throughout the brain; others to a humoral principle mixed with blood; others considered it a general nervous disease, or some pollution of nervous or animal spirits. In sum, the school of Charcot held that hysteria was a permanent neurosis, characterized by fixed stigmas, that was revealed by episodic manifestations. In Argentina, Dr. Eduardo Wilde, writing in 1896, was completely skeptical about the success of all known treatments for this "hateful and intricate neurosis."[32]

Although doctors began occasionally to diagnose men with hysteria, the condition continued to be seen as primarily a women's disease. The reason for this, besides the connection to the womb, was that women's natural propensity to feeling and showing emotion, which was both biological and social in origin, predisposed them more than men to hysteria. To fulfill their noble mission in life, women had been endowed with great sensitivity and emotion. Any unpleasant and painful impressions affected the emotional centers of their brains, causing the strong emotions that were an important factor in the genesis of hysteria. The brain reacted by exaggerating or perverting the body's actions. Thus, an attack of hysteria was described as the reaction of the part of the brain that received emotional impressions.

Sorting out crimes committed in a state of hysteria from crimes committed in a state of passion was difficult. The criteria for distinguishing the two can be seen in the case of a woman who murdered her husband in 1898.[33] She was Italian, aged between twenty-five and thirty, had had several abortions and a son who had died, and had evidently been treated unjustly by her husband. Although many of her acts preceding the murder—such as pounding on the wall with her fists and attempting suicide—seemed to indicate violent emotion, it was the medical examination ordered by the court that confirmed that the woman had suffered from hysteria.

In the trial of María Cristina d'Ambrosio, the forensic doctors Delfín Pacheco and Agustín J. Drago, who were charged by the judge with examining María's "mental faculties and general condition" and reviewing her antecedents and the results of previous examinations, concluded that she had hysteria, specifically, that she was an intermittent *alienada histérica*. This report was compelling to the judge, and he decided that she was not responsible for killing her husband and sent her to the asylum to be cured. But he decided this on the basis of her illness, rather than treating her crime as one of passion, even though there were details of the case that could have supported the latter defense. Such an analysis would have meant that she would not have been sent to a mental asylum.

María's husband had wanted to go to Brazil and abandon both her and the store that she owned. She told him he could go, but that she did not want him to sell the store, which he could legally have done. He had been brutal toward her in the past and had assaulted her with a knife. Immediately preceding the crime, he had denied her ten pesos to pay for her medicine. Just a few days before she killed her husband, María had been looking for a revolver and shouting, hitting the wall with her fists, and banging her head on the bed frame, and had tried to commit suicide. María's husband had had her examined by a doctor from the Hospital Rawson, who warned him to watch out, because his wife was capable of injuring herself or someone else if she had another "nervous attack." The doctor told the court that he had "fulfilled [his] professional duties" by warning the husband and had not returned to see María again. A few days later, the couple had a "strong exchange of words"; she became "exasperated" and felt "weary and desperate" over the state of her married life. At this point, she ran and got her husband's revolver and shot him. She was immediately remorseful and voluntarily confessed her crime to the police.

Shortly after committing the crime, María, then in jail, was examined by Pacheco and Drago, who decided that she had a nervous temperament and a slight deviation of the nose, but "no other personal or degenerative signs." They continued to examine her over the following months. She did not recall her immigration to Argentina, her marriage, or many other events in her life. She could only remember her husband's abuse and thought that he was still alive and would be coming for her soon. Her movements were automatic, as if she lacked any will, and she suffered from vertigo, trembling, sleepiness, and crying, all of which were aggravated by the treatment of hypnosis. María conducted herself well in jail, according to the guards, and she was reportedly neat and clean. To the doctors, however, she seemed to be permanently disturbed and indifferent to her surroundings. In jail, she went from being a hysteric to a woman with hysterical insanity (*locura histérica*). After María was transferred to the Hospital Nacional de Alienadas, she seemed to respond to treatment and returned to being just a hysteric. Her clarity of thought, sensibility, and animation returned, and she began to speak with the "intellectual level of a person of her degree of culture."

Although María did not exhibit the spastic facial movements or tic convulsions accepted as signs of hysteria, and although she had not lost weight or the functioning of organs, the doctors found her body's sensitivity reason enough to continue to think that she suffered from hysteria. In some parts of her body, sensibility had totally disappeared, and in other parts, it had greatly decreased. Both superficial touch and deep sensibility in these areas seemed anesthetized. She did not feel it when her extremities, abdomen, neck, face, and scalp were pricked with a pin. "We went as far on several occasions," the doctors wrote, "as to pierce a fold of her skin with a pin, and far from it hurting, she said that she felt a sensation of light burning or of heat where she was being touched. A similar insensitivity to warmth or heat was found. For example, she was insensitive to the flame of a match and to a spoonful of hot water touched to her skin in various regions." María had numb areas all over her body, but parts of her abdomen were hypersensitive. Her complaint of a constriction in her throat and a lump rising from her stomach to her upper chest was a typical symptom of hysteria, the doctors noted, the "wandering womb."

In another case, from 1901, that of Marcelina David, the judge decided that a woman convicted of adultery and suffering from hysteria should go to jail. The examining doctors' declaration that her hysteria was "of no importance" left the judge the freedom to sentence her to one year in a penitentiary.[34] Following her transfer to the correctional after her husband had charged her with adultery, she underwent a medical examination, the standard practice. The examination did not support Marcelina's own explanation of her condition as epilepsy and asthma. Instead, what the doctors found to be significant was her "marked nervous temperament with some manifestations of forms of hysteria, such as hypersensitivity of the pharynx; a sensation of drunken hysteria; and some heart palpitations." From Marcelina's statement to the police, the doctors would have known that she claimed to have been physically abused by her husband and abandoned twice. The fact that her husband had forced her to bury an aborted fetus secretly at home, without telling the police, had led to yet more arguments between the spouses. Finally, she had left home, taking with her one of their two children, furniture, and clothes. Her husband had asked the police to detain her, but initially they had refused. Only when the husband returned to the police with the charge that his wife was living in concubinage and had been seen publicly with her lover were the police willing to arrest her. Interrogated in the correctional, Marcelina claimed that her husband had thrown her out of the conjugal house. Although she had been living in the same room with another man, she said that she had not been his concubine but had been taking care of his child and a sick woman as well. If she and the man had seemed to be married, it was for appearance's sake. In this case, even though the medical diagnosis indicated hysteria, the doctors concluded that the woman was "healthy and satisfied with her life" and was unaffected by her hysteria. Both doctors and judge refused to take Marcelina's hysteria into account in the charge against her of adultery. While hysteria frequently played a role in criminal cases, most judges discounted it as an extenuating circumstance.

Writing in 1917 on "passion and crime," the Argentine criminologist Eusebio Gómez excluded hysteria as one of the conditions that produced the kind of mental disturbance that extenuated a criminal act. True, the imbalances experienced by hysterics in their organic functions and sentiments could move them from exaltation to depression. However, if a hysteric committed a bloody, vengeful act, it was not excusable, because the act was not the "disinterested and noble reaction of a normal personality," Gómez wrote.[35] Although when compared with other cases, María's killing of her husband seemed to fit the legal and medical model of a crime of passion, which would have been an extenuating circumstance, she was diagnosed with hysteria, which did not give her this advantage. Whereas a husband's anger, jealousy, or "just pain" was readily understood as the motive for a crime of passion and admitted into evidence, often at face value, a wife's reaction to similar situations was judged as indicating that she suffered from a medical condition that did not necessarily get her off the hook.

Hysteria was often confused with epilepsy, and vice versa, especially in women, and most women's epilepsy was described as hystero, or uterine, epilepsy. During the first half of the nineteenth century, doctors still debated whether hysteria was merely just a variety of epilepsy. Experts generally agreed that a hysterical person might also suffer from epilepsy, and that the attacks might at times be hysterical and at other times epileptic. Furthermore, hysterical and epileptic symptoms occurred so much in tandem that it was impossible to distinguish between them. In the second half of the nineteenth century, doctors renewed their efforts to distinguish between hysteria and epilepsy. Emotional factors were increasingly linked to hysteria, whereas in epilepsy, the trend was to look for organic causes that might have affected the brain. Charcot's work at the Salpetrière in the 1870s trying to distinguish between the two diseases, which was continued by his student Richer, eventually led to the two diseases being thought of as separate entities, and hysteria became a kind of counterpart to epilepsy.[36]

EPILEPSY AND AN ATTACK ON THE PRESIDENT

Epilepsy changed the flesh, allowing the nervousness and irritability inside the body to erupt outward, and sometimes causing its victims to commit criminal acts like murder. Because epileptics suffered continuously, Morel wrote in 1857, they had an increased amount of irritability in their nervous systems, which found an outlet in the flesh for their "perversion of their ideas and feelings, and in moral lesions." Irritability, then, was at the base of the epileptic character, and suffering produced and magnified this characteristic. While epilepsy usually manifested itself in convulsive attacks, falls, vertigo, and loss of consciousness, Morel described another type of the disease that he called "larval epilepsy." This was a masked form of epilepsy that could exist as incomplete or aborted attacks, and was not necessarily accompanied by attacks of ordinary epilepsy. Both types could mitigate responsibility for criminal acts.[37]

In the early nineteenth century, the causes of epilepsy were regarded to be as various as "fright and sorrow, masturbation, drunkenness, difficult menstruation, childbirth, teething, vexation, blows on the head, and artificial isolation." Treatment of epileptics at the Salpetrière under Jean-Etienne-Dominique Esquirol in the 1830s included bloodletting, cathartics, baths, cauterization, and various antispasmodic and "secret" medicines. Later in the nineteenth century, doctors still used zinc, silver, bromides, and the *seton*, a thread or horsehair introduced under the skin with a needle. Doctors noted that epileptics' attacks could be contagious to healthy people. Prolonged exposure to epileptics, as well as to hysterics, justified the suggestion that these people be separated off from other patients.[38]

Epileptics reportedly shared similar physiognomic signs, degenerative stigmata, and psychological traits with born criminals and the insane, according to the Lombrosian School. The characteristics common to these groups included "left handedness; blind and unconscious perversity; weak intellectual resistance; great facility for reflexive acts and weakness of inhibitory acts; changes of character; headaches; quarrelsome humor; exaltation; tendencies toward suicide; tremors; and weaknesses." These shared characteristics meant that epileptics, like criminals and the insane, were a special type of human being, with a special type of flesh, whose criminal acts excluded moral responsibility. Lombroso argued that in epilepsy, all the characteristics of the morally insane, that is, born criminals, were found in increased amounts, and that epilepsy represented an exaggeration in the lines of criminality. Innate criminality, or moral madness, was a variant of epilepsy. Epileptic delinquents had a whole set of distinctive characteristics of the flesh too, such as prominent and robust chewing muscles; neck muscles that translated into a preponderance of organic and motor life over psychic and intellectual life; and an ellipsoidal form of the nostrils and a crooked nose.

Lombroso, however, went much further in broadening the biological, social, and cultural role of the epileptic by positing cerebral irritability as the common organic cause of both intellectual and psychic power, and nervous disorders. This theory allowed Lombroso to associate both genius and criminality with epilepsy. Research had shown that epilepsy was a localized degenerative irritation of the cerebral cortex, yet the cortex was also the substratum of the mind and its functions. Hence, one could say that the creativity of genius was a form of degenerative psychosis belonging to the group of epileptic diseases. Genius and epilepsy, according to Lombroso, had many features in common: hereditary affliction, inclination to criminality, frequency of suicide, religiosity, and vagabondage. The absentmindedness of great men could be explained by an epileptic absence. Napoleon was for Lombroso the epitome of combined genius and epilepsy—seen in his egoism, brutality, and duplicity. The key to both genius and epilepsy was excess.[39]

Epilepsy was the crucial attenuating circumstance in the trial of Ignacio Monges, who attacked Argentina's president, Julio A. Roca, on May 10, 1886.[40] Monges's attack on Roca proceeded in a seemingly casual manner, with Monges milling around with the crowd in the Plaza de Mayo on the day Roca was to open Congress. When Roca approached, accompanied by his ministers, Monges picked up a piece of paving stone lying in the street and smashed it against Roca's head as he passed by. The brim of Roca's hat deflected the blow, however, and the president was even able to deliver part of his address to Congress. Criticism of Roca had been rampant before the attack, but afterward, he had the public's sympathy. Within a few days of the attack, a "Rally of Indignation," twenty thousand people strong, filed by Roca's house to pay him homage. Addressing the crowd, Roca said that the republic, not he, had been most harmed by the attack, because it had suffered the shame of violence directed against its president.

An intense campaign against Roca had been under way since before the presidential elections of February 1886, when Roca imposed Miguel Juárez Celman on the country as president (1886–90). Roca and Juárez Celman were mutual supporters and brothers-in-law, and Roca's support of Juárez Celman for president had angered the old *porteño* parties, which felt defrauded by the victory of a provincial. The opposition in Buenos Aires to Juárez Celman, and by implication to Roca, was fierce and was directed by Dardo Rocha, who was supported by liberal former president Bartolomé Mitre's group, Catholics, and various discontented persons. Monges was a supporter of Ocampo for president, and had friends in, and maybe belonged to, the "Dardo Rocha Committee" of San Telmo. In fact, even as President Roca stood bleeding, with much of the crowd crying "Viva Roca!" there were people shouting "Viva Dardo Rocha!" and "Abajo Juárez Celman!" Monges was shouting too, "Muera Roca!" until a policeman put the handle of his truncheon between Monges's teeth. In a way, Monges's attack was just a prelude to the problems that the team of Roca and Juárez Celman were later to experience. Discontent with Juárez Celman produced a revolution in only four years, called the July (1890) Revolution, which forced him out of office. This was the revolution that Lucio Cascallares Paz and María Bidone romanced their way through, while Monges spent it in prison, carving out maté gourds.

As a career soldier in Corrientes, Monges had known Roca from the battle of Naembé of 1871, when Roca served as a lieutenant colonel and Monges as an officer in the Corrientes militia, under Colonel Reyna. Monges had also fought in Paraguay, in the struggle against López Jordán, and finally in the revolution against the government of Santiago Derquí, the second president of the Confederation, in Corrientes in 1878.[41] In 1878, Monges was already second chief of the battalion "Libres" and fought with them in the battle of "Las Tunas," under Coronal Acuña. Monges fought as a sergeant major in the revolution that Coronal Reyna organized in 1880 in Paso de los Libres, but the enterprise failed, and Monges went to the Brazilian city of Uruguayana and established a general store. He ran into trouble with the local authorities, however, and had to leave, abandoning all his property, but hoping to recover it by diplomatic means. With the help of one of his previous superiors, he established himself in Buenos Aires in 1882 and worked successfully for a tram company there, and then for a brick factory in La Plata. But a few months prior to his attack on Roca, he lost his position distributing a newspaper, either *La Protesta* or *El Debate*, after only six hours on the job because of an attack of epilepsy.

Monges's military career and political views were not considered unusual; he did not, for example, belong to any anarchist or fringe group. In fact, his act was similar to the episode in a caricature that the periodical *Don Quijote* published just two days prior to Monges's attack — of Roca lying dead, assassinated, in a carriage in a square! Needless to say, the police questioned the periodical's editor. The caricature, the editor explained, implied that Roca was not stepping down from power after six years, as the Constitution required, but rather was continuing to govern, using Juárez Celman as a front. The editor had been criticized previously for his bold caricatures and had assured his readers that the police would not question them this time, as they had in the past. Evidently, anger and disappointment about his own affairs led Monges to decide to kill Roca, believing, he testified, that in so doing he would both "save the *patria* and gain liberty for Argentina" and "improve his situation with a change in government, or die in the attempt." He was totally without remorse and publicly expressed disappointment that his attack on Roca had failed to result in the president's death.

Nothing exceptional having been turned up in Monges's past that would have pushed him into an assassination attempt against the president of the country, especially with such an ineffective weapon as a stone, medical and legal investigators focused on his epilepsy. The essential question was whether Monges's type of epilepsy, which had yet to be determined, could be regarded as an extenuating circumstance.

In an unusual omission, the judge in this case did not order any medical examination of Monges. Doctors gave testimony as simple witnesses, but they did not conduct an official examination and did not diagnose Monges's illness. Monges's lawyer, the eminent Jorge Argerich, had to plead with the judge to order a medical examination, and then when the judge did so, the report was delayed six months for personal reasons in the examining doctors' lives, which paralyzed the case. Finally, in February 1887, the judge received the medical report. The question that the doctors, Fernández and Aravena, had been instructed to address was whether, at the moment of the criminal act, Monges was conscious of his actions, or whether he had suffered mental disturbances. The doctors reached four conclusions. First, that Monges was indeed epileptic and suffered from grand mal. He showed its characteristics of epileptic aura, loss of consciousness, vertigo, convulsive falls, and epileptic coma. During his attacks, Monges was absolutely incapable of committing any punishable act, because he fell down fulminating; his convulsions affected his members, and he was not fit for anything. On the other hand, he had not recently had the numerous attacks that were required in order to excuse him from responsibility. Second, Monges showed no signs of larval, or latent, epilepsy or epileptic vertigo, and was responsible because he remembered the attack and showed no remorse. Third, Monges existed at a maximum level of irritability because of his epilepsy. He was dominated by his nervous system, and he lacked will. In other words, his organic state could produce no counterweight to his impulses. Fourth, in spite of the first three findings, Monges's responsibility was nonetheless reduced because of his epilepsy.

In spite of his epilepsy, the doctors decided that Monges was not a degenerate, because his epilepsy was not inherited, but rather had been acquired through an accident that had happened thirteen years prior to his attack on Roca. He was organically healthy, with no deformities, that is, nothing that would indicate degeneration; he had no delirium and no hallucinations. As a result, Monges still had a strong intellect; he was literate and read whole books. He had a good memory, a normal character, affective faculties, and healthy, sober, and nonepileptic antecedents.

Epilepsy, the doctors explained to the court, appeared in people in a variety of intensities with varying results. Each gradation had its own characteristics, symptoms, and tendencies. Larval epilepsy was the form most commonly found in criminal attacks and was characterized by hallucinations of sight and hearing; lack of motive for the crime; extravagance; incontinence of urine; and remorse.[42] On the day of Monges's attack on Roca, the doctors explained, an "explosion" had occurred in Monges's nervous system, which was already in a state of complete irritability due to his epilepsy, and a discharge had to occur in order to ease it. "When two-thirds of the people see that the ruler is bad, he must [be made to] disappear," the French mystic Allan Kardec had said, and Monges, who was a convert to Kardec's spiritism, believed this. In a man whose "tyrannical nervous system was ready to explode," the doctors explained, the mere sight of Roca, the person whom Monges deemed responsible for his bad luck, had set him off. His will could not stop the process, because it was paralyzed by epilepsy. His conscience was not functioning fully, and his moral liberty was thus restricted. On the other hand, Monges had not been suffering an attack of epilepsy at the moment of the attack, nor had he had a recent previous attack. He did, however, have an attack on the night of his aggression against Roca. In this case, he should not have been conscious of his act, yet Monges was conscious—and had no hallucinations or remorse. The defense lawyer, Jorge Argerich, disagreed with the medical report, but was on shaky ground when he tried to refute the doctors' findings, even though he appeared to be well versed in the work of the European experts Henry Maudsley and Benedict-Auguste Morel.

In the reports on several examinations of Monges, he emerges as an interesting mix of mid-nineteenth-century man of the *campo* and a man of the new age of spiritism and positivism. Perhaps intentionally, the doctors' 1886 description of Monges calls to mind Martín Fierro, the famous outlaw gaucho figure from Argentine literature, the first part of whose story was published in 1872. A typical Fierro figure, Monges was a man of the *campo*, illegitimate, an ex-soldier down on his luck, and a fugitive who was in trouble with the law and had to flee. Scared and ashamed, all he really wanted to do was to be able to earn a living and love his son. But "his roving life [had] not allowed him to smooth out his temperament and thus his restless spirit [had grown]." He had accepted his arrest for his attack on Roca like a man and showed no repentance. Moving from rural crime to urban crime in Buenos Aires, Monges had chosen a victim at a very high level.

On the other hand, Monges was also a spiritist. Kardec's *Le Livre des esprits* (The Book of the Spirits), published in 1859, was in Monges's book collection, as were fifteen pamphlets on spiritism and a treatise on freemasonry. Like other spiritists, Monges would have used the descriptive and prescriptive answers that Kardec claimed he had received from spirits as models to live by. Monges was a member of the spiritist society "La Humildad" and had a note in his pocket from the society. He had been certain that he was being pursued by a spirit, and the note from the society reassured him that he was safe. Like many other nineteenth-century intellectuals, Kardec was concerned that scientific advances were eroding religious spirituality and Christian morality. Kardec's spiritism, which was widespread and popular, provided an understandable complement to modern positivism, and in this, his philosophy bore some similarities to that of another utopian, who was both a contemporary and a compatriot, Auguste Comte, the founder of positivism. Kardec had medical pretensions and hoped that doctors would choose to use spiritism to better understand mental illness. While doctors were hostile, for Monges, Kardec's spiritism resonated with his epileptic condition, which he at least partly blamed for the high degree of adversity he had encountered in his life. Spiritism, though, according to the doctors, was known to have negative effects on people, and a number of spiritists had already ended up in asylums.[43] In Monges's impressionable imagination and his predisposition because of his nervous illness, the doctors said, spiritism had found fertile soil.

Doctors provided a final examination of Monges, requested by the judge of the National Department of Hygiene, to determine whether he was mentally able to stand trial. With the submission of the department's report, the trial broke down into a debate between the legal and medical professions. The judge had wanted a simple yes or no answer to his specific question, but the director of the department and author of the report, Antonio F. Piñero, a distinguished alienist, instead told the judge that Monges was not responsible for his crime. The judge demanded that Piñero redo the report; Piñero refused, saying that to make the kind of report that the judge wanted would be "capricious, false, and even punishable," and that the judge's refusal to accept his original report was a "rebuff." The judge and prosecutor were livid, not only because they considered that the department had overstepped its bounds and failed to answer the question it had been asked, but also because it had, in the prosecutor's words, "tried to make the court into an organ to reform the 1886 penal code along positivist lines."

This interesting finale to Monges's case well documents the ambivalent attitude toward positivism seen in many criminal cases. On the issue of Monges's epilepsy, the five judges in the appeals court voted four to one against using the medical report. In the lead judge's opinion, the medico-legal report was not scientific, but merely philosophical and individual. What had been asked of the forensic doctors was "scientific meaning"; what they had delivered to the court was "moral meaning," whereas the judges themselves were the only ones in the position to pronounce on moral meaning in cases. Experts could never be judges. Furthermore, the extenuating circumstance of epilepsy was not recognized in the law. Monges was indeed an epileptic and a candidate for certification of insanity, but was not presently an irresponsible person in the legal sense. The only applicable provision in the penal code was to replace the punishment of *presidio*, or hard labor, with confinement in a penitentiary because of Monges's illness. In asking for the reduction of the sentence, the defense lawyer was applying positivism to judicial doctrine. This was not in the spirit of the judges' assessments, nor in the spirit or the letter of the law. If the crime had been consummated, it would have been "assassination" in the old code and "homicide with treachery" without extenuating circumstances in the 1886 code, both punishable by death. Four judges voted that Monges should get the maximum punishment for "attempt," which was imprisonment in a penitentiary for an undetermined time. The fifth judge voted for nine years' *presidio* or, better, penitentiary. With this split vote, which meant that the appeals court's sentence could not exceed ten years, Monges was sentenced to ten years' *presidio*.

The fact that all epileptics could at some point in their lives experience sudden attacks of homicidal violence, and that even when they were not having attacks, the disease was incubating future violence, placed epileptics in the category of criminals. As the new school described the relationship, criminality was a variety of epilepsy that had been purged of some neurotic manifestations, especially of its convulsions. Epileptics constituted a category of psychopaths who had no brake on their will and no ability to honor the social pact. "Their desires," Dr. G. Sittoni wrote in 1899 in a study of epilepsy in America published in *Criminalogía Moderna*, "are irresistible impulses; their passion was emotion, convulsion, reaction; pleasure exalted their sentiment and transformed it into rage, a nervous automatism and consequently psychic." Even when they seemed to be "normal," they were always under the influence of their disease. Epileptics could remain innocuous for years and then turn into ferocious assassins suddenly because of the latent accumulation of cerebral lesions, Sittoni contended. That is, simple epilepsy could transform itself, through its own evolutionary degenerative maturation, into complete epilepsy. In reality, all the varieties of simple epilepsy were believed to take the form of complete epilepsy.[44]

Some professionals believed that epileptics, like born criminals, were never morally responsible for their acts; others, such as Henri Legrand du

Saulle, Benedict-Auguste Morel, Vittore Bonfigli, and Ambroise-Auguste Tardieu, added a qualifier and said that epileptics were responsible if they had coldly calculated their crime and had a motive. Crimes were believed to occur both during epileptic attacks and during the ordinary life of epileptics. Thus, both the convulsive manifestations of epilepsy and the ordinary psychic life of epileptics had to be examined. There was thus no such thing as innocent epilepsy; there was always the possibility that an epileptic might be dangerous to society.

NEURASTHENIA

With more attention to medical conditions and more diagnostic theories and tools, some diseases tended to become in vogue, such as neurasthenia, a kind of professional burnout. This was a sure sign of modernity. However, in a more serious vein, neurasthenia also predisposed its victims to degeneration. Neurasthenia was first identified as a disease in the United States by G. M. Beard in the 1860s and linked to the "nervous modernity" of North America. Connected with intellectual life, the disease mainly involved the exhaustion of the nerve cells, evidenced by fatigue and weakness. Popularized in Europe by the Italian physiologist Angelo Masso, "fatigue" theory held that nervous exhaustion interfered with governing the passions. The cause could be anything from simple stress to insanity. Nervous energy was a precious commodity and was not to be squandered or misdirected. Unlike hysteria, neurasthenia was an acceptable and even a valuable illness for men, and it became a main male disease in the later nineteenth century. Though neurasthenia could affect women too, it was most common among well-to-do and intellectual men, especially those in the professions. The male patients in the private practice of the famous nineteenth-century neurologist Jean-Martin Charcot came from the middle and upper classes and were far more likely to be diagnosed as neurasthenic than as hysterical. Among professional men, often doctors, according to Horacio Piñero writing in 1900, the disorder was attributed to overwork, sexual excess, anxiety, ambition, sedentary habits, or the use of alcohol, tobacco, or drugs. Its symptoms were blushing, neuralgia, vertigo, headache, tooth decay, insomnia, depression, chronic fatigue, and fainting. In accord with the new sciences that enjoyed quantifying, fatigue could be measured as well. Since intellectual work was active, it produced "excremental" material. Just as with urine, for example, the material produced by the brain could be measured, both quantitatively and qualitatively. If an examiner did this before and after mental work, he could evaluate a person's mental aptitude.[45]

Satirists mocked neurasthenia as nothing more than "laziness." The author of a popular article in 1906 thanked the disciples of Pasteur for the bacilli of cholera, leprosy, typhus, and tuberculosis but begged that research stop there and that neurasthenics be told that they were not ill. Fantasy had created new evils, he wrote, like neurasthenia, *surmenage* (overworking), appendicitis, and others that were seen in Paris and were the latest fashion plate for distinguished patients. Poking fun both at doctors, who were perhaps inventing new diseases in order to get more patients into their clinics, and at patients, the satirist wrote that whereas Christianity taught that laziness was a sin, doctors said it was caused by two microbes, and that since Argentina was a democratic country, Argentines had a right to enjoy this disease![46]

Cures for this "nonexistent" disease came in for some ribbing in a cartoon series from 1906. The doctor in the script suggested to his patient that he avoid any heavy work, like moving his library; engage in poetic pursuits; and provoke someone to a duel. Other cures included telling his servant to yell fire at night, which would excite the patient, but in the end provide him with a good sleep; insulting phone operators; and getting a good cold. In another article, an anthropomorphized planet suffering from earthquakes was described as a neurasthenic because of its unpredictable conduct. The planet even decided to imitate the "Negroes of Root's country," a reference to the United States and its envoy Elihu Root, and started to do the cakewalk. In the medical advice column in another issue of the weekly *PBT*, neurasthenia was attributed to the consumption of condiments, such as vinegar, that excited gastric secretions. Finally, in an advertisement for Banqueros cigarettes entitled "Renacimiento" (Rebirth), a rich count contemplating suicide, because he is "tired of life," lights up a Banqueros cigarette for the last time and decides to live because of its rich aroma.[47]

When Dr. Luis Agote was charged with violent behavior in 1898 and diagnosed with neurasthenia, the public undoubtedly had some chuckles at his expense. A noted physician and public health expert, Agote fitted the stereotype of the disease as a hard-working professional. He had become director of the National Department of Hygiene only a year after graduating from the Faculty of Medicine at the University of Buenos Aires in 1893. Two years later, presumably stressed out, Agote approached his colleague Viñas, the head of the office of administrative control, who was seated at his desk, reading his newspaper.[48] Agote was angry about Viñas's attacks on the department, and on himself, published in the newspaper the day before. Agote was head of the *lazareto* (leper hospital) on the island of Martín Garcia and many of Viñas's accusations implied corruption in Agote's administration of this institution. In his letter to the newspaper in April 1896, Viñas referred to abuses, mistakes, and criminal operations. "The Hygiene Department," he wrote, "shows a perversion in its business and an intolerable disorder." Agote's worst offenses, according to Viñas, included giving business contracts to people who charged more than the going rate; charging his personal trips to the department; using the departmental ship to transport families instead of charcoal to the *lazareto*; allowing doctors to act as managers of pharmacies; allowing doctors to practice without a license; using the telegraph for his personal business; tolerating uncertified folk healers; inventing jobs in order to make special hires; and allowing department employees to trade illegally in ship disinfectants.

Agote reportedly addressed Viñas in an aggressive tone of voice, saying: "I'm going to give you some advice. Don't touch my family in your accusations because, if you do, I've had it! I'm not [even] going to ask you for an explanation for your behavior, since it would be like asking a servant for an explanation. You dirty Spanish bastard, you!"

"Go to the Big Mother Whore who gave birth to you," Viñas responded.

Agote thereupon drew his revolver and fired at Viñas.

At his trial, Agote claimed that he had asked Viñas politely to desist in his accusations, and that it was Viñas who had been the aggressor, with Agote only pulling out his gun to defend himself. Viñas claimed that Agote had fired first. Agote, who explained that he carried a gun for self-defense because he often traveled to Brazil and Martín Garcia, said that he had had no intention of injuring Viñas, even though the bullet had gone through the back of the chair where Viñas had been sitting.

Agote pleaded innocent on the basis that the shot was a spontaneous act resulting from a nervous fit. The judge then asked for a medical examination of Agote. The court doctors learned from him that his father and siblings had experienced nervous attacks. Upon examination of Agote himself, the doctors found that he suffered from flatulent dyspepsia, liver attacks, insomnia, hypersensitivity, heightened reflexes, a burst blood vessel in the left retina, nearsightedness, and nervous exhaustion. Agote had been harmed by his dedication to intellectual labor that demanded excessive mental effort and tension, the doctors explained. He had become thin and pallid, with a depressed digestive system; stooped, with a vacant look, without vivacity; with migraine, aloof, indifferent, and hypochondriacal. Finally, he suffered from an organic depression that affected his nervous system. "When this depression is prolonged," said the doctors, "the vigor of the nerve cells diminishes, and they become sensitive to the slightest disturbances." The doctors concluded that Agote, overly dominated by his exhausted nervous system, had made an impulsive movement that resulted in a contraction of his muscles and an unintentional firing of his gun. Viñas's words were "so violent, atrocious, and indecent that they would have made the most intimate and delicate cords of the heart vibrate with indignation," Agote said. "Viñas hurled his words against my face like a slap. These words produced in me a spirit of irritation and rage." In his own defense, Agote quoted from the Siete Partidas, a thirteenth-century Spanish law code that continued to be cited: "When a man fears for his body, he loses his head; he changes color; he can move the continent."

The prosecutor pressed for a harsh sentence, classifying the crime as attempted homicide; the defense lawyer argued for a lesser sentence, classifying the crime as the discharging of arms; and the judge opted to drop the case due to lack of evidence against Agote, in what was probably the most politically astute move. But Viñas appealed, especially as he had been fired from the department and had lost a year and a half of his salary. In the end, however, the judge absolved Agote.

CONCLUSION

The theory of degeneration was a useful and nearly all-encompassing means of diagnosing the ills of individuals and societies in the modern mass environment of the later nineteenth century, and it was considered an innovative way to analyze human behavior. Physicians and criminologists not only struggled to apply the theory to their patients and subjects but attempted to use it as an explanation for the success or failure of entire nations and civilizations. Degeneration dug itself into the *porteño* population in the late nineteenth century in a variety of ways—through racial and national degenerative features, and diseases such as hysteria, epilepsy, and neurasthenia. In terms of nation-building, degenerative conditions were seen as a particular threat because, as Lucas Ayarragaray argued in 1887, it was mainly in the "high social classes" where the devastating affects of modern society were felt. People who were dedicated to intellectual work, to politics, to the professions, seldom, he wrote, had good health.[49]

Two of the more important caveats in this focus on the degenerative condition and its manifestations were, first, that such theories delayed the search for other causes of civilization's ills, and, second, that treatment involved extremely radical cures. Such theories could be substituted for social and environmental explanations for poor economic and social conditions, and for perhaps treatable mental disease. For example, although public hygienists were campaigning to clean up *conventillos* and factories in the late nineteenth century, to move cemeteries outside the city center, to build sewers and improve latrines, and so on, they could still say, as Wilde did, that degeneration in the constitution of the city's working class resulted more from workers' own vices and excesses and lack of regimen than from poor living and working conditions and the monotony of factory work.[50] A cure seriously suggested for degeneration seemed to presage the atrocities of the early to mid twentieth century in Europe. "Regeneration," the counterpart of degeneration, it was suggested, was to be accomplished, not through moral improvement, but through physiological purging. That is, improvement of the "race" was no longer to be accomplished through religion, but rather now through evolution, selective marriages, and the castration of born criminals. Just as purgings of the body relieved it of excess blood and so on, the purging of society would eliminate unwanted elements and degenerates. This was considered to be nothing more than preventive medicine, which, it was argued, was not limited to transmissible diseases but rather could be more broadly applied to "preserve the human race from all causes of physical and moral degeneration." The problem with allowing individual acts of transgression, even minor ones, to go unchecked was that they would inevitably spread their degenerative nature to the entire race. What was one day an individual and limited offense, it was argued, could easily be converted the next into a broad social evil. In this reality, then, there was more to be feared from degeneration than from "transitory plagues and contagions," because degeneration was less reversible.[51]

5 Eliminating Threats to the State

While people of color, hysterics, epileptics, and neurasthenics were perceived as exhibiting physical degenerative characteristics that made them less apt to contribute positively to the building of the Argentine "race" and more apt even to commit crimes, it was the moral degenerate, the person who had no moral sensibility, who was seen as posing the larger threat to the modern world. These were people who committed atrocious crimes and felt no remorse, or who rejected their society and committed suicide. They had no respect for the republic or for themselves, not even enough to have a reason for committing a crime or for wanting to end their lives. Degenerative characteristics could be found at all levels and heightened awareness of them led Argentine professionals to take a hard look at the state of justice and the reputation of its practitioners.

Based on social Darwinist notions of natural and artificial selection, the logical solution to the threat of degeneration was to eliminate degenerate individuals. If the true social function of medicine was the biological defense of the human species, oriented toward purely selective ends, José Ingenieros argued in 1902, society needed the "immediate and sweet destruction of incurables and degenerates" to preserve itself. The elimination of incurables and degenerates, in addition to blocking the possibility of the hereditary transmission of bad characteristics, saved society from having to waste precious resources in caring for "parasites." Proponents of such methods agreed, however, that the time was not right for such an extreme measure. Although Ingenieros advocated elimination of society's "waste and rejects," he acknowledged that it was a project for future generations.[1]

The turn of the century witnessed the growth in many countries of the conviction that degenerates, both men and women, should be sterilized or eliminated, although by the least painful means possible. Professionals argued, first, that the science of law ought to conform to the science of biology. Just as nature had the exigency of liquidation, so should law, if it were to be a true science. Any penal disposition that conflicted with a law of physiology, chemistry, physics, or psychology had no more science than the name, the Argentine jurist Carlos Olivera asserted in 1900. Writing fourteen years after the passage of the country's first national penal code, Olivera argued for reforms that relied less on prisons. Incarceration merely multiplied the cases of violent death by the most "toxic" (that is, contagious) elements of society, he argued, hardening the spirits of criminals and making them into martyrs. Liquidation might be revolutionary, but progress only came about through revolution, Olivera argued. While it was true that the idea seemed "irreverent," and that sensitive people might be horrified, their horror would disappear when they saw the benefits of a more hygienic society.[2]

Prolonging the life of anything that harmed society, be it physical disease or degenerates such as "criminals and epileptics," just created social disorder, the Argentine criminologist Rodolfo Benuzzi argued in 1902. Benuzzi praised criminal anthropology and positivist science's commitment to a physiological, rather than moral, approach to degeneration, focusing on analyzing and classifying degenerative types, and defended his radical ideas. Reformers should be open to these ideas, which might seem radical now, but which were no more so than César de Beccaria's proposal to abolish torture to exact confessions had been in the 1760s. Given that there was always objection to innovation, Benuzzi was ready to persevere and face the objections of people who disagreed with him about the policy of liquidation. His plan to build a healthier population included the selection of marriage partners based on health factors and the castration of born criminals. Eventually, it was hoped, the result would be a population free of degenerative features.[3]

Such extreme solutions as castration and elimination were denounced as "absurd or impossible." The category of degenerates was too large, the Argentine doctor Benjamín Solari argued in 1902, based on contemporary lists that included "epileptics; alcoholics; the insane; criminals; people ill from a perversion of conscience or the senses; and racially all the neo-Latin population who, according to criminal anthropology, were subject to an organic and moral decadence through heredity"; mestizos and mulattos likewise tended to degeneration, according to the Brazilian doctor Raimundo Nina Rodrigues in 1894.[4]

This chapter focuses on those perceived as potential candidates for elimination, the real "dregs" of society, people with no redeemable virtues. First, we have Pedro Castro Rodríguez, who murdered his wife and daughter in 1888. His motive was either a weak suspicion of adultery or a desire to get his wife's money. Second, we have Luis Castruccio, who insured his servant and then killed him, also in 1888. His motive was greed. Third, we have the suicide of the discouraged Leandro Alem, an important Argentine statesman, in 1896. All three were seen as suffering from inherited and/or environmental mental degeneracy. Three major psychiatrists—Luis María Drago, José María Ramos Mejía, and José Ingenieros—rendered opinions on their mental states and concluded that they had degenerative characteristics.

In the two 1888 murder cases discussed below, degenerative characteristics played an important role in judgment and sentencing of the criminals. The defendants, Pedro Castro Rodríguez and Luis Castruccio, both committed horrendous crimes and were apprehended at approximately the same time. Both men received death sentences, which, out of respect for "civilization," courts commuted to confinement in a mental hospital for Castro Rodríguez and to a prison term for Castruccio. Both were educated immigrants, the former from Spain and the latter from Italy. There was an important difference between the two criminals, however. The court determined that whereas Castro Rodríguez showed the stigmata of a degenerate and deserved hospitalization, Castruccio did not.

THE PERFECT DEGENERATE

Pedro Castro Rodríguez's murder of his wife and daughter in Olavarría on June 5, 1888, came to be featured by late-nineteenth-century criminologists as the epitome of degeneracy, both because of its atrociousness and because of Pedro's lack of remorse.[5] The fact that Pedro was a priest may have also added to people's horror. Moreover, Pedro had no medical extenuating circumstances, as determined by a lengthy forensic report.

Pedro had had a confrontational relationship with the Church, beginning in Spain and continuing in Argentina, perhaps because his father had forced him to enter the priesthood in spite of his having studied medicine for two years. In terms of the medical history of the family, Pedro's sister, who had also been forced to enter the Church, was described as "always hysterical, with a slight hysteroid color." Pedro had immigrated to Argentina after an armed altercation with a cleric in Spain. In Buenos Aires, he was openly hostile to the archbishop and shocked him by his conduct at a boys' school that he had established in Barracas al Sud. After the archbishop forbade Pedro to say Mass or wear priest's garb, he apostatized and married Rufina Padín in the Methodist Church, had a daughter by her, and joined the "reformed Argentine Church," presided over by the well-known priest Castro Boedo. Later, Pedro returned to Catholicism, "simulated repentance," and accepted an appointment as parish priest of the town of Olavarría, but he apparently continued the relationship with his wife and daughter.

One day, as the police learned from Pedro's correspondence and private papers, because he believed his wife guilty of adultery, wanted her money, or both, Pedro took advantage of an attack of Rufina's asthma to administer a strong dose of atropine camouflaged with licorice and served on a piece of bread. In spite of vomiting and heart palpitations, she attempted to flee. Pedro grabbed her by the neck and began hitting her on the head with a hammer. Terrorized, their ten-year-old daughter ran to his arms, but he took her brutally in his hands, anchored her between his legs, and violently forced poison down her throat. He watched her struggle with death for the next six hours. After pulling the cadavers of his wife and daughter into the parish church, Pedro squashed them into a single coffin, wrote a death certificate for a single body, "a very fat woman whose body had been sent to him from the *campo*," had the casket buried, and continued to say Mass in the church as usual for several months.

There were several reasons why the examining doctors, Drago and Ramos Mejía, found Pedro, who at first sight seemed merely "common and of low origin," an example of a "late stage of degeneration"—a far more interesting scientific specimen. First, the features of his head indicated advanced degeneration. It was a head covered with coarse, abundant skin, "which in some movements ma[de] coarse folds in his neck, recalling the excessive skin of certain animals." He had a narrow forehead, prominent eyebrows, "like the celebrated Neanderthal cranium with its multiplicity of simian characteristics," and a wide, flat face, with visible asymmetry. He had a thin mouth and lips, a long curved nose, fleshy asymmetrical ears, small eyes, large asymmetrical teeth, with premature loss of his molars, and a common and unintelligent look.

Pedro's hands, considered next in importance after his head as the most useful organs to the progress of the species, exhibited several simian characteristics. His fingers, although long, had flat, thick tips; his index finger, although it was "human," had a narrow oponibility; the space between his thumb and forefinger was narrow, whereas it should have been more than forty degrees. He had small nails, and since he had chewed them, a coarse rim covered the ends of his fingers. In sum, Pedro's unrefined and abnormal hand could never be mistaken for the hand of a "cultured, intelligent, and morally well-constituted man."

Pedro's physical insensibility, the next area of examination, showed the doctors his moral insensitivity. Transmission of all types of impressions, physical and moral, were slowed by Pedro's flesh because of his weak organs and systems, which resulted in mental inertia and slow reactions. The range of insensitivity of degenerates ran from slight to deep idiotism, as described by the Italian Giuseppe Sergi in 1900. Between the two extremes, there existed an immense variety of degenerative states. Along with the slowness and atrophy of sentiments went "weakness of memory; difficulty in forming images and associating ideas; unfocused and dull perceptions and apperception; and a lack of will and inhibitory power that signified energy, and moral and intellectual activities."

The examination for sensitivity done on Pedro began with the end of the third finger and continued upward, using Weber's esthesiometer. The doctors measured the sensitivity of Pedro's fingers, the tip of his tongue and nose, the nape of his neck, the end of his metacarpal, the ball of his thumb, and his lower forearm. Recognizing that these measurements could sometimes vary a great deal, the doctors took into account Pedro's age and social condition, the delicacy of his skin, his anemia or hyperemia, and the temperature of his body and the environment. Pedro had reduced general tactile sensation of volume, form, direction, and consistency of objects, and reduced local and topographical sensation. Some of his senses were also dull. For example, his right ear could not hear a watch at twenty-five centimeters, or his left ear at twenty. He had difficulty tasting pepper and bitter substances, and his sense of smell was dull for some odors. Pedro's dullness, concluded the doctors, had its source in his weak nervous system.

Even though Pedro's crime, on its own, indicated his moral level, the forensic doctors considered other factors in order, they said, to be physiologically complete. For example, they used Richard von Krafft-Ebing's observation that the most famous delinquents "lacked [even] the most elemental sentiments of human nature," which fitted Pedro's case well. Pedro's description of his deceased wife, which was repeated throughout the public commentaries and court records, supported Krafft-Ebing's observation. "She didn't stop looking ridiculous for a moment," said Pedro, "when I was dragging her body into the church. She was my fat [metida en carnes] wife, and dragging her body, taking her by the feet, her skirt got wrapped around her head in such a way that I had to laugh at her grotesque figure." Shocked, the doctors reported that Pedro had not expressed a word of remorse for his wife or daughter, and that he confessed his crime with complete tranquility. On the contrary, Pedro perfectly exemplified the "puerile vanity of criminals," their excessive egoism, often cited by criminologists as typical of the worst criminals.

Besides his "frightening moral insensitivity," Pedro displayed a penchant for luxury in his correspondence and had been criticized by his parish for excessive partying.[6]

In spite of the doctors' recognition that Pedro was "relatively enlightened," in that he had studied medicine, literature, theology, natural history, and chemistry, they found his intelligence "less than average." His father's gout had caused defects in Pedro's nervous system. Doctors knew that gout, the cause of which was bad nutrition, could develop in following generations into diabetes, dyspepsias, obesity, insanity, nervous disorders, idiotism, deformities, sterility, and even criminality. Pedro, the doctors argued, was clearly an example of the final stages of degeneration: he must have been sterile, since he had only had one child in spite of his wild lifestyle, and he had committed a heinous crime.

For Pedro's responsibility to be mitigated or negated, the doctors had to find evidence that he had suffered a mental disturbance, passion, or insanity. The doctors quickly eliminated the first condition of acute mania and imbecility, because Pedro did not fit this diagnosis. They also eliminated passion, because the long death scene of the murder victims was inconsistent with the nature of passionate impulses. Moreover, a passional criminal immediately repented, while Pedro had remained cold and unrepentant. In fact, ignorance of sentiments such as piety and charity formed the basis of natural criminality. Furthermore, Pedro did not have the "appeal and attractiveness, fire, nervousness, and sensitivity" of the passionate person. Rather, he was, in stark contrast, the "born criminal," "ugly, degenerate, cruel, and lethargic." He had physical degenerative abnormalities, which a passionate man did not. The doctors also eliminated insanity. The most likely types of insanity in a case like this, they said, originated with a delirium of persecution, an alcoholic delirium, or larval epilepsy. The doctors eliminated feelings of persecution, because no evidence existed that anything had clouded Pedro's reason, and he was expansive and a charlatan, unlike persecuted people. The doctors also eliminated alcoholism, because Pedro was never reported to be a drunk and he showed no trace of the dementia that followed drunkenness. Finally, he had not suffered an epileptic attack, they said, because he remembered everything that had happened. Pedro could have tried to simulate any of the above conditions, but his degeneracy made this unlikely. The doctors concluded that Pedro was totally responsible for his actions. He was sentenced to death, but was allowed to go instead into a mental hospital.

This was an act of clemency, because forensic doctors had evaluated him as sane, a born criminal, and totally responsible for his actions, thus deserving of prison. However, Pedro had the physical stigmata of degeneracy and morbid heredity through his father's gout, which was enough to gain him hospitalization.

THE MORALLY INSANE DEGENERATE

In contrast, the criminal Luis, because he did not exhibit the physical stigmata of degeneracy and did not have morbid heredity like Pedro's family gout, could not conclusively be found insane.[7] The doctors' ambivalence paved the way for the death sentence. The medical examination of Luis that reached the verdict of his possible insanity took a year and perplexed the court. The characteristics that pointed to the possibility that Luis might be morally insane, not shared by Pedro, were his masturbation, pederasty, and refraining from heterosexual coitus.

The origin of Luis's criminality bore out the often-voiced criticism that immigrants' greed was undermining social stability in Argentina. Modern times brought an increase in mental illness, new inclinations and passions that confused reason, and ambitions that only a few could satisfy.[8] Luis Castruccio, who had emigrated from Genoa, Italy, to Buenos Aires in 1878, had endeavored to "make [it in] America" through life insurance fraud. This was a relatively new crime, in that little had been written about it, and Luis's victims had no notion of life insurance, as explained by those who survived his attempts on their lives and by witnesses. The abuses of life insurance were already known, though, in police circles, where it was reported to "excite sordid passions and incite crime." Life insurance presupposed knowledge of a "science of numbers that allowed the calculation of probabilities; a civil state regularly led; tables of mortality; a self-assured spirit of association; government that guaranteed public security; impartial justice; a well-rooted spirit of family; and a knowledge of laws of political economy."[9] Luis was fourteen when he arrived in Argentina, and within a few years, he was scheming the death, by chloroform, of various young male servants in his employ in order to profit from a life insurance scam. He finally succeeded in 1888. After he had insured the life of his servant Alberto Bouchot Constantín for 10,000 pesos and contracted to marry Bouchot's sister, Luis poisoned Constantín with arsenic and suffocated him. Luis was such a cold-blooded murderer that he attracted the interest of criminologists, and with the opening of the Institute of Criminology at the National Penitentiary in 1907, Luis became one of the first prisoners studied. He was still alive because, although he had been con-

demned to death, the president of the republic, Miguel Juárez Celman, had
commuted the sentence to prison in 1889 (elaborated on in chapter 6).

The first issue that the doctors had to sort out was whether Luis suffered
from dementia and/or from insanity (*locura*). Popular medicine and the penal
code both lagged behind new research and adhered to the older theory that
the two conditions were the same, and that both were caused by the molecular disturbance of the cerebral mass. According to the older theory, the causes of disturbances took a wide variety of forms and included "excesses of temperature, drink, prostitution; heredity; consumptive illnesses; wounds and
blows to the head; bad digestion; tobacco snuff; ambition, pride, fear, love,
anger, shocks; vicissitudes of family and fortune; humiliations, hypochondria,
epilepsy, melancholy, masturbation, uterine furor (nymphomania), and a
thousand other things." The symptoms of insanity were "extravagance,
impetuousness, and fantastic plans; and a lack of respect, memory, and rationality; excessive rage, joy or complete dullness; tears; total silence; anxiety;
insensitivity to heat and cold; dry cold skin; bad odor; crossed teeth." Insanity
was popularly treated with vomitives, purgatives, sedatives, baths, and exercise.[10]

The 1886 penal code also did not distinguish between conditions like
dementia and insanity, and it only referred in general to "locura, somnambulism, absolute imbecility, or complete and involuntary drunkenness." More in
tune with modern studies on insanity, the doctors in Luis's case argued that
whereas dementia had quite obvious characteristics and was "just idiotism
acquired under the powerful influence of factors such as [old] age and alcoholism," locura was the result of some definite intellectual disturbance or
delirium, which was often hidden, even from patients themselves. Inspired by
the new sciences, the doctors explained to the judge that it was an absolute
necessity that they use positivism and criminal anthropology to evaluate Luis,
even though the 1886 penal code did not contain any of these principles.
They chose to do this both because the theories and techniques were worth-
while, they said, and also because it would favor Luis's case, since the new sciences accepted that moral insanity often proceeded from morbid heredity or
organic influences and could annul a person's free will.

Drago's 1888 work *Los hombres de presa: Antropolojía criminal*, quoted by
the examining doctors in the case, explained that the condition of moral
insanity was best defined as dominated by "moral dullness." Moral degenerates who had committed criminal acts had no repugnance or remorse for their
crimes. With their natural morality rarely surfacing, they rejected what was
beautiful and good, and concern for others, and were motivated by personal

interest. They often spoke about honor, order, religion, philanthropy, morality, justice, and patriotism, but they lacked the sentiments. The lack of a moral
sense, of sentiments of honor, and so on made these people easy targets for
the influences of morbid heredity and the environment and meant that they
had no moral liberty and were truly prejudicial to the collectivity.[11]

Luis's cruelty and his lack of repentance, grief, or any other affective faculty supported the above description of the nature of moral insanity. Far from
showing repugnance for his crime, Luis had had to repeat his scheme several times before succeeding in killing one of his chosen targets. He showed no
remorse when he first confessed to the police. Even as he was being led off to
prison, all he thought about was how soon the insurance company would pay
him. The only thing that he had to say about his victim was that Bouchot had
been saved a lengthy painful death because of his own, Luis's, scientific hur-
rying along of the death, "just as Othello had done when he killed Des-
demona."[12] Luis's chosen weapon of poison, used against a person he had
recently met and toward whom he had no ill will, underscored his moral degeneracy.

The evidence considered by the doctors in determining Luis's condition
included a long list of his catastrophic antecedents, which could also support
a diagnosis of moral degeneracy. It was a known scientific fact, after all, that
madness was transmitted through heredity. Luis's uncle had hanged himself
in 1872 in a mental asylum in Genoa, Italy. His father had committed suicide
by throwing himself in front of a train in 1884. His only brother had returned
to Italy after this, leaving Luis alone in Buenos Aires, and his mother had died
in childbirth.

Luis's lawyer used these catastrophes to argue that Luis had been congen-
itally predisposed to insanity, and that this predisposition was exacerbated and
converted into the illness by the sexual aberrations noted by the doctors. Early
on, Luis had decided to abstain from coitus. It seems that he had made a vow
of abstinence to protest his father's refusal to allow him to enter the priesthood. In Luis's own words, his objective was "to cut out at the root [his] pro-
creative powers and extinguish completely [his] branch . . . annulling the
power of love completely." In addition, he had a strong aversion to women. In
his suicide plan of 1887, which he did not act on, he left a note bequeathing
his property to the Italian Hospital in Buenos Aires, but only on the condition
that the funds not be used to support the women's ward, because, as he
explained, women were "harmful and annoying."[13] Luis's male servants
described him as a pederast, a vice that reportedly accompanied dementia.
When examining Luis in the penitentiary, the doctors noted that he was "ef-

feminate," because of the way he "walked and moved his body," and because of the "beauty of his manners and the relative meticulousness of his clothing with respect to the other inmates."

A long-term habit of masturbation, also considered a sexual "abnormality," had exacerbated Luis's condition. Masturbation, in particular excessive masturbation, was considered to be a serious disease or disease state. As it was described in a popular medical manual, the "disease's" symptoms were difficult digestion, paleness, weakness, recurring illness, trembling limbs, involuntary pollutions, loss of memory, kidney pain, head pain, cough, consumption, and hypochondria. The treatment that was suggested to sufferers was to stop masturbating; separate youths from bad company; avoid obscene books and conversation; and institute strict surveillance of schoolchildren of both sexes.[14]

In addition to being discussed as a disease, masturbation was also considered an organic and behavioral sign of hereditary degeneration, similar to the stigma of asymmetrical ears, which could lead to more serious diseases in the masturbator and to criminal acts. As with the effects of mental fatigue, doctors described masturbation as reducing the brain's energy and weakening the body, thus increasing the chances of a hereditary degenerative feature emerging from the bodies of susceptible individuals. According to doctors, onanism left children with a weak personality and no initiative, left adults fatigued and dulled, and disposed people to suicide.[15] An inveterate masturbator supposedly showed his condition in his weak spirit, his fatigue, and his inability to fend off inclinations to crime.

Masturbation reportedly made its "victim" insensible to reason, which clearly allowed it to be considered as an extenuating circumstance when assigning criminal responsibility. On the other hand, masturbators had the responsibility of self-control. Although professionals recognized masturbation as a common activity, not necessarily leading to crime, they warned that people who did not try to curb the habit were contributing to their own demise. The doctors noted that the foreskin on Luis's penis was "large and elastic, and that with the slightest pull, the glans indicated that he was either a frequent masturbator or had schemed to meet the legitimate needs of his organism in some other way." In spite of the overwhelming evidence that Luis might well be one of these inveterate masturbators, unable to fend off inclinations to crime, the doctors rejected the idea that Luis was a masturbator. Their reason was very interesting. Luis was not a masturbator, they wrote, because if he were, the disease would have left traces on his "intellectual level and cerebral functioning," areas in which he was quite normal.

Again, in spite of evidence to the contrary, the doctors also decided that Luis was not morally insane, which undercut the defense lawyer's assertion that Luis had been born with a "faulty moral complexion" and had turned to crime "obeying the impulses of his sick brain." The doctors based their decision on the fact that Luis had had a motive for his crime and because even though he had questionable antecedents, Luis himself showed no sign of morbid heredity and in fact was probably using his catastrophic antecedents in an effort to simulate insanity. First, the morally insane generally lacked a motive for their crimes. This was logical, the doctors said, because such people experienced hallucinations of sight or hearing and irresistible impulses that were completely pathological and translated into aggressive acts. The morally insane were driven by a general or partial delirium and committed crimes unconsciously; hence, they were not responsible. Luis, however, had had money as a motive. Moreover, his cerebral functioning was good. He had total memory, association of ideas, the ability to make judgments and give satisfactory answers, and could engage in eloquent mental gymnastics.

Second, Luis himself showed no signs of morbid heredity. Moreover, his insistence on talking about his family's suicides and his self-definition as a crazy person—when he said that only a crazy person would insure the life of someone he did not even know or contract marriage with that person's sister whom he also did not know, made the doctors suspect that Luis was trying to simulate insanity. He was also probably trying to simulate insanity when he was first being observed by the doctors in prison. They tried to be secretive, observing him through a small pane of glass in his cell door, but he heard them coming, "so he adopted an affected and confident air, walking around his cell with an open book in his hands, . . . affecting truly comical attitudes." The doctors knew this was dissimulation, because after a while in prison, Luis dropped this behavior. Moreover, his case was totally unlike those of the "certifiably insane."

The forensic doctors concluded that Luis was not evil for the sake of it, like children who tormented animals or mothers who aborted their pregnancies in order to preserve their beauty, or like Pedro in the previous case, who had poisoned his wife and daughter, but rather that he was evil for the sake of greed. Their examination of Luis took one year, which they explained to the judge was necessary because of the seriousness of the case. Basing their work on Lombroso's 1876 work *L'uomo delinquente* and Drago's 1888 *Los hombres de presa*, they informed themselves about the identification of a *loco moral*. In weighing the evidence from their studies and examinations of Luis, the doctors concluded that while Luis had the characteristics of lack of repugnance and remorse for crime and the moral dullness that identified a morally insane person, his cranial measurements were normal, his features were symmetrical, and his physionomical traits were regular. On the other hand, according to Lombroso, morally insane people could exist who did not have these characteristics. This had in fact been proven in a European study in which it was found that out of twenty-four morally insane "criminals," only ten had anomalies of the cranium. The doctors decided that Luis was such a person, that is, a morally insane person without the stigmata of a born criminal.

In their report to the judge, however, the doctors were not completely conclusive, saying:

> If Luis's cruelty, his lack of repentance, and his absolute lack of moral sense—in spite of having complete intellectual integrity and having coldly premeditated a criminal act that resulted in a real advantage for him—constitute *locura moral*, then, Judge, Luis can be accepted as a *loco moral*. But in the present case, we can well believe, following Lombroso, that the morally insane like Luis are confused with criminals. We believe that Luis must be included in this group, and thus [judged to have] enough moral freedom to establish complete responsibility for his crime.

The doctors' lack of a definitive judgment on Luis, which greatly annoyed the judge, merely reflected the confusion at the time between the insane and criminals.

There were many theoretical problems that had to be ironed out in the new sciences, and judges were continually coming up against what many believed were facetious arguments and theories made up to excuse delinquents from being punished. The judge and prosecutor were angry in Luis's case because the doctors waffled. The defense lawyer was angry, arguing that if there were scientific doubts in a case, the accused should be absolved. How could a court sentence a man to death, he demanded, when there was doubt? Penal science and mental medicine were still investigating insanity. Experiments had been conducted in France to try to distinguish between insane ideas and logical ideas in order to be able to resolve the problem of identifying the morally insane. But the experiments had proved "surprising and almost embarrassing" when no difference between insane and logical ideas could be noted.[16] When major European scientists such as Lombroso (1876) and Tarde (1886) contradicted each other, and when the medical profession admitted that there was confusion and reason for scientific doubt, then Luis had to be given the benefit of the doubt. This was especially the case, the lawyer protested, because Pedro Castro Rodríguez, whom he described as one of the century's worst criminals, had just received the court's clemency without even being considered insane.

Whether or not Luis was morally insane was a moot point, though, because the appeals court refused to accept Luis's form of insanity as an extenuating circumstance for or exemption from responsibility for his criminal act. Their reasoning was a strong attack on the new school of criminal anthropology and on positivism, and it illustrates the nature of the opposition to the new sciences. According to the court's interpretation, the insanity referred to in article 81 of the 1886 penal code, which listed the legally accepted exemptions, was the kind of insanity that suppressed the consciousness of criminality. This kind of insanity had its main cause and place in the spirit. In this kind of insanity, one of two things happened. Either one of the intellectual faculties became dominant over the others, or the tie that united the faculties was weakened in such a way that each intellectual faculty was abandoned to its own impulse. In both cases, the spirit lost reason, that is, the spirit lost the faculty to discover unity, linkage, order, and harmony in things—because, when the interior order of the faculties was missing, the spirit was incapable of recognizing order and unity in the exterior world. In sum, the spirit was *real*. Positivist theory, in contrast, the court criticized, made the spirit into an *abstraction*. According to positivism, human life was ruled only by changes in the organs and functions of the body, especially of the brain, and not by the spirit. Because positivist theory was governed by materialism, rather than spiritualism, the judges wrote, it was totally contrary to Argentina's penal legislation, which rested on moral order and free will. The death penalty for Luis was confirmed, based on the medical report that he was not insane, that is, omitting the doctors' caveat, and on his use of poison, his malice, and his premeditation.

Luis's sentence was commuted to a prison sentence, however, so that twenty years later, José Ingenieros was still able to analyze him. With twenty years' more experience and study, Ingenieros could confidently talk about Luis's degeneracy. Even though much time had passed, his crime had not been forgotten. Later, in the penitentiary, his imbalance changed into frank mental illness, under the clinical form of "chronic hallucinatory polymorphous delirium." His insanity became clearer; he was dominated by delirious polymorphous ideas and sensory and coenesthetic hallucinations. His mental state had deteriorated slowly and he had adapted to prison well, so he had not yet been taken to the Hospicio de las Mercedes at the time when Ingenieros was doing this analysis. Wanting to reconstruct Luis's psychology, Ingenieros had tried to get hold of the voluminous court case from the tribunal archives, but was unsuccessful.[17]

For Ingenieros, Luis's crime and his psychology seemed to typify Argentina's immigrant environment. First, Luis came from a poor background but had received some education. A little education was worse than none, however, in that it only served to "intoxicate" immigrants' spirits, "awakening in their imagination the desire for wealth." Although the desire for wealth was natural in an immigrant country, it was fatal for people like Luis, because his degenerative mentality impeded him from becoming a productive worker and getting rich as many immigrants had done in Argentina. Pressed to compete and do as well as his compatriots, Luis was "forced" into following a different route to personal wealth. Because of his psychic deficiency, he did not have the ability to "save and progress." Even in his choice of the means of murder, one could see his illness. He delighted in pulling off a complicated and novel act. His attempts to use chloroform were novelesque. After his first failures, he could have chosen another method, but he continued to use chloroform "with the perseverance of an artist modeling clay." Besides the lack of a moral sense, Ingenieros noted in Luis a "criminal vanity." It was clear from what Ingenieros later wrote about criminal vanity in connection with the trial of Tullio Murri (discussed in chapter 6) that this characteristic was a fatal flaw that particularly disturbed Ingenieros. In Luis's case, evidence of his vanity emerged when he proudly claimed that his crime was "suave, meditated, and scientific," and that he could tolerate ten years in prison, because it was an adequate amount of time to devote to his studies. What he regretted most was that the insurance company had won the claim in only eight days. In Ingenieros's view, besides being a congenital amoral person, Luis had long been a mental degenerate, which had probably been inherited. His advantage, however, was that he was "intellectually lucid," which masked his lack of intelligence and malformed moral sense.[18]

When Luis first entered the penitentiary, the section for the delinquent mentally ill in the Hospicio de las Mercedes did not yet exist. Thus, it was not unusual to find the mentally ill among the prisoners. Inmates such as Luis were, in fact, an attraction for visitors to the penitentiary. There were criminals who were morbidly interesting, such as one of Luis's contemporaries, the famous criminal Pagano, a homicidal epileptic who went mad in jail and had to be chained. Luis, on the other hand, interested people because he entertained them. He was described by Ingenieros as picaresque and pleasantly loquacious, and he had a genius for communicating aberrant ideas. In 1907, when the Institute of Criminology was founded, Luis became one of its first subjects. Ingenieros and other doctors observed him first in the printing work-shop, where he was not an efficient worker and engaged in soliloquies in a loud voice that did not make any sense, although he seemed kind and nice. In the workshop, Ingenieros wrote in 1909, he submitted to discipline, but his mental disorder was obvious. He much preferred his solitude and hallucina-tory conversations to associating with the other inmates. As a student at the "convicts' school," Luis was reported to do his work well, though he wrote with "pompous phrases and lots of adjectives." Luis once asked if in a repub-lic, the people were sovereign. The answer was yes, and Luis replied that he could not conceive of sovereigns without subjects and that he did not know who the subjects of the Argentine citizens were. To get to know his mental defects better, Ingenieros and the other doctors asked him to answer in writ-ing some questions that he was told would serve for his pardon. When asked why Bouchot had died, Luis replied that it was the result of natural illness and that the attending doctor had said that it was produced by indigestion and headaches that had caused cerebral congestion. Regarding his own health, Luis told the doctors that he suffered from the effects of bad spirits, electrici-ty, and magnetism, which recalls Monges's interest in spiritism. Neither Monges nor Luis, however, were really in a marginal group in their beliefs, because studies of spiritism, magnetism, and so on were all established inno-vations of the period. Drago's interviews with Luis revealed that Luis was an atheist. "The only hell is not what the hypocrite in the Vatican describes," said Luis, "but the central fire that does more evil to the living than to the dead." Tiring of the penitentiary, and determined to be pardoned and released, Luis spent a great deal of time writing requests, not only for pardon but also for indemnification from the government for the time that he had spent incar-cerated. His obsession with getting out of the penitentiary eventually led to his transfer to the Hospicio de las Mercedes.[19]

THE SUICIDAL DEGENERATE

Pedro and Luis, degenerates of moderate means and somewhat educated, ended up as criminals, threatening the republic. So too did suicide victims. The increase in suicide in the late nineteenth and early twentieth centuries was viewed as an indicator of the level of well-being of society and a warning that there was a flaw in the model of development that Argentina had chosen. The choice to commit suicide was considered to be a negative judgment against Argentina, Víctor Arreguiné wrote in 1905, and thus an unpatriotic and anti-social act.[20] Suicide also reflected both urban and immigrant problems and contagion and degeneration. The fact that the largest number of suicides occurred among males aged sixteen to twenty-five was not only a product of demography, determined by the disproportionate number of young adult male immigrants, but also an indicator of the general health of the economy and society. The suicide statistics also reflected the phenomenon of imitative contagion, which the Argentine physician and director of the Sanatorio de Santa María in the city of Córdoba, Fermín Rodríguez (the son), described in 1905 as a "moral epidemic whose prophylaxis [was] difficult and whose intensity and propagation [depended] on the diseased state of the universal conscience." The worse the general conscience was, the more suicides there would be. Suicide was more morally contagious in certain situations, especially in *conventillos*, where the general level of living was poor. The suicide rate, especially among young people, also reflected degeneration. Youth were especially susceptible to the "projectiles of inheritance and environment," and youth suicide was thus a good predictor of things like latent alcoholism and larval epilepsy. Inheritance and environment included parental alcoholism, masturbation, hysteria, epilepsy, rheumatism, tuberculosis, typhoid fever, sex with prostitutes, and the reading of bloodthirsty and immoral pamphlets. Degenerative diseases, such as gonorrhea, syphilis, and neurasthenia, prepared the ground for suicide, which moved in on sufferers like a "traitor, taking advantage of the general ill health of their organisms, their weakness, sexual impotency, and insomnia."[21]

Two factors in Buenos Aires society led Argentine scientists to maintain that suicide in Buenos Aires was distinct from the phenomenon in European cities, where much of the suicide research had been conducted to date. First, Arreguiné speculated in 1905 that among the many European immigrants to the republic, a disproportionate number might well already have had the seed of suicide in them before they left Europe, increasing the number of potential suicides in Argentina. In fact, they might have emigrated precisely because they saw emigration as a last chance to make good and their only alternative to suicide. If their fortune did not change after immigration, they were thus already on the starting block toward suicide, so to speak. It was also considered probable that immigrants had higher hopes than native-born Argentinians, making the disappointments they experienced greater.[22]

The second factor was Argentina's ambivalence about European civilization and progress. On the one hand, people argued that suicide had increased owing to the republic's lack of civilization. On the other hand, the very civilization being sought, itself corrupt and antithetical to national identity, might be a cause of suicide. In this case, the problem was encased in the negative effects of "excess," which was a kind of blanket concern in the late nineteenth century. An excess of civilization, and the problems and yearnings it created, could be just as harmful as a lack of civilization. In a way, Argentina's colonial past, its advanced stage of development, and its heavy European immigration may have allowed Argentines the luxury of feeling that they could criticize Europe. What also came into play, however, was Argentina's own history as a new nation. The Argentine gaucho, a kind of "noble savage" who was associated with anti-civilization and in whose society suicide was allegedly absent, epitomized the ambivalence. Lucas Ayarragaray argued in 1902 that suicide was "entirely foreign to the psychology of our gaucho." Being physically and mentally healthy, gauchos did not translate their problems into "melancholic desperation, typical of civilization, but rather into immediate and vigorous action." In contrast to the gaucho, people in cities, "neuropathics and the exhausted," products of the sedentary life of luxury and excess, were more susceptible to suicide. With the advance of progress, however, Ayarragaray direly predicted, this noble part of the Argentine national character would disappear and suicide would move into the countryside, "a painful tribute that the weak and exhausted will pay in the hazardous struggle for life that civilization imposes on us."[23]

Suicide attracted the attention of political and professional elites in the second half of the nineteenth century for several reasons. First, suicide formed part of the growing study of pathological mental conditions, based on the work of the French physicians Philippe Pinel and Etienne Esquirol from the first half of the century.[24] New statistical data indicated that suicide was a growing trend. Second, the conceptualization of suicide as a contagion or epidemic, similar to social phenomena, repositioned private voluntary death as a public danger. Third, scientists' confidence that such social phenomena could actually be controlled, because they were either partly or wholly biologically based, led to increased investigation and analysis of suicide. Finally, the growing tendency toward suicide confirmed the degeneracy of contemporary societies and Western civilization.

Publication of suicide statistics in France in 1827, England in the mid 1850s, Italy in the mid 1860s, and Germany, Prussia, and Bavaria in the early 1880s made it possible to see the increase in suicide.[25] Government offices collected data that allowed scientists to examine the correlation between suicide and gender, age, civil status, religious affiliation, and wind direction, and preferences as to method, location, season of the year, and time of day. These studies also elaborated suicide's relationship to homicide; wars; political and economic crises; mental illness and alcoholism; heredity and ethnicity; pas-

sion, honor, and shame; and onanism, epilepsy, hypochondria, and neurasthenia. By the end of the nineteenth century, scientists were labeling suicide
a "universal plague," which was said to reflect "a coming universal wish not
to live."[26] In eleven European countries, the average rate of suicide increased
by 64 percent between 1840 and 1877, and by 14 percent between 1877 and
1912. Although the increase slowed after 1877, it remained appreciable.[27]

Alarming as the increase in suicide rates appeared to be, the real danger,
the French scientists Esquirol, Gabriel Tarde, and Paul Aubry argued, lay not
in the number of people lost to society, but in people's imitation of acts of suicide and the "contagious depression that [suicide] propagate[d]," leading to
degeneration. Like diseases such as typhus, the contagion of suicide "weakened the strength and courage of those who breathed it in the air." When they
experienced setbacks in daily life, they became overwhelmed by dismay and
could not handle it and spread their infection.[28] A further disturbing aspect of
contagion, the Argentine Miguel A. Lancelotti argued in 1914, was that a relationship often existed between suicide and homicide, with the homicide
being committed first, followed by suicide out of remorse or to escape the consequences of one's crime.[29]

Some professionals saw suicide as having pathological origins, and autopsies of suicide victims that showed brain lesions supported the organic view.
The Italians Enrico Ferri and Enrico Morselli argued that suicide was always
an expression of mental illness, the result of a disorder in the body's organization. Others saw suicide as a freely chosen act, such as Frenchman Émile
Durkheim, who argued in the early 1900s that social causes, not pathological
ones, and imitation were responsible for suicide. Esquirol argued in the early
nineteenth century for the intermediate position that while suicide was not
actually an illness such as mental alienation, it was "analogous" to it.[30]

While organic and inherited conditions could cause suicide, so could environmental factors, and the suicide rate could be read as a commentary on the
contemporary world and a challenge to the values upon which modernity and
progress were based. Morselli argued in 1882, for example, that the struggle for
existence and of human selection provided fertile ground for the growth of
suicide as an answer for weaker members of society who could not cope with
the stresses of civilization and could not satisfy their desires. Civilization's
"runaway science, technology, and urbanism" instilled a sense of "power-
lessness" into people, the English psychologist Havelock Ellis wrote in 1881.[31]
Other analysts, such as the Frenchman Maurice Halbwachs in 1930, however, blamed not civilization and progress themselves, but rather the conditions
under which states were moving toward progress. Society's fragmentation, he

argued, deprived people of support at the same time that it "kept them in a crowded situation where the chances of injury and wounds were multiplied." Durkheim had already earlier blamed suicide on the lack of social integration and on the weakened bonds attaching people to society. These analyses took an elitist and insidious direction in promoting the view that the suicide rate would be reduced if people just accepted their place in the social hierarchy and adapted to the demands of progress. That is, the cause of suicide did not derive from flaws in the model of the industrial revolution and a laissez-faire economy, but rather from people's inability to accept and adapt. The argument concluded that suicide should be seen as an enemy of the established order and the favorite social model.[32]

In 1881, the suicide rate in Buenos Aires had been only 11 suicides (not including attempts) per 100,000 inhabitants. By 1897, this had increased to 37. While an accurate construction of reliable comparative statistical tables is almost impossible for this period, the perception, at least of *porteños*, and undoubtedly it was based on hard data in some form, was that Buenos Aires had a higher suicide rate than London, the classic city of suicide, and that the Argentine capital had earned the name of "the Minotaur of suicide" for a good reason.[33] In a comparison of just two years, in order to show the increase of suicide in the city, Buenos Aires had 36 suicides in 1881—30 men and 6 women—out of a total population of 327,323. In 1897, the number was 267— 184 men and 83 women—out of a total population of 715,052. Arreguiné, the source of these figures, warned that they were incomplete and suggested increasing them by 5 percent because of families' tendency to hide suicides and because some suicides, perhaps many, were reported as other kinds of deaths or as having unknown causes. Fermín Rodríguez expressed alarm in 1905, especially at the increase of suicide in the susceptible sixteen-to-twenty-year-old age group.[34]

Arreguiné also provided statistics on presumed motives of suicide, comparing the city of Buenos Aires (between 1884 and 1895) with the province (between 1891 and 1900). The "miscellaneous or unknown" category was the largest for both: 593 cases for the city of Buenos Aires and 903 for the province. In descending order for the city, the other causes were: "tired of life"—351; "financial"—161; "mental derangement (alienation)"—149; "passion"—120; "physical problems"—120; "alcoholism"—23; and "fear of punishment"—7. In descending order for the province, the causes were: "mental derangement"—224; "physical problems"—202; "passions"—180; "tired of life"—145; "disappointed love"—124; "business problems"—78; "alcoholism"—77; "poverty"—64; and "bad treatment"—42.[35]

Of the cases available for consultation in the National Archives covering 1860 to 1903, 155 involved male suicides; 25, female; 58, attempted male suicides; and 31, female. Of the 85 cases examined, "honor" was by far the main justification given for the suicide (20 cases). "Mental illness" (17) and "poor physical health" (17) followed; then "tired of life" (9) and "poverty" (9); "alcohol" (6) and "failing business" (2), and a general category in which family disappointments were cited in the majority of cases (13). Men most often used firearms in their suicides, and women most often took poison, used revolvers, or threw themselves into wells.

Just as degenerative terrain could cause other kinds of deviant behavior, it could also cause a tendency to commit suicide. An unmarried twenty-three-year-old Italian woman, María Carnevale, with twenty years' residence in Argentina and no money, goods, or family there, lived and worked in a house of prostitution on Calle Necochea in La Boca. In 1881, she slit her throat with a razor, accidentally left in her room by one of her customers, an Englishman. She was first sent to the General Hospital for Women as a detainee, and then to the Hospicio de Dementes. The medical-legal report confirmed that she had suffered an attack of mental illness brought on by "a monomania" and that her dementia was caused by an excess of alcohol. She had an illness that made her choke and her whole body trembled. The suicide attempt had all happened quickly. She had been in bed, nude, when she fell on the floor and started screaming that she had a devil in her throat. She wanted to bolt, nude as she was, but then she seemed to calm down, and the other prostitutes went back to their work. At this point, she ran for the razor and slashed herself in the throat, saying that she had a devil, a *mandinga*, in her body and to bring a priest to get the devil out. She was treated at the pharmacy and then questioned by the police.[36]

A fourteen-year-old servant girl who threw herself into a cistern after she was reprimanded by her employer in 1882 was diagnosed as degenerate. After the reprimand, the girl asked to leave her employer, yet when her mother came to get her, the girl insulted her so viciously that the mother asked the police to place the girl with the Defense of Minors Office. The girl was thus trapped between a disgruntled employer, a parent who could not handle her, and the Defense of Minors Office. This was when she threw herself into the cistern. She survived her attempt and explained that she had felt impelled to jump by a force superior to her will. Investigating doctors described her as having "slightly crossed eyes," a "vagueness," and a twitching in her fingers and arm. In addition, her cranium was not perfectly formed and was of the kind often found in epileptics. Her antecedents included a mentally ill, alcoholic father, who was in an asylum. The doctors diagnosed this attempted suicide as due to a melancholic impulse (*raptus melancolico*), and she was put at the disposition of the Defense of Minors Office.[37]

Both single men and single women were more likely to have suicidal tendencies than married people. This phenomenon had been noted early on when suicide statistics had first become available. Fermín Rodríguez was one of the physicians who researched the motives for the suicide of single women whose maternal organs were not yet being put to proper use in pregnancy or nursing. As we have seen, anomalies of the female reproductive system were held responsible for a whole range of female actions. Rodríguez held that hysteria, believed to be connected to the uterus, was usually evident in female suicides. He explained that while he did not support the idea that "woman [was] a womb served by organs," suggested by Samuel Jean Pozzi in his treatise on gynecology published in 1890, Rodríguez did support the view that the "genital apparatus of women represents the principal essence of the female organism, and that the normal state of women was pregnancy or nursing." Moreover, he argued, women's "organization" did not adapt to the social environment in a parallel way to men's. Women's organization remained stationary, while men's advanced, which created an imbalance that hurt them both. Positioned between "the two extremes of nubility and menopause," he wrote, single women, since they had not yet realized their primordial function of maternity, easily became unbalanced.[38] The absence of maternity explained their hysteria, the absence also feeding off the effects of heredity, arthritis, tuberculosis, alcoholism, and syphilis, which had prepared the way for their bodies to be affected by the "seeds" of hysteria latent in their parents.

Seventeen-year-old Teresa Cardeviola threw herself into a well in 1882 because she felt ashamed that she had offended her fiancé, but she was rescued by her family. Declining to dance with him the previous evening, because no one else was dancing, she had made her fiancé angry, and her sister remonstrated with her that she had done something bad. Without thinking, Teresa said, she had thrown herself into the well. In the investigation, it was learned that Teresa suffered from epilepsy. This was precisely the situation that Rodríguez had described, namely, that Teresa's epilepsy had prepared the way for her hysteria, described in her case as her "state of nervous excitation with slight restless movements." According to this analysis, represented by Rodríguez and others, even the slightest disturbance to the female organism could provoke suicide, especially if the terrain had already been prepared by heredity.[39]

Statistics from later in the century confirmed that single people committed suicide more often. In Buenos Aires between 1889 and 1897, there were 919 suicides of single people (defined as older than age fourteen), 683 men and 236 women. This was out of a total of 1,547 suicides whose civil state was known.[40] The index of the suicidal tendency of singles per one million inhabitants was 659 for men and 423 for women. These were very high indices compared with 393 for married men and 160 for married women. Single men's motives, according to Rodríguez, involved poverty, illness, alcoholism, and being tired of life; while women's motives were fear of punishment, unrequited or impossible love, illegitimate maternity especially among servants, bad treatment, and family disagreements. Poverty did not figure among women's reasons, he said, because women could always survive through prostitution. Alcoholism also did not enter into it, because women were not apt to be alcoholics. Rodríguez speculated that the index of 423 suicides by single women per million inhabitants in Buenos Aires was probably one of the highest known. He compared it to France, where the index was 80 per million, although this figure reflected all of France, and not just Paris. In both Europe and Argentina, remarkably fewer suicides occurred among married people. However, it could be that in the case of honor suicides, the fact that married people had a mechanism of protection that single people did not have, namely, depositing, was a factor lowering the suicide rate among married people. The ability of a husband to place a wife who had allegedly dishonored him in a house of deposit to assuage the shame she had caused him might have gone a long way toward dissuading him from committing suicide. The wife would have found it difficult to commit suicide while being watched and also might have found some solace from the other inhabitants and staff. It was widely recognized, however, that a married woman's children were the main reason why she was unlikely to commit suicide.[41]

THE DEATH OF A STATESMAN

Leandro Alem, founder of one of Argentina's most important political parties, the Radical Civic Union, might also have been a victim of degeneration, inherited from his father, when he committed suicide in 1896. The episode generated a great deal of study and also a great deal of imitation. Alem's mode of suicide, with a firearm in a carriage (*carruaje de plaza*), was copied by no fewer than eighteen *porteños* in a single year![42] In terms of his heredity, Alem began life at a disadvantage—at least one source reported that Alem's father suffered from mental disturbances. As a child of eleven, Alem saw his father shot by firing squad and his corpse hanged from a gallows in the Plaza

Independencia in 1853, for having been a supporter of the dictator Juan Manuel de Rosas and an agent of Rosas's police, the Mazorca. Six thousand spectators reportedly watched the scene, including Leandro, who fainted. As one of Leandro Alem's biographers wrote, this was the point at which "the seed of rebellion was planted."[43] In medical terms, the seed that had been planted in Alem aggravated his inherited degeneracy. He also reportedly carried in his antecedents Arab blood, which was not unlikely, given his Spanish origin. Medically interpreted, this implied pathological passion. His biographers referred to Alem's "Islamic passion of the caudillo" and said that "his speech had the proverbial sensuality of the Musulman chief"; he was said to have "saffron flesh [*carnes azafranadas*] like the martyrs of old Spain."[44]

After Alem graduated as a lawyer in 1869, he served Argentina as a diplomat in Rio de Janeiro, Brazil, and Asunción, Paraguay. He became a national deputy for Buenos Aires in 1874 and ran against Carlos Tejedor for governor of the province in 1877. Tejedor won. It was a tumultuous election, with neighbors in the parish of Balvanera shooting at one another and with dead and wounded. After the gunfire, the police carried out a registration of arms in private homes in the parish. Alem's house was on the list, but he would not allow the police to enter, claiming the inviolability of the domicile. However, the judge, who was repulsed by the disturbances, argued that the inviolability of the domicile was not an absolute principle and that it could be overturned for reasons of hygiene and public security. "We do not want to upset the peace of the family," he wrote, "but we cannot let society be hurt, whose rights must be put over those of individuals." When the police finally succeeded in entering Alem's house, they found seventeen carbines and forty-two bayonets. Alem claimed that he had been in danger for some weeks from armed men outside his house yelling "Death to Alem!" and death to Aristóbulo del Valle as well. Alem, del Valle, and Hipólito Yrigoyen, Alem's nephew, had formed the short-lived Republican Party in 1877.[45] Alem vehemently opposed the nationalization of the city of Buenos Aires, and when this happened in 1880, he withdrew from politics. Returning to politics in 1889 as the favorite of the younger generation, he founded the political party Civic Union in 1890 and led it until 1896. Support grew to overthrow the government of Miguel Juárez Celman in protest against high inflation, which was hurting the middle class, and a corrupt political system in which the incumbent customarily picked his successor. When a stock exchange crash wiped out middle-class savings, hatred of the oligarchy grew. By July 1890, the leaders of the Civic Union had enough support to rebel against Juárez Celman.

The rebellion was put down within three days, but Juárez Celman was forced to resign, and Carlos Pellegrini became president. The so-called Revolución del Parque failed, in that its leaders did not get to take power, but it was the precursor of much subsequent Argentine social and political development, and notably of the triumph of radicalism in the elections of 1916, when Hipólito Yrigoyen won.[46]

Elements of the ruling elite succeeded in co-opting many of those affiliated with the Civic Union, and Alem broke with the party and created the Unión Cívica Radical. Subsequently, Alem was sent into exile to Uruguay and imprisoned for six months for subversion. He had arguments with people in government and with Hipólito Yrigoyen, and witnessed the failure of his ideas. In September 1894, when an imputation of impropriety was made in Congress, Alem jumped up roaring against the supposed instigator. In a rage, Pellegrini responded: "May the gods allow me to eat your raw flesh [carne cruda] for the evil that you've done me!" The "blow of the Titan split his armor and Alem fell wounded." This may have been the betrayal that Alem mentioned to his friends before he died. He was the "Don Quijote" of Argentine politics, always tilting at windmills, "sad and explosive," "impetuous and bold," the Argentine biographer Agustín Rivero Astengo wrote. He was also materially poor and suffered from "sick nerves," hypochondria, alcoholism, depression, and gallbladder attacks.[47]

Alem's suicide at the age of fifty-four was carefully planned. On July 1, 1896, he got into his carriage at about 10:30 P.M., having invited his friends to a final appointment. A jolt during the ride, which triggered the gun that he was holding against his head, prevented him from ending his life among them. The shot occurred at the corner of his street, Sarmiento, and Rodríguez Peña, and was only heard by the driver. The carriage continued on to the Club del Progreso, the designated place for the appointment with Alem's friends. When his friends opened the door of the cab, they found Alem, his face covered with blood. A crowd of thirty thousand people accompanied his body to the Recoleta cemetery, where he was buried in the vault of the Revolutionaries of 1890.[48]

The issue that experts needed to face, in the interest of order and national honor, was whether pathologies had caused Alem to commit suicide or he had taken his life of his own free will. In spite of degenerative factors in Alem's life, doctors had reason to believe that his suicide had been freely chosen and was due to his high sense of honor. Alem's final message, his "political testament or will," addressed to the public, fell completely within the context of a freely chosen defense of his honor:

> To live sterile, useless, and depressed [after having given all that a man can human-
> ly give, and in the end, my efforts have exhausted me], it is preferable to die. I deliv-
> er [to you] what remains to me, my last blood, the rest of my life. My causes . . .
> are perfectly known. If I am mistaken about this, it is something that I cannot feel
> nor remedy now. From my boyhood, I have struggled from below. It is not pride
> that dictates these words, nor is it weakness [in these last moments]. It is a deep
> conviction that I have in my soul. . . . I deliver then my labor and my memory to
> the judgment of the people, for whose noble cause I have constantly struggled.[49]

Alem had sacrificed his flesh out of honor. A caudillo and a man of the
campo, to whom the act of suicide was anathema, a biographer wrote, Alem
was the last person imaginable to commit suicide. But Alem felt that his
honor had been tarnished; that he had sacrificed for the people of Argentina
and had then been abandoned by them. He stood alone, a "widower" in a
sense, vulnerably alone, like many other suicide victims. He was confronted
with changes to which he could not adapt. The analysis was that creeping civilization had affected Alem, and that he had chosen to commit suicide rather
than fight. As a biographer wrote, Alem had not understood the "new spirit,
the evolution of things." "Disillusioned by [his] failure" to successfully promote the Radical Civic Union, "Alem committed suicide," David Rock
writes. "For almost ten years after Alem's death in 1896, the Radicals were little more than one among a string of minor factions."[50]

THE DEGENERATION OF JUSTICE
AND ITS PRACTITIONERS

In popular legal culture, there was ample space for criticism of the state's justice system. Since the theory of degeneration was a kind of worldview, it is no
surprise that it was applied to systems and professionals. The Argentine justice
system, no less than individuals, was one of the theory's victims. A common
complaint of jurists was that their colleagues relied on the turn of a phrase
rather than on hard arguments to argue their cases, or what Estanislao Severo
Zeballos in 1902 called the "deplorable decadence of forensic style." An analysis of the erudition in criminal cases shows two basic styles. The first style
relied on classical references, which even the admirers of erudition called a
"blind cult of the past." As an example, in an 1891 adultery case, the litigating
wife's lawyer told his client's story this way:

> From the first, things were bad in this marriage. Both spouses made a mistake. It
> was not, certainly, the home of Philemon and Baucis that was constituted under

the auspices of this union. Like Jupiter in the Greek legend, eternally posing as Olympian Paris [sic], always lying in wait for gallant adventures, Don José made his debut by killing time, sowing infidelities in the heaven of the nuptial couple. With the passing of time, this perpetual Don Juan of melodrama, in place of reacting by adapting his conduct to his marriage commitment, became recalcitrant and a hardened sinner. This "lovelace" of a husband reached the point of inspiring serious fears in his wife. Any woman would do for his lecherous appetite, which, like the barrel of the Danaides, he could never fill to the brim.[51]

An alternative style used more recent references. For example, in 1882, in his defense of María Bidone, whose reputation was on trial, the attorney, Jorge Argerich, cited a prosecution of Émile-Clement de La Roncière in France in the 1830s for the alleged rape of Marie de Morell:

> If the honor of Marie de Morell were to have succumbed like María Bidone's, if you would declare her guilty at the age of sixteen, if you would absolve La Roncière, [then] do it—with a frenetic and triumphant pleasure—and [then] honorable people would repeat these words with desperation: To what does it serve to love good? Thus, Judge, I hand over to you, not really the fate of my client and his daughter . . . , but also something more elevated and fraternal; the fate of Justice itself![52]

Even the criticism of lawyers' oratory was mock erudite. Attacking María Bidone's fake "youthful purity" in 1882, the prosecutor, Nicolás Casarino, accused Maria's lawyer of constructing a

> novel, where the facts are made up and the characters live in a magic world, with all their defects and qualities; and the scenes of life happen with an adorable naturalness . . . when the Bidones reach the end of the day and contemplate their frustrated hopes, literature is their reserve. People fall before its deceitfulness. People believe in the incomparable power of the phrase. Words can change facts. Words can be so eloquent and stirring that they move people to defend themselves, like in the Greece of Demosthenes, or to fight for their civil liberties, like in the eighteenth-century France of Mirabeau. In the courtroom, we must scorn the phrase, because our mission is not to please or charm the court, but rather to convince it. We must ask for cold reason to be the arms of combat. Logic must be our invulnerable shield. We must use arguments and proofs before the judge, and abandon the ornate rhetoric and the finery of the language. . . . The phrase is a veneer; let us not confuse the brilliance asked of acts with the brilliance asked of art to obscure or disfigure that truth.[53]

Charges of corruption and political interference are indicative of more serious flaws in the justice system. Carlos A. Aldao charged in 1898 that Argentine judges were as inert and indolent as the rest of the nation; Ernesto Quesada warned in 1899 that "our state of justice is a dishonor for Argentina";

and A. Gancedo lamented in 1901 about "our sick state of justice." In 1902, President Roca (1880–86, 1895–1904) also singled out the Argentine judiciary for criticism. "Justice, the fundamental base of social organization, the highest sign of civilization in a people, has fallen into discredit in Argentina. Without good justice, it will not be possible to inspire confidence in work, capital, or immigration." Foreigners also made derogatory comments, such as Homer Greene in the United States, who questioned whether there was any justice at all in Argentina, and the British legate in Buenos Aires, who said that Argentine courts were "deplorable."[54] The Argentine professional journal *Revista de Derecho, Historia y Letras*, edited by Zeballos, regularly reported and analyzed these comments. The problem was that without a good system of justice, Argentina could not claim to belong among the "civilized" nations. Not only was the republic subject to international ridicule, but its "honor and national sovereignty" were in danger when Argentine judges' decisions were disputed by foreign judges. Incompetent and corrupt judges, President Roca said in 1899, had already been responsible for the "decrease in the number of immigrants, the suspicion and removal of capital, the commercial lack of confidence, the country's stagnation and backwardness, and the lack of Argentine prestige abroad." Because judges occupied an exceptional position in society, their public conduct, their private actions, indeed, their entire lives had to be exceptional. Moral authority was not something "won at the races," Zeballos wrote in 1902, but rather was earned by maintaining good character while fulfilling one's duties, which might cause "wounds" but would nevertheless inspire respect. If public men, like judges, wanted to preserve their decorum and independence, they had to be able to retain their respect through setbacks, but the majority capitulated, with the demoralizing excuse that everyone did the same thing. "This is the environment that judges have," Zeballos said, "now that they have left the guild of lawyers and today are not distinguished in Argentina for their wisdom or respectability."[55]

Political interference in the justice system was partly to blame for judges' lack of good conduct, Zeballos charged. Government exacerbated the public's scorn of lawyers and judges by filling vacancies according to favors, not merit. Political appointments had allowed a "mass of inferior elements" to "infiltrate" the Argentine court, and there was no organization of lawyers to watch over the discipline and the honor of the profession. The press commonly did not restrain itself in criticizing these political appointments.[56] The profession needed to be respected by the public, by government, and by judges and lawyers themselves. In turn, judges had to honor Argentina, which was officially dishonored abroad especially in matters of justice. Judicial irregularities dishonored national justice, which dishonored the *patria*. Herrera even called for a court of honor in 1899 to try lawyers themselves, saying that the practice of law took more than common human dignity, gentlemanliness (*caballerosidad*), scrupulousness, and delicacy.[57]

CONCLUSION

Degeneration theory can be analyzed as a general description of what was wrong with Argentina at the turn of the century. New Worldism and independence, republics and liberal governments, and European immigration and capital were supposed to rejuvenate Argentina, yet many in the country's professional and political elite saw one another and their society as degenerate. This was not atypical of the epoch, but Argentines attached a unique definition to modernity, and the social evidences of degeneracy that it produced were thus also unique. The concept of modernity, which was often blamed for degeneracy in other countries as well as Argentina, included models that were copied from Europe and that were brought from Europe by immigrants. The models were criticized for propelling Argentina down foreign and thus inappropriate paths. Imported social customs created desires that could not be satisfied. On the other hand, what was native was also a cause of degeneration, namely, the indigenous and mestizo elements in society, what Emilio Daireaux, a Frenchman transplanted to Argentine soil, called "the substratum of social degenerations" in Argentina in 1888. These races, he said, did not have the energy to improve their condition. Argentines did not need a foreigner to tell them this. Vice and excess, perversity and dissimulation, utilitarianism and materialism all contributed to the physical and mental deterioration of the species.[58]

6 Passion in a State of Reason

Thus far, individual rights have been seen as having had to give way to the good of the whole. Wives' rights took a back seat to the marital authority of their husbands, reinforced by civil and penal law and by concepts such as honor. Pregnant women's physical and financial needs took a back seat to the demands of shame and public interest. Individuals were subjected to invasive identification techniques in the interest of public hygiene and security. Personal rights gave way to the need to root out degenerative terrain dangerous to the state, and the more degenerative of those people were recommended for elimination. When it came to passion, however, we find the situation changed. Passion as an individual right was allowed to take precedence over the needs of society. Sooner or later, it affected everyone, and even affected the way in which the state saw itself judging the individual. Passion was not merely tolerated; modernity actually depended on passionate man as an antidote to encroaching materialism and utilitarianism.

Passion was similar to degeneration in that both were pathologies, and their symptoms sometimes became confused; however, they stood at opposite ends of the spectrum of human conditions. Passion allowed for a variety of interpretations, whereas no flexibility existed in the interpretation of degeneration, though there could be sympathy for the degenerate individual. Passional man had no physical stigmas, while degenerative man was marked.[1] Degeneration summed up all that was bad; it did not ennoble. It had no redeeming features and always reflected human failings. Passion, on the other hand, had redeeming features and generally denoted something basically good about the person it "victimized." If the accused in a criminal trial demonstrated passion, the court showed some leniency. If not, there was little hope of extenuation. The murderer Pedro Castro Rodríguez, whose case is discussed in chapter 5, for example, having failed the test for "passion" in 1888 because his symptoms and characteristics did not measure up to those of a passionate man, was labeled a degenerate.

PASSION AS A MEDICAL CONDITION

Medical doctors viewed passion as simultaneously a normal and a pathological condition, making passion unique and distinct from other pathological conditions, such as epilepsy, which doctors never considered "normal." Forensic doctors and jurists frequently cited passion as an extenuating circumstance in criminal cases. This made passion part of both the production of criminal behavior, through its effect on the mind and body, and of the reason for mitigating punishment for that behavior, because of its undermining of the human will.

In some ways, the passions and the emotions were similar, in that both involved sentiments and led to intense feeling or action. The passions, though, differed from simple emotions in that they could endure much longer. Characteristic was a fixation on an idea or person, and only such a fixation could be transformed into a passion. Passions, as special forms of affective life, could cause violent ruptures in the mechanisms of a person's physiological constitution. Passions were emotive and physiological, then, and in addition, specifically human. Only man had the capability of reflection, it was believed; animals, children, and primitive people had outbursts or impulses, but not passions.[2]

The scholarly treatment of passion elaborated on the theme that, as a true disease, it should not be punished. In the 1840s, Professor M. J. B. Orfila at the Sorbonne argued that it was "scandalous" to convict a person who had suffered an attack of passion, and Dr. J.-B.-F. Descuret pointed out that the very etymology of the word *passion*, from the Latin verb "to suffer" indicated an illness of the body and spirit.[3] The Spanish jurist Joaquín Francisco Pacheco argued in 1856 that to doubt that passion was a true illness was "ridiculous." The paroxysm of passion figured in the same category, he wrote, as monomania and partial madness. Obviously, a clear link existed between what we might today think of as psychological states and their somatic manifestations. The relationship in the nineteenth century, however, actually identified the passions as entities existing in the body that "got sick." Professionals located them variously in the diaphragm, the heart, and the nerve centers.[4] The important point was that a passionate man did not "have" a passion; he "was" the passion. The passion was part of his flesh; it came with his flesh.

Medical treatises and the forensic reports from criminal cases tracked the path of damage that an attack of passion could inflict on the body as a pathology. The internal damage began, according to some doctors, in the brain, spinal cord, and nervous system. According to other doctors, the damage could begin anywhere, since the passions were distributed throughout the whole body, although a "nervous elaboration" had to occur for an act to pass from virtual to fact. The damage began when a passion awakened a strong reaction in the nervous system as it tried to adapt. Supposing that a passion awakened a strong reaction in the epigastric center, the next step involved agitation in the nervous system as it tried to adapt to the disturbance. In attempting to remain in harmony with the nervous system, the body's organs reacted. Thus, there was a rupture between the nervous system and the other apparatuses of the body, a "true hemorrhage of sensitivity," in which the organs deviated from their physiological state and caused changes to occur in the body's temperature, blood circulation, and heart rhythm, basically sending the body on a skittish path from excitement to exhaustion.[5]

Descriptions of the wreckage left by this medical condition appeared in Argentina in disparate sources such as home medical manuals and scholarly medical treatises meant for professionals. Common symptoms for such passions as anger, fear, melancholy, and hypochondria included apoplexy, aneurysm, and congestions for anger; madness and liver and heart disease for fear; delirium and insanity for melancholy; and palpitations and stomach, liver, and heart disease for hypochondria. In women, the passions caused suppression of menstruation, menorrhagia, and the nervous disorder of chorea. The generic home remedies for passion included cold baths, salt baths, vomitives, purgatives, and relaxants, and removal of the object that had "caused" the passion.[6]

With its deathly trail, passion existed in bodies with the tangibility of a disease. It was an "aberration of intelligence," Pacheco wrote in 1856, "as powerful as any physical and material force." It was "moral violence done to the soul, just like physical violence applied to the body." Passion exhausted the body and the will. "If we keep in mind that the functions [of the organism] can only be sustained at the expense of nervous energy," the Argentine doctor Lucas Ayarragaray, on the staff of the Hospital of Alienados and the National Department of Hygiene, explained in 1887, "we can see that an enormous amount of nervous energy is needed to sustain a passional existence. In a passional existence, the organs get tired; the nervous system is disturbed; the constitution weakens—exactly as in a sick person with a long illness, or a 'monster' who has to sustain supernumerary organs. In sum, too many intense stimuli pervert the functions of the organism or annihilate them."[7]

Like a disease, passion "attacked" the body from within, excited by stimuli from without, exhibited symptoms and crisis points, and had cures. Like the common cold, passion was common to most people, and as José Ingenieros wrote in 1905, passions were "reactions belonging to innate mechanisms," the work of "our physiological constitution." Almost everyone could at some time or another find himself succumbing to them. The criminologist Eusebio Gómez, director of the Penitenciaría Nacional, added in 1917 that the human characteristics associated with passion, such as "exaggerated vanity and extreme susceptibility," were in some ways normal.[8]

Passion's violent assault on the body intersected with the justice system in a very real way. Because a consequence of passion was paralysis of the will, passion could be invoked to extenuate or entirely remove personal responsibility for criminal acts. Many experts held that people under the influence of passion had no more will, and thus no more moral responsibility, than people suffering from madness, or *locura*. The presence of passion removed liability, meaning that there was no crime. "What converts us without our [being at] fault into an instrument," Pacheco explained, "[also] cleanses us and exempts us at the same time of any stain, of all responsibility, as human and moral agents. The man who, without liberty, commits homicide, does not have any more blame than the sword itself, the instrument with which he caused the wound." Passionate crime, most of the experts agreed, was characterized by the delinquent's remorse after the crime, indicating that basically there was a fund of positive sentiment toward passion in the medical and criminological fields and in the 1886 penal code.[9]

PASSION AS A LEGAL PRINCIPLE

Passion figured large in court cases at a point in time when judicial discourse intersected with judicial practice, and judges accommodated the medical and legal arguments about the influence of passion and often found extenuating circumstances. Judges stopped short of exempting delinquents totally from punishment, however, even though the law allowed them to do so. Although there was a growing medicalization of criminal behavior, and neuroses, epilepsy, hysteria, and so on were introduced to explain violent acts, passion held onto its place as an important contender for the ear of the judge.

The Tejedor Code reflected the latest midcentury views from Europe that passion produced "moral numbness," "involuntary blindness," and "paralyzed the will and erased a person's responsibility." References to human disturbances became more explicit in the penal code of 1886. The first three articles of the four that applied dealt with exemptions. First, a state of "insanity, somnambulism, absolute imbecility, or complete and involuntary drunkenness" could *exempt* a delinquent from punishment, in general when the act had been "determined and consummated in any perturbation of the senses or intelligence, not imputable to the agent, and during which he [had] not been conscious of the act or its criminality." A second group of delinquents could be *exempted* if they had acted "impelled by irresistible force, physical or moral." A third group were spouses who had been surprised by their consorts "in the flagrant crime of adultery" and had suffered "justifiable pain," who were *exempted* if they had "[wounded] or [killed] both or one of the guilty parties." The fourth article had to do with the *reduction* of a person's responsibility for a crime when in a state of "irritation or furor" that was not the person's fault, but that did not make the person "lose total consciousness of what he was doing." To summarize, when criminals committed crimes in a state of insanity and related conditions, including drunkenness, disturbance of the senses, irresistible force, and in the case of flagrant adultery, they could be exempted from punishment, and a criminal committing a crime in a state of "irritation and furor" had reduced responsibility.[10]

Argentine jurists pressed the legal system to respond to the new thinking about passion as a medical condition and its influence on criminal acts. As a lawyer admonished his colleagues in a case in 1904, "Give way to the enlightened people of the century and examine with them the criminal, the environment, and so on, thus driving away the phantasms of classicism that Beccaria already thought were old in the mid eighteenth century." The principle involved here was that the state of passionality deprived the subject of the quality of free will, and his penalty thus had to be reduced.[11]

Argentine jurists found, though, that passion was not an easy concept to argue, in spite of its general acceptance as a legitimate element in certain kinds of crimes. First, it was difficult to argue, Eusebio Gómez wrote in 1917, because a passionate attack did not always lead to a crime being committed, since not everyone sought vengeance in times of passion. Thus, one could not really say that passion "caused" crime. Second, passions often had two sides, which made them difficult to evaluate. The passion of love, for example, was noble and social, yet exalted love could become dangerous. The passion of hatred was ignoble and anti-social, yet hatred of a common enemy was honorable. The passion of honor, sometimes held to be the most "respectable" passion, often led to infamy. Political passion, which was considered morally healthy for a state and necessary to offset utilitarianism, could divide nations and cause human destruction. In other words, the same passion had the power to lead people to both "heroism and villainy."[12]

Third, and most important, passion was difficult to argue because it intersected with the controversy over the validity of the concept of free will. The basic premise of a penal system for classical jurists was that free will had to exist in order for a justice system to confer punishment on an individual. Positivist criminology challenged this notion, viewing free will as an "illusion" that resulted from ignorance of a person's antecedents. Crime was merely an anti-social act that originated with the intervention of stimuli from the external world, which produced different reactions in different people, in accordance with their psycho-physiological characters. Thus, whether a person had free will was not at issue. Human beings were not the sole arbiters of their actions, capable of choosing between good and bad, and morally responsible. Rather, human nature differed from individual to individual, making it necessary to treat delinquents as individuals and develop classification systems for them, as Lombroso did.[13] The justification for the punishment of criminals was based not on the presence of free will, but rather on the need for "social defense." When passion was added to the picture, empirical evidence showed that passion did not always have the same effect on free will in all cases. The problem was that the passion argument, to be used by courts, either had to annul free will in all cases or leave free will intact. Although sometimes lawyers could avoid this pitfall by arguing that the problem lay in the concept of free will, rather than in the concept of passion, the dilemma often arose in criminal trials.

Positivists, although they used arguments of passion, looked more to pathologies to explain crime. Whether a criminal acted out of passion was in a sense irrelevant since, according to positivist criminologists, such as Lombroso, Ferri, Garofalo, Tarde, Lacassagne, and Fouillée, *no* criminal was responsible for his actions, because he lacked free will. All crime, regardless of the effect of passion, indicated pathology. For example, delinquents lacked the moral sense that made crime repugnant to "normal" people. In addition, delinquents lacked foresight about the prejudicial consequences of their acts, in terms both of the likely punishment for them and of what the public's attitude to them might be. Passional criminals did differ from other types, however, in that their pathological condition was transitory. Evidence of the transitoriness was the sheer violence of passional crime and the passional criminal's remorse. Passional criminals only momentarily suffered from dulled inhibitory centers and then were filled with repugnance for their acts.

Of course, opponents of positivism totally opposed the invocation of passion in judicial arguments. The Argentine medical doctor Samuel Gache (1886) and the jurists Enrique B. Prack (1891) and Godofredo Lozano (1901) warned that excusing criminals on the basis of their attacks of passion was absurd, nonsensical, and totally wrongheaded. To maintain that criminals did not have free will, and thus were not responsible for their acts, undermined the entire justice and penal system. To maintain that they were merely sick would send criminals to asylums rather than jails, with only doctors to oversee their release back into society. Science could not in any way prove that free will did not exist, and although conditions such as climate could influence free will, they could not replace it. In fact, free will did exist for most people; the exceptions that lacked it, according to Prack, were the insane, hysterics, and epileptics. Moreover, Prack argued, while positivists *denied* free will, they *acted* as if it in fact existed. For example, they refused to accept punishment for the insane; the reason for this had to be that positivists believed that the insane lacked free will. According to Prack, society absolutely needed the existence of free will—denying it was just like trying to explain the universe without the existence of God: if free will did not exist, people would have to invent it. The positivists, then, were hypocritical; they negated the existence of free will but simultaneously at least appeared to need its existence.[14]

Caught in the midst of these controversies, court discourse on passion tended to become mired in arguments over free will. In thirty-two fully sentenced cases between 1871 and 1906 that involved wounding, homicide, or attempted homicide, judges and lawyers frequently explained criminal acts as a result of passion. In well over half, clauses such as "disturbance," "irresistible force," and "irritation or furor" were invoked in judging and sentencing the delinquent. Anything that could bring about these disturbances—be it passion, disease, drunkenness, or even the devil—could be used to extenuate the crime.[15] Exaggerated warnings about the impending end of the justice system reflected the increased use of clauses of "irresistible force" and so on. In his treatise on passion and crime, Eusebio Gómez, for example, criticized lawyers for abusing the excuse of passion and introducing a "false dramaticity" into cases to facilitate the defense of their clients. He argued that judges, uninformed about criminal anthropology, too often accepted this dramaticity.[16]

THE PASSION OF "JUSTIFIABLE PAIN"

In the later nineteenth century, the "justifiable pain" concept was invoked with respect to particularly dramatic crimes of passion. Passion in this case, when a person was overcome by a "blind rage" or an "irresistible force" at the sight of his or her spouse's flagrant adultery, allowed judges actually to exempt the criminal from punishment.[17] When murder resulted, the choices in sentencing in these cases were capital punishment, which had been retained in the 1886 penal code for the killing of family members; the maximum prison sentence of twenty years; or a lesser prison sentence, depending on how passion was taken into account. If it was proved that the crime had been an act of passion, then the death penalty was not invoked.[18]

According to Joaquín Escriche, writing in the mid 1870s, "justifiable pain" for a husband meant seeing with his own eyes the staining of his honor—"that particular honor that husbands acquire[d] the day of their marriage and that a very special judgment [made] them lose when their wife dishonor[ed] them." Husbands also suffered "justifiable pain" when their wives scorned their marital authority, insulted them, or infected them with gonorrhea.[19] There was no question in many people's minds that a wife's adultery was the worst dishonor for her husband. It did not even have to be proven; judges accepted circumstantial evidence. Thus, even a husband's mere presumption of his wife's infidelity was sufficient to cause him "justifiable pain."

"Justifiable pain" was usually applied only to husbands, although the law covered the possibility of wives' "justifiable pain." Wives' pain did not appear in the discourse of actual cases, however, most likely because wives were not supposed to be offended by their husbands' adultery. Of the women who killed their husbands "out of passion," one was condemned to death in 1856, a sentence that was commuted to ten years' imprisonment. A second received a sentence of imprisonment in perpetuity in 1914 for killing her adulterous husband, because her "justifiable pain" had not involved any "surprise." She was released for good conduct after fourteen years' *presidio* and died soon afterward.[20]

Although the penal code of 1886 did not state that "justifiable pain" justified killing the offending spouse, legal experts did argue that such murders needed no justification. First, the fact of "surprise" was enough to excuse the homicide; it did not matter that it was not self-defense. As Rodolfo Rivarola wrote in 1910, even though the act was not done to preserve the husband's or another's life, the law gave one the legal right to kill in such circumstances.[21] Second, the "intensity of the pain" justified homicide. As Gómez explained in 1917, the law only took into account the "intensity of the pain; not the nature or quality of the passion of jealousy." Spousal love did not enter into the equation; it was not necessary for the feeling of "justifiable pain."[22] Third, jealousy that reached a passional level was a disease, like madness, and justified homicide. Passional jealousy created illusions and hallucinations, in the form of an obsession in degenerates, and of an outburst of anxiety in epileptics. Jealousy stemmed from both primitive instincts and the modern world. It recalled primitive instincts of savage love, violent struggle for females, and the suppression of rivals. On the other hand, it also reflected the "perversions that contemporary civilization, with its retinue of vices, had imprinted on sexual life." Jealousy arose from the "fever of luxury," excessive egoism, vanity, and utilitarianism. From it came suicide and crime. It always accompanied love; the purest of loves carried within itself the bitter seed of terrible passion. Jealousy was the earthly "virus" of divine love.[23] This passion was intense, persistent, and generally unmotivated. Only one idea dominated: the possible loss of the loved one.

Sexual honor differed according to the type of union, and the invocation of justifiable pain as a defense thus did too. Fundamental to all unions was man's desire for the unlimited possession of woman. However, in irregular or concubinary unions, a man's reaction to infidelity or abandonment, Gómez argued, obeyed the sentiment of vanity, which was obsessive and passional. He had conquered the woman for reasons of vanity or luxury, like a Don Juan. If he lost her, he attacked; he saw vengeance as the only solution. Thus, when couples living in concubinage and their lawyers tried to invoke the law of "justifiable pain," they usually failed.[24]

By the early twentieth century, there was a movement in Argentina to abolish the clause "surprised in flagrant adultery" from the penal code as an attenuating circumstance from punishment for wounding or killing a spouse and his or her consort, as had been occurring in Europe. The clause created too many cases of injustice, Rivarola argued in 1910, because the law allowed a husband to coldly premeditate the death of his adulterous wife, even though he had tacitly consented to her conduct, and then claim "justifiable pain."[25]

Other jurists argued that the attenuating circumstances of "surprise" and "justifiable pain" needed to be retained, although in a revised form. The Argentine Norberto Piñero, for example, argued in 1898 that there could not be a single adultery law, since conjugal relationships differed, depending on a person's socioeconomic class. When dealing with the lower class, for example, it had to be realized that men sometimes chose dishonest women as wives, consented to their wives' adultery, or drove them to it by abandoning them. In such cases, the judicial system had to ensure that the judge had complete freedom to assess the acts and deny the husband exemption from responsibility. Though Piñero favored reform of the law, he firmly upheld a husband's basic right that "every man [had], especially of a certain social class, to be protected from responsibility when he [had] acted because of the excitation that his wife's adultery had produced in him."[26] Well into the century,

it was argued that to abolish the adultery law was to go against Argentine custom because most people accepted that a wife's adultery was the greatest
injury she could inflict on her husband.

The passion of jealousy and husbands' "justifiable pain" produced heated
debate in court cases, such as one from 1870. Eusebia, introduced in chapter
1 as having been deposited by her husband Pascual in a rented room during
their court-decreed separation, ended up dead when Pascual killed her in
cold blood, suspecting her of adultery.[27] In many cases, a husband in this situation would get a reduced sentence, especially if it could be proved that his
wife had provoked him.[28] But the judge in Pascual's case was not convinced
that Eusebia had committed adultery and sentenced Pascual to death. We
pick up Pascual's story here with his daily visits to Eusebia's place of deposit
and with his secretive nightly visits in which he reappeared in disguise to
stand outside her building and spy on her. At times, he thought he saw a
man's shadow in his wife's room. His suspicions grew and he decided to move
her, but she roundly refused to go. He enlisted the help of an ecclesiastical
judge and got a summons, but then he could not find her to deliver it! He was
desperate. When he did find her—a couple of drinks later—he stormed:
"Eusebia, stop and listen, since you haven't come back to me, I'm going to
make you pay to the last drop of blood." He grabbed her by the waist, threw
her down on the ground, jerked her head back, and slit her throat. She died
instantly.

The defense lawyer argued that, first, Pascual had not acted out of hatred,
a desire for vengeance, or criminal intent. Rather, he had experienced a sudden violent passion, an irresistible fit of jealousy, brought on by his drinking.
Moreover, he had been provoked to violence by his wife's repudiation of him,
her denial of his marital authority and his conjugal rights, her incitement of
his children against him, and her disobedience of his order forbidding her to
see a certain man. All Eusebia's acts, Pascual's lawyer argued, were intended
to irritate the passionate character of her husband. As frequently happened in
criminal cases, the lawyer in this case introduced his own sociological commentary in defense of his client. He argued that a corrupt government and
society had to expect that people like Pascual would surface. It was no surprise, he said, that Pascual had committed this murder "when cultured men
who should be setting an example for people like Pascual put a dagger in his
hand and plied him with wine and food to gain his vote and let him commit
illegal acts with impunity."

Rejecting the defense lawyer's plea, the judge argued that Pascual was not
entitled to claim the extenuating circumstance of passion for the following

reasons. He had committed the crime in public in broad daylight, in cold blood, with premeditation, and in the presence of his daughter; he had used a knife, a weapon fit only for the "worst Neapolitans"; and he had all the more obligation to society and to his victim because he had finished a year of medical school. The public nature of the act, as in previous cases, played an important role in the judge's evaluation. The premeditation was also crucial to his judgment. The last reason, that Pascual had a greater obligation to society because he was educated, is especially interesting and reflects the fact that conditions such as social class were both extenuating and incriminating circumstances.

The judge's sentence of death was uniquely severe and somewhat anachronistic, although the appeals court upheld the decision. It was to be "death by firing squad in the public plaza of Lorea, to be published in the newspapers and posted on the most visible walls in Buenos Aires, towns, and districts of this judicial department." Clearly, the judge intended the sentence to be exemplary. Members of the more enlightened public launched a protest, however, perhaps because they believed in Pascual's right to express his passion through murder, perhaps also because they objected to the use of the death penalty. A petition for commutation dated August 22, 1870, went to the judge with thirty pages of signatures and was successful; the executive commuted the sentence to twenty years' *presidio* on September 15, 1870. A well-known Argentine intellectual spearheaded this campaign. The writer Josefina Pelliza de Sagasta (d. 1888), who collaborated on *La Nación* and *La Ondina* and who, with Juana Manuela Gorriti (d. 1892), founded *La Alborada del Plata*, actively solicited signatures for the commutation of Pascual's death sentence. These were the feverish days of growing involvement of women authors in social movements, and Josefina must have been pleased when *La República* complimented her for her humanitarianism.

PERSONAL RESPONSIBILITY FOR PASSION

By the late nineteenth century, courts had become more committed to searching for scientific reasons for outbursts of passion that resulted in crime, although there were instances when a criminal was held responsible for producing his own passion. In the next case, from 1894, the court doctors performed a thorough medical examination of the estranged lover, and the court engaged in serious discussion of passion's possible influence and whether the criminal could have controlled his passion—all this even though the man did not actually succeed in killing any of his victims.

Enrique Campanelli had spent several years of his young adulthood in the early 1890s in deep suffering over his love for Agustina Barat.[29] Recalling Descuret's association of passion and suffering helps to explain the denouement of Enrique's mental fixation on Agustina, or monomania. He was set to marry Agustina in 1894 as soon as he received a character reference from Italy. When the letter arrived, however, Enrique found that Agustina had chosen to escape from his entreaties, we are not informed exactly why, by entering a convent. Or perhaps her family had put her there. Driven by his now unrequited love, Enrique went there, removed her bodily from the convent, made off with her in a carriage, and was arrested by the police for abduction. The case was dismissed, but Agustina's family no longer supported the marriage and threatened to disown Agustina if she married Enrique. With his one idea of marrying Agustina clouding his reason, Enrique returned to his lover's house at night with two revolvers and shot Agustina's family while they were eating dinner. Agustina's eight-year-old brother later recalled that he had been eating potatoes when his sister's boyfriend shot him; he suffered a wound to his left lung. Agustina's father sustained two gunshot wounds and contusions on his head and face where Enrique had beaten him with the butt of the revolver; the mother had a chest wound. Agustina's married sister had forehead and shoulder wounds and a younger sister had a shoulder wound. The family members were treated first by doctors at a nearby pharmacy, and then by the *médico de guardia*, Francisco Sicardi. Though Enrique had managed to do a fair amount of damage, none of the wounds were serious enough to incapacitate the victims for more than thirty days.

Jorge Argerich, a prominent lawyer and a member of an old Argentine patrician family, took on the defense of Enrique, even though he did not usually take on cases of this type. He did so because he felt strongly about the law's obligation to look into Enrique's psychology and passion. He wanted to prove that Enrique was truly "lovesick" and not just faking it. Argerich eulogized Enrique, comparing him to Renaissance Tuscan troubadours. Enrique's problem, argued Argerich, was that his "imagination had no brake or limit." His flesh could not contain it. Rather, Enrique had the "flesh [carne] of passion"—a passion that was in the same mold as "Faust's vacillation on Margarete's threshold." Enrique was helpless in the face of his passion for Agustina; the thought of her "made his eyes lose themselves in the void." Her voice was like that of Sarah Bernhardt in Racine's play *Phèdre*, although Argerich asked the court's pardon for this "artistic heresy." If events had happened differently, Argerich argued, there would have been one less nun and two more happy people in the world. Perhaps if Enrique had married, he said, his violent passions would have been tempered by the "tranquil love of the home." Instead, the court had to realize that it was dealing with a "confused man, in the middle of [contemporary society's] life of regulated [that is, harnessed] passions."

The forensic doctors found that Enrique was "dominated by a pathological amorous passion, a fixed idea," and that "he always satisfied his limited aspirations within [the boundaries of] his romantic character." In addition, the doctors concluded that, judging from conversations with Enrique and an examination of his intellectual, moral, and affective condition, his brain had "some signs of weakness, few acquired notions, and a weak will." Although he did not show signs of mental alienation, they concluded that it was probably in his background.

The medical report was inconclusive, however, because science could not prove absolutely that Enrique had lost his reason due to mental disturbance. The fact that he had fled after shooting at Agustina's family seemed to indicate that he had been in his right mind and aware that he had committed a crime. Nor did the medical report show any form of mental alienation; it could only be supposed. Moreover, if it had truly been passional love that had confused Enrique's mind, then how, medically speaking, had this occurred, given that Agustina—the object of the passion—had not even been present on the night of the shootings.[30] Enrique had had the opportunity to dominate his passion, but instead he had used his will to cherish and fuel it; this made him partially responsible for lack of energy and foresight. Nevertheless, because of the influence of passion, he was not totally responsible and did not belong in jail.

Even though the judge viewed the category of "passional crimes" as much abused, and argued that people had a duty to dominate and repress passions, he agreed with the defense lawyer that passion had indeed been a factor in Enrique's case and sentenced him to five years' confinement in a penitentiary, rejecting the prosecutor's plea for imprisonment in perpetuity, but, on the other hand, not exempting Enrique from punishment. Enrique had not shown premeditation and malice; he had never confessed an intent to kill; and the wounds he had caused had not incapacitated his victims for more than thirty days. Actually, the maximum sentence that he should have received in this case, where the injuries were so minor, was one year or less of imprisonment; the fact that the sentence was five years indicates that the judge viewed Enrique as having had some responsibility for his passion.

Well into the twentieth century, criminologists and law codes continued to support the defense of murderers on the basis of passion. As seen in the criminal cases, though, it was difficult to find criminals who could fit the model and who were acceptable to judges as victims of passion. Yet the perception existed that the number of crimes judged as passional was increasing and/or that more cases were being decided this way. Eusebio Gómez, who featured the case of Pascual in his book on passion and crime, suggested that this was because lawyers had found an easy way to win their cases and that the public had become more indulgent of passional criminals, perhaps calculating that at some point they themselves would need to take advantage of the attenuating circumstance of passion.[31]

THE PASSION OF THE ELITE

Passion became more complex as one moved up the class ladder, especially into public officialdom. As public officials and representatives of public office, members of the elite often had a source of honor that other classes did not have, which they might express passionately. On the other hand, they were more responsible for their passion because of their education, level of civilization, and obligation to the social good. The Club Sud América was not concerned with the law in 1887, but merely catering to its members' passion for gambling. Pedro Arata, discussed below, allegedly revealed himself to be strongly passionate in 1892 when he showed more interest in his passion than in resolving social questions. Ernesto Madero was not interested in the traffic jam he caused during Carnival in 1901, but only in asserting his power over an insolent policeman.

In 1887, a police officer named Beascochea made a surprise raid on the Club Sud América, a legally constituted social corporation, for gambling.[32] Enraged, the club president filed a case of violation of domicile against Beascochea, who, he wrote to the judge, had treated the house as if it were a "pigsty or immoral gaming house" and had carted its members off to jail with the "surliness of a Chinese mine foreman." The elite club members— lawyers, brokers, stockbrokers, notaries, merchants, ranchers, educationists, all neighbors in the parishes of Monserrat and Concepción—claimed superior "urbanity." Feeling that his passion was more legitimate, Beascochea argued that it was his job to "protect public morality and the purity of customs," and that the club's case against him was an "affront to him as an employee and man." Lack of urbanity was not a crime, he argued. Furthermore, the club members were "guilty of stimulating immoralities that they, so zealous of their honor, condemn[ed] in the lower classes." In fact, he argued, as long as the law prosecuted people of the lower classes for indulging in the "degrading passion of gambling," which went on all around them, members of the elite who gambled in "sumptuous" surroundings should be prosecuted as well. In fact, for these men who were called *hombres decentes*, the immorality was greater; precisely because of their position, they were more strictly obligated to behave and live correctly. In recognition of their status, Beascochea had arrested them, not for gambling, which would have caused them shame, but rather for "disorder." The sentence in the case is unclear, but it did not please the club.

Two respected chemists each argued in 1892 that the other had acted inappropriately out of passion, and they accused each other of provocation.[33] Dr. Atanasio Quiroga accused Dr. Pedro N. Arata of being a man of strong passions and injuring his reputation, and Arata defended himself saying that Quiroga had provoked his (Arata's) passion. Both had solid reputations to protect. Arata held important administrative positions as chief of the Oficina Química Municipal and vice president and acting president of the Consejo Nacional de Higiene. Quiroga had been named in Congress as a "sage" (*sabio*) and had received awards from the Consejo Superior Universitario and the faculty. Their anger unfolded when Arata refused to become part of a commission in a poison case headed by Quiroga. Quiroga had reportedly tried to ignore Arata's "shop war" (*guerre de boutique*), even though he knew that Arata was spreading damaging rumors about him. But when Quiroga learned that Arata had refused to participate in a review of the poison case because of his personal hatred, meaning that he had little interest in clarifying the question of "social order," he realized that "Arata was a man of strong passions." Quiroga charged that Arata's report was unscientific and was just a vehicle for Arata to "spill his bile" against Quiroga. Arata, through "diabolical art, harassed Quiroga, without the least provocation," portraying Quiroga to the judge as "ignorant, immoral, passionate (biased) in the extreme."

In the end, Quiroga and Arata reached an accord in October 1892, saying that the whole thing was a misunderstanding based on a mistake made by the court clerk who had written a word incorrectly in Arata's testimony. The discourse in the case on the provocation of passion is especially interesting in that it took place at the level of the very professionals who were judging other people's cases. As I have argued elsewhere, the fact that no one could escape from pathologies such as passion made the late nineteenth century an interesting laboratory for individual self-examination and social experimentation.

Rancor between the judiciary and the police has been noted in chapter 2 in a court's objection to a police sting operation, and in chapter 3 in a court's rejection of police efforts to fingerprint and measure suspects. A 1901 case involving the judiciary and the police that rocked Buenos Aires, making head-lines for several days, also involved class and passion.[34] Judge Ernesto Madero charged Antonio Ballvé, a police officer, who had ridiculed him one night during Carnaval in February, with contempt and abuse of authority, although Ballvé had been acting under orders from the police chief, Francisco J. Beazley. The rancor between Madero and Ballvé was an expression of class warfare, as well as of professional infighting. For a policeman to cast asper-sions on a judge in the flesh was to dishonor the office of judge. Madero jus-tified his action, saying that it was his duty to report a crime against the *mag-istratura*, and that it went beyond him as an individual.

At 10:30 P.M., Madero had been in his carriage in the parade line on the Avenida de Mayo that was directed to turn onto Calle Buen Orden. Madero had asked to be allowed to continue on the Avenida de Mayo because he was on a "judicial errand," but Ballvé, who was directing traffic, denied Madero's request. Two policemen forced Madero's carriage to make the turn by grabbing the horses' reins. Furious, Madero jumped out of the carriage and planted him-self defiantly in front of the horses, yelling at the policemen that he was "going to blow [their] brains out." He was later described by observers as "visibly nerv-ous," which fostered the idea that he might well have been inclined to harm the policemen. Again, according to observers, Ballvé spoke almost affection-ately to Madero and chided him about the public spectacle that he had pro-voked. Madero, who appeared to have completely "lost control of himself," observers said, answered that Ballvé was to blame. "I am a *juez del crimen*. I have to take a deposition from a witness who lives on Avenida de Mayo between Buen Orden and Lima. You can't stop me." Ballvé claimed that this was just a pretext. The dominant mood was one of anger and derision. The crowd that had gathered by then took Ballvé's side and criticized Madero for holding up the parade. Totally humiliated, Madero and his two daughters continued on Avenida de Mayo on foot, while Ballvé took the carriage "prisoner."

Apparently, Madero had had other altercations with the police, and Ballvé threatened to show Congress the evidence, further angering Madero. This pattern of conflict was used to further damage Madero's reputation. Once, he had gotten on a crowded tram and refused to get off when asked, again invok-ing his character as judge. Another time, he had gone to the police station where his son was making a deposition, yelled at the personnel, refused to take his hat off, and taken away his son, leaving the deposition unfinished. On a third occasion, Madero had entered a police station and taken away four youths who were being detained for having bothered a young woman who was alone on the street.

According to the newspaper reports, the incident provoked animated controversies in all circles. In court, the judge supported Madero, saying that the police should have respected him, rather than "insult[ing] his honor in front of people anxious for free spectacles and predisposed to jeering." The press of Buenos Aires, national and foreign, sided with the police, however, and *El País* even conducted a poll of local jurists, who either offered no opinion or argued that judges and police were supposed to work together as a team, that the police were not the judiciary's subalterns, and that judges did not have *fueros*, or personal privileges. Ballvé was freed.

THE PUBLIC'S PASSION AND THE JURY SYSTEM

Rarely did a concept encompass so many dimensions and figure in so many arenas as did passion. It was not only a medical condition, an extenuating circumstance, and even ennobling, but an interference in many determinations that the political elite had to make in organizing a national government, and thus a dilemma to the state. This can be seen especially in the debates that took place in this era on the jury system and the death penalty. The Argentine constitution of 1853 mandated a jury system, but politicians and professionals balked at creating one, and proposals to do so were defeated in the legislature in 1873 and 1884. Although the new sciences that were coming from Europe were largely well received in Argentina, the jury system was not considered to be a part of the modernization of criminal justice. There was general distrust, as if the jury system were some kind of "exotic plant" that would never be able to put down roots in Argentina.[35] As much as Argentine statesmen talked about incorporating Argentina into the civilized world as quickly as possible, they held back when it became a question of adopting something that they felt did not fit in with Argentine nature and customs.

Defenders of the jury system pointed out its many advantages over the Argentine judge-centered judicial system, whose inquisitional nature and secret instruction of cases have been noted in the Introduction to this book. In contrast, the jury system was public. With the introduction of a "conscience" in its legal procedure, Argentina, it was argued, would be "in harmony with republican principles," where trials were oral and public, and where judges *followed* cases, rather than *led* them. Judges would provide the "scientific" factor, while public curiosity, which was good because it was like another court, would provide the "moral" factor. The jury had a proven track record in Great Britain and America, and France (for a time), Japan, and Spain had juries. Argentines were advised to do the same; the alternative was to live like a subject under a monarchy, like "less than a subject of Napoleon III." Adoption of the jury system would mean another case of copying a foreign model, but in this case, it was argued that it was not an artificial adoption. Rather, it "responded to a natural necessity of modern civilization and even helped to bring inferior groups out of barbarity." The association of the jury system with civilization was also noted by jurists, who saw it as a powerful tool of liberal governments in forming political customs, educating and raising the moral level of citizens, and allowing the public to oversee criminal justice.[36]

In spite of the criticism of Argentine judicial practices, congressional opposition to the jury system remained firm. The opposition was mainly based on a lack of confidence in Argentine character and level of civilization. Especially in criminal matters, people doubted that the jury system would work in Argentina. Jurists argued that Argentine character was unsuited to the jury system, since Argentines did not have the habit of self-government and were indifferent, or even averse, to their responsibilities. Moreover, because of the nature of Latins—their "passional outbursts of sympathy or hatred" for defendants—criminal trial by popular juries was impracticable. Some jurists also saw a disturbing secretiveness in the jury system, in that the reason for a verdict always remained "hidden in the conscience of each juror," while, with a judge, people knew the verdict's author and the reasoning behind it. Others argued that the popular jury was not "respectable" for democracies and Latin republics, and that with a mixture of ignorance and education, it would only produce anarchy. However, a permanent, specialized jury in criminal cases consisting of lawyers, doctors, and "good men" was another thing.[37]

Foreign immigration and rural migration turned Buenos Aires into a particularly improbable environment for institutions of popular justice. Positivists especially strongly doubted whether an unenlightened, potentially volatile population could ever judge well. José Ingenieros, for example, wrote in 1905 that anyone who saw a jury function in all its glory as a theater would become its enemy. Part of what had confirmed his opinion was his own experience as a spectator in a Turin, Italy, courtroom at the turn of the century.[38] Just as professional and political elites made a habit of visiting penitentiaries and asylums abroad, they also made it a habit to attend trials. While visiting Italy, Ingenieros saw the greatest show "playing," the trial of Tullio Murri who had killed his brother-in-law, Conte Francesco Bonmartini, in Bologna in 1902, reportedly in order to free his sister, Linda Murri, from her unhappy marriage. "No theater spectacle [could] compare to this mise-en-scène,"

Ingenieros wrote, "and it [was] free." He criticized the spectators as "idle men of criminal temperament, mental degenerates," unable to file into the court-room "in an orderly fashion with their tickets and getting trampled in the rush; distinguished women . . . titillated by the scandal and pornography. This was the audience." Of course, Ingenieros was himself a member of the audi-ence, but he had a scientific reason for being there. Then there were the lawyers, the men who played to the jury. These were charlatans engaging in tournaments of commercial oratory, defending whoever paid them the most; law students learning to accept a circus spectacle as criminal procedure; and "blackbirds," that is, devotees of criminal cases. Finally, there was Tullio, who had committed the crime for reasons of personal vanity, in order to become the hero of a great drama, a martyr who had sacrificed himself to free his unhappy sister. His act was said to be a "beautiful passional gesture." The spectators were degenerates, however, and Tullio was the worst kind of crim-inal because of his vanity. There was nothing noble about passion in Ingenieros's view. The criminals, Tullio and Linda, had to sit in the court-room while lawyers made their secret life known in the most lurid style possi-ble in order to please the jury and spectators. Most offensive to Ingenieros, there was no scientific judge, not even a "mediocre" one, to evaluate the social and biological causes of the crime. Presenting scientific evidence to a jury, wrote Ingenieros, was like getting a country bumpkin to judge the tech-nical merit of a psychiatric report. No. The only way that a jury system could work was in a country where each man was "a sage and a saint." Finally, Ingenieros wrote, the jury system was dangerous; because of its theatricality and the publicity of trials, it fomented criminal vanity.

As new advances were made in criminal justice, the concern for scientific judgment of cases became more widespread. Ignorant of the arguments based on science, positivism, free will, and disease, the public was ill equipped to judge cases. While some jurors could assess extenuating circumstances such as drunkenness, acute dementia, or offenses to honor, for most, the subtleties slipped by, especially in assessing conditions such as latent insanity and larval epilepsy. For the public, these conditions were a "dead letter," and they were also ignored by some "judges, who, not withstanding the progress of medical and anthropological sciences, continued believing that 'when one is crazy, one is crazy to the tips of one's fingers.'" Even without the jury system, pro-fessionals pointed out, the Argentine public had a hand in judging crimes. The masses prejudged crimes in an indirect way through moral pressure, much as the midwife María Baby was judged guilty by a newspaper of the crime of abortion.[39]

Some legal professionals regarded the adoption of a jury system as a way to involve the public more extensively in the judicial process; others saw it as a direct route to decadence and corruption.

THE STATE'S PASSION AND THE DEATH PENALTY

The implementation of the death penalty seemed to be at odds with scientific, objective, unimpassioned justice. Executing people, even though it was done according to law, was nevertheless an "evil of passion" on the part of the state in response to the evil of an individual, Joaquín Escriche argued in the mid 1870s.[40]

Sentiment against the death penalty increased throughout the nineteenth century, building on the views of the Enlightenment thinkers Montesquieu and Rousseau and the classic criminologists Beccaria and Bentham, the latter being the most radical abolitionist. In the early 1830s, Argentine courts were directed to use capital punishment sparingly, both for humanitarian reasons and to "economize on American blood," although these beginnings were submerged in the summary justice and capital punishment of the Rosas era (1829–52).[41] Provincial legislatures generally abolished the death penalty for political crimes after the fall of Rosas and outlawed the gallows and exempted women from the death penalty in 1859. Observers credited these reforms to the country's abhorrence of the Rosas tyranny's atrocities—not the least of which was the execution by firing squad in 1848 of the pregnant Camila O'Gorman for eloping with a Catholic priest. The reforms were also consistent, however, with a broader international movement against capital punishment. In addition, a provision that commuted the death penalty went into effect in 1868, when the maximum penitentiary sentence was increased from ten years to twenty. In 1870, Pedro Goyena, Bernardo de Irigoyen, and others, proposed the abolition of the death penalty, but their proposal was voted down in the legislature.

The Tejedor code retained the death penalty (articles 99 and 100), justifying it on the basis of the "present state of civilization," contemporary customs, and the lack of other methods of repression. The code limited it to homicides without extenuating circumstances and, in addition to women, exempted people under the age of eighteen and over seventy. Since only one guilty party per crime could be executed, fate (*suerte*) decided which person would be executed in cases involving multiple criminals. The 1886 penal code retained the death penalty for murders committed with premeditation or malice, for payment or with extreme cruelty, and by drowning, arson, or poison, as well as for cases of parricide, which included father, mother, child (legitimate or natural), and any other immediate relative and spouse. Unless there were extenuating circumstances, the death sentence was applied to traitors and pirates. Defense attorneys knew ways to prolong cases, however, by requesting large numbers of expert witnesses on the basis of mental alienation and so on. After two years had passed, the death penalty could no longer be applied.[42] The death penalty was limited in 1906 and eventually removed from the second national penal code of 1921.

Argentines related abolition of the death penalty to national honor. Capital punishment failed to deter crime adequately, making the state seem ineffective; and it was uncivilized, making the state seem as brutal as a criminal. José Mármol argued in 1897 that because the death penalty was a poor deterrent and a cruel means of dealing with criminals, it reflected badly on the judiciary and the nation. "What affected people was not the punishment [or the blood] [itself], but rather the cruelty of the law, and thus the moral effect of the lesson was lost on society."[43] In fact, argued Alfredo M. Gándara in 1884 and Mármol in 1897, it could boomerang and increase public immorality, because bloody spectacles hardened perverse hearts and only inspired compassion and repugnance in weak ones. People accustomed to seeing blood could become insensitive, and an insensitive person could not be virtuous. Moreover, the death penalty might actually have been increasing crime, because some criminals saw glory in the gallows. Other criminals, however, remained unaffected, because the executions they witnessed were so rapid that they soon forgot about the spectacle. Attempts to justify capital punishment with theories of criminal anthropology were based on the view that the death sentence was just one of many forms of natural selection. It was not an efficient means of selection, others argued, because it could only be efficacious by generalizing it to all useless individuals or those prejudicial to society, which was impossible. Society would have to kill the insane, epileptics, tuberculosis victims, and all those who could transmit a fatal pathological seed to future generations. The fact was that there were no exact criteria for those who should be sacrificed.[44]

Second, the death penalty was considered inappropriate for a civilized nation and thus brought dishonor on Argentina. Argentina should give the Old World an example of civilization, Mármol wrote in 1897, and do away with the death penalty. Even for crimes against the head of state, such as when an attempt was made on the life of the Argentine president, Domingo F. Sarmiento, in 1873, the defense lawyer argued against the death penalty, saying that it was old-fashioned to "look for a cure through cruelty," and that it was useless as a legal means to prevent crime.[45] First, it did not follow humanitarian principles, argued Gándara in 1884 and José Luis Muratore in 1902. In the social contract, man did not give away his life. The death penalty did not benefit society; rather, it demoralized customs and led to the replacement of humanitarian sentiments with ferocity and insensitivity. Capital punishment was also not egalitarian, in that it did not provoke the same horror in everyone. The criminal might even be in shock and not feel anything when he was executed. Moreover, the death penalty could not be graduated or divided. It hurt the family by "eternally staining it with dishonor," which meant that it was actually a personal penalty. If the death penalty was unnecessary and unjustifiable, as Muratore argued, then it was certainly inappropriate for a civilized nation. Capital punishment was supposed to eliminate the element in society that disturbed harmony, but the basis for the elimination was debatable. If it were done according to the danger the criminal represented to society, Muratore wrote, it meant that the law was only punishing the physical damage done by the criminal, not the moral damage. To get at the moral damage, the criminal had to be imprisoned in order to convert him into a healthy element. If, on the other hand, society could judge that the criminal would never be regenerated, then death would be justified. If this was not possible, though, then the death penalty had to be viewed as just a vestige of the law of retaliation typical of uncivilized countries, rather than a scientific method of selection.[46]

What argued for the retention of the death penalty was that prison and other institutions of incarceration were appallingly inadequate and places of contagion. Again, Sicardi's images from 1903 capture the squalor of these institutions. On his night visits to prisons, he found the prisoners a "legion of larva that [did] not seem human," "syphilitic prisoners, with ulcers on their noses and mouths, who have been contaminated in prison."[47] Professional criminals were mixed in with "incipient" ones. In 1897, Mármol derisively called the contagion idea "silly," saying that people acted as if the criminal's breath was so poisonous that its very mixing with the atmosphere was to be feared, but others argued that mixing in jails precisely made it possible, not only for germs to propagate physiologically, but for moral contagion to spread. An "overflow into society of purulent and contagious germs, that physiologically and morally poisoned, brutalized, depressed, and corrupted" was pictured as the result. Others argued that incarceration should not even be an option for incorrigibles. Carlos Olivera wrote in 1900, for example, that society should not waste its resources maintaining the "organisms that harm[ed] it." Going even further, he said that society should not even maintain insane asylums, because these people were irreparably lost, while it allowed poor people and children to die. The latter would contribute in time to increasing the population or power of the country, whereas the former would never be able to contribute anything.[48]

On the other hand, modern, panopticon-style penitentiaries, with a place for the spectator, built on the cellular model and imbued with the ethics of work and education and the scientific study of prisoners were thought to avoid many of the problems of old-style prisons, even contagion, and to be more conducive to the regeneration of criminals. The cellular prison secured criminals, not with chains or the guards' severity, but with cells that could be viewed from a central location. Argentina's Penitenciaría Nacional, which opened in 1877 under the directorship of Enrique O'Gorman, became a model of the panopticon in South America, and items made by the inmates were sent to the Paris Exposition of 1878 to show its educational and productive possibilities. At first, though, the mixing of sentenced and unsentenced prisoners continued even in the panopticon. This situation improved in the period 1904–14, especially because the national penitentiary was given international exposure when Ingenieros established the Institute of Criminology there in 1907, reportedly the first diagnostic clinic for criminals in the world. In the early twentieth century, in addition to the separation of prisoners and increased work and study programs, the prisoners were treated with the latest criminological techniques. Anthropometric measurements, psychiatric examinations, and lengthy investigations of prisoners' backgrounds were made. The national penitentiary had taken on a life that stood in stark contrast to old-style prisons, with their dancing, guitar playing, and communal living. Guglielmo Ferrero, Cesare Lombroso's collaborator, and Gina Lombroso, Lombroso's daughter, while on a professional and educational tour of South America in 1908, gave high praise to the administrative staff of the national penitentiary in Buenos Aires, especially for its commitment to the work and education program for prisoners. Ferrero even added that the Buenos Aires penitentiary was one of the most interesting places he had visited in South America. He was especially impressed with the high level of reform of a prisoner serving a term for killing his wife who gave an impressively knowledgeable lecture on pre-Columbian America to his fellow inmates. In a letter to her father in 1908, Gina wrote that the Argentine penitentiary could not have been more successful had its founders "extracted all [Cesare's] knowledge from [his] head," and she opined that it was a shame that Italy was not able to compensate her father with an institution as prestigious as Argentina's penitentiary.[49]

For the incorrigibles, however, there was still the penal colony in Ushuaia, from which the prisoners were not supposed to return. Abolitionists argued that the new-style penitentiary was a good alternative to the death penalty. In fact, the penitentiary's "silence and solitude," isolated cell life, and hard labor were seen as possibly more effective than the death sentence. A man did not mind death, it was argued, but he did mind "slavery, the loss of his freedom, and his conversion into a beast" who had to "make amends to society with his sweat." The 1886 penal code included the penalties of confinement to cells and group labor. In *presidios*, the prisoners performed public work outdoors while chained; in penitentiaries, the inmates worked indoors without chains. All types of incarceration, including prisons, adopted the same regimen in 1904. Modern incarceration was supposed to impose orderly personal and work habits, regenerate the criminal, and discourage any future criminal activities. It also meant that in order to repair the damage done to the victim and his family, the criminal was forced to live incarcerated in a place where he could do no more damage.

Even with the campaign against capital punishment and with the construction of modern penitentiaries that made incarceration more "scientific," the death penalty continued to be solicited by prosecutors and judges for atrocious crimes. Most times it was commuted to a penitentiary sentence, but executions still took place, such as that of Cayetano Grossi, who was put to death by firing squad in the Penitenciaría Nacional on April 6, 1900, for the crime of infanticide. Often the argument for capital punishment was that exemplary punishment was necessary to contain people's passions. For people who attacked "honor, laws, and the most intimate sentiments of man," Francisco Netri argued in 1902, only the punishment of death was sufficient, especially in cases such as parricide.[50] In addition, people felt that it was really the only way to deal with "incorrigibles." In the view of positivists, such as Osvaldo Piñero, writing in 1888, for example, the death penalty was a "must," because *all* criminals were morally and physiologically incapable of repenting or reforming. The reason that these people were delinquents in the first place was because they were organically degenerate and the victims of morbid heredity that made them different from most men. The utopian classical criminologists were criticized for their opposition to the death penalty. Such a stance did not benefit humanity. Pious sentiment as regards criminals should not be allowed to be the norm for the conduct of society, because it was out of sync with individual behavior. Not even life imprisonment could ever advantageously replace the death penalty, because criminals were not affected by being locked up. In fact, it had been proven in countries such as

England that the death penalty was effective in decreasing crime. In sum, abolitionists' humanitarian sentiments were misplaced.[51]

In a criminal case in 1888, capital punishment was even argued to be "doubly just"—first, because it protected society by selectively eliminating a bad element; second, because it was not vengeance, but an "act of humanity for the accused himself." No one escaped death. If a criminal received the death sentence, the only thing that happened was that death got to him sooner. But the advantage for this criminal was that he had time to repent, to get ready for the last moment, and then it was all over with him in a second. He had a "chance to show a tear before God and courage before men." In this sense, the death sentence almost absolved its victims. It not only protected society but "bathed with its rays the man who must die." Besides, most prisoners died in prison anyway; it was simply that the public did not see this.[52] In an Italian study, for example, out of one hundred prisoners sentenced to fifteen years in prison, eighty died while they were serving their sentences, and those who were eventually released were debilitated. Abolition of the death penalty merely altered the *external* form of death.

It was this external form of death, in fact, that seems to have been important to many defenders of the death penalty. It was the opinion of many distinguished criminologists that the death penalty was necessary and had to be executed in public for it to be effective. In Argentina, although the death penalty for women had been outlawed in 1859, prosecutors and judges still called for it in criminal cases. In 1860, a Córdoba court sentenced a woman to be garroted for the crime of infanticide and for her cadaver to be suspended for six hours for public viewing, though this was later commuted to nine years' imprisonment.[53] This was one of the times when public dishonoring was called for and deemed, at least by some people, to be effective. The Spanish penal code of 1870 made execution a public and defamatory spectacle by conducting the victim to the scaffold in a black tunic in a special carriage. Incarceration also contained some dishonoring mechanisms. On his visit to the Sierra Chica penitentiary in 1899, Pedro Gori reported that inmates who had committed bloody crimes had to wear red uniforms. The regulation that prisoners were put in solitary confinement for thirty days on the anniversary of their crime each year was also meant to publicly defame.[54]

Although both supporters of the death penalty and abolitionists invoked honor in arguments about the death penalty—the latter contending that it was dishonorable to use it, and the former that it was dishonorable not to do so—by the end of the century, there was a reluctance to actually employ capital punishment, even though it might still be called for, because of dishonor.

Reprieves were only granted after the case had been appealed, however, and often only on the brink of the execution. In the case of the poisoner Luis Castruccio, cited in chapter 5, for example, the appeals court confirmed the death sentence on December 5, 1889. The sentence was to be carried out by firing squad in the penitentiary at 4 P.M. the following day. There were no more appeals available, except to the president of the republic, who at the time was Miguel Juárez Celman. On December 6, he commuted Luis's death sentence to prison. It was not because he did not believe in capital punishment, since he said in his decree that the punishment was just. Rather, his clemency was based on the need for honor and passion to follow the correct path in Argentina so that it could be considered part of the group of civilized nations.

Juárez Celman began by acknowledging the receipt of petitions for clemency from "distinguished Argentine ladies," and his reason for acceding to them is interesting. These women had been "moved by a noble sentiment of piety" to ask for clemency. Piety was a scarce commodity and not to be allowed to go to waste in society; moreover, it was very important to the nature of women, who in turn were important to family and state. It was ill advised, then, not to acquiesce to it, because if women's piety were not rewarded, it would remain "futile," which was contrary to the well-being of society, as we saw in chapter 1. Juárez Celman acknowledged, furthermore, that his constituency would not be pleased with his decision, and that he would have to face the public's unsatisfied "vindictiveness," that is, the public's desire for the state to express passion against the vile, cruel criminal Castruccio. But, he said, that was what the penitentiary was for, for keeping the public safe from such criminals, and that safety and not vindictiveness was what was important. Finally, Argentina had a regional and an international role to play, and it would be a stain on its honor for the state to put a man to death in an act of passion. Argentina was a co-celebrant with Brazil in a celebration in honor of the new Brazilian Republic, which was to be held on December 8, 1889. If Argentina staged a "bloody execution" on December 6, near the eve of Brazilian festivities, it would be seen badly. It would be better for an act of clemency to precede the festivities, which would both add to the public's rejoicing and show Argentine sympathy for the arrival of free institutions in the United States of Brazil.[55]

CONCLUSION

Passion was widely alleged by the Anglo-Saxon as well as the Latin world to be a part of Latin identity. The shared opinion of these diverse worlds was that passion was a negative characteristic, although more subtle evaluations of it were also introduced. There were ramifications of the Latin "abuse" of passion, it was argued. For example, Estanislao Severo Zeballos suggested in 1898 that passion hampered the proper imitation of European models, which Argentina needed for development. In addition, passion did not provide a good basis for judgment and action, especially in politics. Passion was also a hindrance to the justice system. When any member of a Latin race sat in judgment on a criminal, a lawyer argued in an 1882 case, he had to be careful, because Latins were easy to impress and dominated by fantasy, so they saw more than what was there.[56] Rationality, so valued in this era of positive science, was out of balance in Argentina, Zeballos wrote, which would explain to future historians the origins of the country's "serious disorders, deficiencies, and anomalies."[57]

Curbing passion was also necessary for global political "health." Decadent nations, ruled by passion, were a threat to universal peace, in that their vulnerability attracted imperialist invaders.[58] The London *Economist* had predicted that European intervention would continue for years to come in South America, as in Africa and China, because of its political disorders, and Zeballos warned that these were "hints to [Argentines] that [they] should not ignore." Argentina's incapacity for political stability was not a question of its lack of development, Miguel Romero argued, but of its "way of being," its *modo de ser*. In accordance with the psychology of the age, Argentina's lack of stability was argued to lie in its "defective" ancestors, the Celts, who had implanted their particular political spirit in the Spanish organism. "History shows," wrote Miguel Romero, "that all the defects of Argentine political character are flourishing sprouts of the Celtic Spanish tree, transplanted to the fertile soil of South America." Although he did not go as far back in history as the Celts, Zeballos noted that in the political crises of South America, the impulse was always revolutionary. "We do not have the character for educating and founding," he wrote, "but we have lots of heroism for assaulting or dying."[59]

There was a dilemma in the above arguments against passion, however, in that some of the social forces springing from the pursuit of progress, such as utilitarianism, materialism, individualism, and dissimulation, posed as many problems as passion. This is why some of the same people who warned about excessive passion seemed at the same time to be nostalgic for it and felt that Argentine identity was being undermined by abandoning it. Zeballos argued that Argentina should defend itself against "utilitarian vulgarity."[60] Utilitarianism showed up in singular ways. For example, women who used the court system to challenge their husbands by bringing cases of adultery and divorce against them were criticized by judges and lawyers for not using passion and sentiment, like tears and sweet words, instead. Obviously, this was one of the safe areas for passion that was nurtured by society. It was also safe and good for men to respond to their passion in defending their honor, even if it resulted in crime. Materialism was seen as a negative effect of foreign influence and of the copying of foreign models. No one wanted progress to erase national identity. An editorial in the *Revista Jurídica* in 1891 complained that "social and political sensualism" and the "fever of speculation and profit" were "enervating the national spirit." The focus on utility was useless and prejudicial to heroism. The Argentine national apathy-inducing disease of encephalitis might well have been ameliorated by a good dose of passion.[61] "Interest," meaning self-interest, and individualism were destroying Argentine ideals. It was the only country at its stage of development, Zeballos wrote, where there was no moral force struggling to direct the flood of materialism and private interest. As important as scientific reason was, an excess of it would degenerate into utilitarianism if it were not balanced with sensitivity. In 1898, Zeballos warned that man was becoming a "machine," and that Argentina was becoming a "factory."[62]

Conclusion

The theories being developed to resolve social problems around 1900 offered an all-encompassing diagnosis of the ills of both individuals and societies at a time of modern innovations and new values, seemingly explaining the success or failure of entire nations and civilizations. The theories were new, but they could nonetheless be used to maintain the status quo. Liberal democrats' support for new theories and modernity was tempered, for example, in the case of women, by a respect for male authority. The possibilities of contagion in houses of deposit was not deemed as important as maintaining a husband's superiority in the family. The use of new laws on divorce was not deemed as important as keeping the gender hierarchy intact. Even though more and more elements of society were moving under secular state control, areas in which the law was discouraged from entering the sacred interior of the family continued to be preserved, so that honor could be maintained. Cures for broad social evils that came in the form of degeneration or contagion, for example, substituted for plans that might better have addressed social and economic ills, leading to suggestions that presaged the Nazi atrocities of the 1930s and 1940s. Contagion was a divisive factor that was especially useful in encouraging the self-management of society. It was recommended that one avoid sights, desires, displays of emotion, and thoughts that might literally corrupt the flesh, in the interest of the good of the whole. This meant that people should act in a way consistent with their class.

On the other hand, the theories led to some interesting formulations of Argentine character. In spite of the success of the centralization of the government, foreign investment that helped beautify Buenos Aires and brought advanced public works to the city, and a comprehensive immigration policy, dissatisfaction with the national character was expressed. More important than "all political, monetary, and administrative questions," C. O. Bunge wrote in 1900, was national character. His point was that it was not enough for a country to have "excellent finances, organization, and hegemony" if the character of its population was "banal, [false], quixotic, inactive, dull," and if it was content with "bread and circuses." It was a mistake to look for the origin of problems in proximate causes, such as the educational system or the lack of preparation for liberty. Rather, Argentina's problems had deep causes, with the root of them being the population. The focus on population was a natural progression for this positivist era in which the conviction dominated that human bodies could indeed be physiologically and psychically improved. What was needed, Miguel Romero wrote in 1901, was to correct the ethnic defects of the national character through selective immigration and naturalization of foreigners, and to reconstruct and discipline collective forces.[1]

The trajectory chosen, followed, and encouraged by Argentinian politicians and professionals for the forward movement of state and society toward modernity then focused on the analysis and transformation of individual and collective bodies. The historiography is now well advanced on how people at the turn of the century anthropomorphized the public works that flushed away the city's waste, cleansed its inner organs, and guarded against miasmas in the air that contaminated through contagion. Society, like flesh, degenerated if it had enough fatal elements in it. The nation itself sustained all the flaws and idiosyncrasies of human flesh. As a "body," the Argentine state was variously described in emotional, even passional, terms as psychologically "wounded," spiritually "poisoned," "feverishly delirious," "demoralized," and "organically perverted." Argentina was "the child of a degenerate mother" (i.e., Spain) and engaged in "siring a race," like a human parent. It was infected with "germs and viruses, with its vital fluid contaminated, and in need of emollients, calming agents, tonics, elixirs, and even surgical intervention in order to cut away the gangrene from its raw flesh."[2] By juxtaposing the problems of the state and those of individuals, these analogies might have helped individuals better to understand the task of the state, but subscribing to these images also conveyed that, in the end, flesh resisted the imposition of orderly systems on both individual and state levels.

Individuals "in the flesh" were necessary to modernity, it was argued, and passion was the best manifestation of the flesh. While flesh did, it was true, sometimes get out of control and challenge authority, allow contagions to enter and exit the body, and harbor degenerative characteristics, it was also an important antidote to the increasing utilitarianism and materialism that was threatening to become dominant at the turn of the century. In some ways, the passional person, even when committing a criminal act, was the perfect citizen. His passion was an outlet, a safety valve for society's inability to understand the mysteries of human flesh. It was an outlet for the expression of traditional social values that were still being honored in their dishonoring—like the punishment of adultery. And it was a source of the extremely useful qualities of confession and remorse for human "excess" and an opportunity to renew the strength of the human will. Passion raised flesh to its most noble level.

Notes

The following abbreviations are used in the Notes and Bibliography:

AGN, TC   Archivo General de la Nación (Argentina), Tribunal Criminal (cited by series, first letter of surname, *legajo*, year)

AGN, Trib. Civil   Archivo General de la Nación (Argentina), Tribunal Civil (cited by index number, first letter of surname, *legajo*, year)

AGN, SB   Archivo General de la Nación (Argentina), Sociedad de Beneficencia (cited by *legajo*, section, year)

APCCA   *Archivos de Psiquiatría, Criminología y Ciencias Afines*

APCMLP   *Archivos de Psiquiatría, Criminología, Medicina Legal y Psiquiatría*

CC   Archivo Histórico de la Provincia de Córdoba

CM   *Criminalogía Moderna*

PBT   *PBT; Semanario infantil ilustrado (para niños de 6 á 80 años)* (Buenos Aires)

RDHL   *Revista de Derecho, Historia y Letras*

RJ   *Revista Jurídica*

RLJ   *Revista de Lejislación y Jurisprudencia*

RP   *Revista de Policía*

Introduction

1. Francisco de Veyga, "Los auxiliares del vicio y del delito," *APCCA* 3 (1904): 293; Estanislao Severo Zeballos, "La crisis del gobierno y del país," *RDHL* 2, 5 (1899): 456.

2. See Eduardo Wilde, *Obras completas* (Buenos Aires: Peuser, 1914), pt. 1, *Científicas*, 3: 101 (written in the 1880s).

3. *PBT* 2, 62 (1905): 72; *PBT* 3, 76 (1906); *PBT* 3, 104 (1906): 21.

4. See Emilio Brusa, "Derecho penal: El tercer Congreso internacional penitenciario y el antropológico-criminal," *RJ* 3 (1886): 1057–58; Baldomero Llerena, "Discurso," *RDHL* 1 (1898): 233.

5. This and following biographical information is from sources containing biographies of Argentine professionals, such as Vicente Osvaldo Cutola's *Nuevo diccionario biográfico argentino (1750–1930)* (Buenos Aires: Editorial Elche, 1968–85).

6. AGN, TC, 1, U, 2, 1882, case against Enrique Ucar for robbing Alfredos Ducasse; Aurelio Bassi, "El proyecto de Código penal: Su exámen," *RJ* 9 (1892): 406–7.

7. Julián L. Aguirre, *Autos y sentencias del juez del crímen . . . (departamentos del Sud y capital de la provincia de Buenos Aires, 1875–1881; Capital 1882–1885)* (Buenos Aires, 1885).

8. Agustín Rivero Astengo, *Hombres de la organización nacional: Retratos literarios*, 1st ser. (Buenos Aires: Coni, 1936), 129–38; Ricardo D. Salvatore, "State Legal Order and Subaltern Rights: The Modernization of the Justice System in Argentina (1870–1930)" (MS), p. 4 n. 3, pp. 4–8 on law codes.

9. Luis María Drago, *Los hombres de presa: Antropolojía criminal* (1888), 2d ed. (Buenos Aires: Cultura Argentina, 1921), 32; Pedro Gori, "La ortodoxia antropológica en el derecho penal," *RJ* 15 (1898–99): 78; "Guerra al delito!" *CM* 1, 1 (1898): 1–2; Oscar Terán, *Positivismo y nación en la Argentina* (Buenos Aires: Puntosur, 1987), 13–14; Ricardo D. Salvatore, "Positivist Criminology and State Formation in Argentina" (forthcoming).

10. Estanislao Severo Zeballos, "Analecta," *RDHL* 3, 8 (1901): 476; id., "El Instituto de Criminología de la República Argentina," *APCCA* 7 (1908); Jorge Salessi, *Médicos, maleantes y maricas* (Rosario: Beatriz Viterbo, 1995), 97.

11. Gina Lombroso, "Instituciones americanas: La Penitenciaría Nacional de Buenos Aires," *APCCA* 7 (1908): 236.

12. Manual Obarrio, "Derecho penal," *RLJ* 11 (1878): 13–14; Emilio B. Prack, "Escuela antropológica criminal," *RJ* 8 (1891): 112–13, 255–56.

13. Brusa, "Derecho penal," 1055, quoting Lombroso.

14. Lombroso noted that criminals did not feel pain, a "disvulnerability" that was called *buena carnadura* in Argentina. Drago, *Hombres de presa*, 47.

15. Godofredo Lozano, "La reforma del Código Penal Argentino," *RDHL* 3, 8 (1901): 378, 380–81.

16. Terán, *Positivismo*, 11, 14.

17. Manuel Carlés, "Atavismo pampa," *CM* 1, 2 (1898): 57–58.

18. Manuel Carlés, "Atavismo pampa," *CM* 2, 5 (1899): 143–44.

19. Salvatore, "State Legal Order,"2, 6; Juan José Montes de Oca, "Derecho criminal," *RLJ* 7 (1872): 422; Eduardo A. Zimmermann, "El poder judicial, la construcción del estado, y el federalismo: Argentina, 1860–1880," in *In Search of a New Order: Essays on the Politics and Society of Nineteenth-Century Latin America*, ed. Eduardo Posada-Carbó (London: Institute of Latin American Studies, University of London, 1998), 138–39, on the court system in Buenos Aires; Raimundo Wilmart, "Nuestro poder judicial," *RJ* 17, 2 (1899): 22–23.

20. Wilmart, "Nuestro poder," 22–23.

21. Joaquín Escriche y Martín, *Diccionario razonado de legislación y jurisprudencia* (Madrid: Cuesta, 1874–76), vol. 4 (1876), 523–53, s.v. "Pena."

22. "Reforma de la Constitución de la Provincia de Buenos Aires," *RLJ* 5 (1870): 405, quoting López; Antonio Dellepiane, "Nuestros propósitos," *RJ* 12 (1895–96): 6; José Luis Cantilo, "El gran problema," *RDHL* 1, 2 (1898): 304; Juan Ramón Fernández, "Reforma universitaria: Concepto filosófico del plan de instrucción pública proyectado," *RDHL* 2, 6 (1899): 214.

23. Carlos Octavio Bunge, "El caracter nacional y la educación," *RJ* 19 (1900–1901): 80–82; Walter S. Logan, "Tribunales sajones y latinos," *RDHL* 1, 3 (1899): 80.

24. AGN, TC, 1, U, 2, 1882, case against Enrique Ucar.

25. "Derecho civil," *RLJ* 10 (1876): 256.

26. Cantilo, "Gran problema," 304–5, 307; Carlos A. Aldao, "Consideraciones sobre la justicia argentina," *RDHL* 1 (1898): 355.

27. Wilde, *Obras*, 14: 292 (written in 1896).

28. José Manuel Estrada, "El patriotismo," *RJ* 13 (1896–97): 77–79, 81 (talk given in 1883).

Chapter 1: Liberalism and the Ego

1. Wilde, *Obras*, pt. 1, *Científicas*, 3: 265–67 (written in the 1880s).

2. Luis María Drago, *El poder marital* (thesis, Facultad de Derecho y Ciencias Sociales; Buenos Aires: El Diario, 1882), 18, quoting Daniel Stern; Francine Masiello, *Between Civilization and Barbarism: Women, Nation, and Literary Culture in Modern Argentina* (Lincoln: University of Nebraska Press, 1992), 102, on feminists' views of the new sciences.

3. Drago, *Poder marital*, 12–17; Asunción Lavrin, *Women, Feminism, and Social Change in Argentina, Chile, and Uruguay, 1890–1940* (Lincoln: University of Nebraska Press, 1995), 201–2, on Drago as a reformer of women's civil rights.

4. Drago, *Poder marital*, 12; Lavrin, *Women*, 124, on anarchist support of women's "sacred mission."

5. Augusto Carette, ed., *Diccionario de la jurisprudencia argentina, ó síntesis completa de las sentencias dictadas por los tribunales argentinos* (Buenos Aires: Lajouane, 1917–21), s.v. "Obediencia."

6. Severo Catalina del Amo, *La mujer: Apuntes para un libro*, 2d ed. (Madrid: San Martín, 1861), 117; this author sometimes uses *honor* and *honra* synonymously. I have not found the date of the first edition. Men's obligation to honor was asserted about Luisoni, a naval official, in AGN, TC, 2, C, 64, 1891, and AGN, TC, 2, C, 68, 1891, case against Juan Lucio Cascallares Paz and Susana Breuil de Conderc for provoked abortion.

7. Estanislao Severo Zeballos, "Discurso," *RDHL* 5, 13 (1902): 461–62, quoting Juan Bautista Alberdi; Mario Bravo, *Derechos civiles de la mujer: El código, los proyectos, la ley* (Buenos Aires: El Ateneo, 1927), 69, 119; Carette, *Diccionario*, s.v. "Violación" (clause 7).

8. Zeballos, "Discurso," 457–66 passim.

9. Ibid.

10. Ibid.

11. Cesare Lombroso and Guglielmo Ferrero, *La donna delinquente, la prostituta e la donna normale* (Turin: Roux, 1893), translated as *The Female Offender* (New York: Appleton, 1898), 151, 157–58, 165, 182.

12. Miguel F. Rodríguez, "El adulterio: Contribución al estudio de nuestra legislación penal," *RDHL* 3, 7 (1900): 393.

13. José Luis Peset and Mariano Peset, *Lombroso y la escuela positivista italiana* (Madrid: Junta de Castilla y León, 1975), 632, 643, 650.

14. Lombroso and Ferrero, *Female Offender*, 148, 150–52.

15. Rodríguez, "Adulterio," 393–94; Donna Guy, *Sex and Danger in Buenos Aires: Prostitution, Family, and Nation in Argentina* (Lincoln: University of Nebraska Press, 1992), 102; id., *White Slavery and Mothers Alive and Dead: The Troubled Meeting of Sex, Gender, Public Health, and Progress in Latin America* (Lincoln: University of Nebraska Press, 2000).

208 Notes

16. AGN, TC, 2, B, 48, 1891, case against the wife, María Blanc Marc, and her lover Silvio Mattei, for adultery, brought by María's husband, Clemente Venancy.

17. AGN, TC, 2, C, 64, 1891, and AGN, TC, 2, C, 68, 1891, case against Juan Lucio Cascallares Paz and Susana Breuil de Conderc for abortion, quoting Ernesto Legomé.

18. Alfredo J. Molinario, "La desincriminación del adulterio en el Proyecto de Código Penal Argentino," *Anales de la Sociedad Argentina de Criminología* 5 (1939): 17–32 passim.

19. Enrique del Valle Iberlucea, "Fundamentos científicos del divorcio," *APCCA* 1 (1902): 471, 479; Bravo, *Derechos civiles*, 26–27.

20. Molinario, "Desincriminación," 17–32 passim.

21. Argentine Penal Code, 1886, 2.1.3.1.123. See Salvatore, "State Legal Order," 11, on the double standard of adultery.

22. AGN, TC, 2, C, 118, 1899, Brunette Wal de Catton against her husband, Julio Gasten Catton and his lover, Agustina Villain, for adultery.

23. Escriche, *Diccionario*, s.v. "Adulterio;" Lavrin, *Women*, 252, on the distinction between male and female adultery.

24. Molinario, "Desincriminación," 30, quoting the Italian Manzini.

25. Luis M. Campos Urquizi, "Solicitud," *RJ* 20 (1901): 63, 65; Marcelino Escalada, "Matrimonio civil y divorcio," *RJ* 5 (1888): 401. The reform plan of Rivarola, Matienzo, and Piñero proposed to decriminalize adultery.

26. Bravo, *Derechos civiles*, 70.

27. Iberlucea, "Fundamentos," 478, 483; Campos Urquizi, "Solicitud," 64.

28. Iberlucea, "Fundamentos," 481–83.

29. Campos Urquizi, "Solicitud," 61; M. Rodríguez, "Adulterio," 403.

30. Bravo, *Derechos civiles*, 69; Sandra Gayol, "Duelos, honores, leyes y derechos: Argentina, 1887–1923," *Anuario Iehs (Instituto de Estudios Histórico-sociales, Universidad Nacional del Centro, Tandil, Argentina)* 14 (1999): 322, 326; Pablo Piccato, "La política y la tecnología del honor: El duelo en México durante el porfiriato y la revolución," *Anuario Iehs* 14 (1999): 273–94, 277–79. Salvatore, "State Legal Order," 11; Manuel Obarrio, "Familia," *RJ* 4 (1888): 157, from a speech to new graduates; Pablo Piccato, "Criminals in Mexico City, 1900–1931: A Cultural History" (diss., University of Texas, Austin, 1997) 130, on a similar heightened concern for personal reputation in Mexico; Lyman L. Johnson and Sonya Lipsett-Rivera, eds., *The Faces of Honor: Sex, Shame, and Violence in Colonial Latin America* (Albuquerque: University of New Mexico Press, 1998), on colonial honor; Ann Twinam, *Public Lives, Private Secrets: Gender, Honor, Sexuality, and Illegitimacy in Colonial Spanish America* (Stanford: Stanford University Press, 1999), 41–50, on colonial honor.

31. Salvatore, "State Legal Order," 12.

32. AGN, TC, 1, A, 6, 1886, case brought by Gerardo Arciello and María Esperanza against José Apicelli for serious injury.

33. Julián Pitt-Rivers, "La enfermedad del honor," *Anuario Iehs* 14 (1999): 241.

34. AGN, TC, 2, B, 1873, Manuel Adano against Antonio Bonfiglio for injuries, 29–35, quoting Quesada; José Luis Duffy, "Curiosidades fiscales: Otro dictámen del Dr. Quesada," *RP* 3, 57 (Oct. 1, 1899): 139–42 passim; J. L. Duffy, "Curiosidades fiscales: Sentencia del doctor Barrenecha," *RP* 3 (58) (Oct. 16, 1899): 151–52 passim.

35. Argentine Penal Code, 1886, 2.1.2.119.

36. AGN, TC, 2, B, 22, 1883, against Clara Barghelli for poisoning of Aquilino Semino and attempted poisoning of Santiago Semino, and against the accomplice, Andrés Pagano.

37. AGN, TC, 1, M, 5, 1871, Ramón Heredia against his wife Gervasia Moron for adultery; Bartolo da Sassoferrato, *Commentaria in corpus iuris civilis (codice e istituzioni)* (Venice, 1567) cited in *Enciclopedia del diritto*, vol. 1 (Varese: Giuffrè, 1958), s.v. "Adulterio." I thank Daniela Lombardi for this reference.

38. Escriche, *Diccionario*, 659–63.

39. Ibid.

40. Escriche, *Diccionario*, s.v. "Depósito de personas" (clause 2); "Asilo de Mujeres 1899," *RP* 3, 64 (Jan. 16, 1900): 260–61 passim.

41. Argentine Civil Code, 1869, 1.9.205.208.

42. Aguirre, *Autos y sentencias*, 637–38.

43. AGN, TC, 1, D, 2, 1872, Luis Fraquelli against Cesario Díaz for seduction of his wife, Francisca Plaza de Fraquelli.

44. Aguirre, *Autos y sentencias*, 637–38.

45. Carette, *Diccionario*, s.v. "Divorcio" (clause 112); AGN, TC, 1, S, 2, 1867, against Enrique Stolle, Manuel Viera, and Carmen Guodanoviche for adultery.

46. AGN, TC, 1, D, 2, 1872, Fraquelli case.

47. AGN, TC, 1, R, 3, 1865–70, Pedro Moreno against Donata de la Rosa for adultery.

48. AGN, SB, 139, 88–89, 97–98; AGN, SB, 51, 192–230; Muriel, *Recogimientos*, 121, 187.

49. Ricardo D. Salvatore and Carlos Aguirre, eds., *The Birth of the Penitentiary in Latin America: Essays on Criminology, Prison Reform, and Social Control, 1830–1940* (Austin: University of Texas Press, 1996).

50. AGN, SB, 179, Defensoría de Menores, 1824–1895, case from 1887; "Buen Pastor," *El Diario* (Oct. 12, 1892).

51. AGN, TC, 2, D, 70, 1902, Pedro Rontin, husband, against his wife, Josefina Durbec de Rontin, and her lover, Juan Bonnafous, for adultery; AGN, TC, 1, B, 5, 1902, Justo M. Jiménez, husband, against wife, Carmen Bernabe, and her lover, Manuel Vazquez, for adultery and complicity.

52. AGN, TC, 1, B, 4, 1872, Felisa Barturbuní and Teodoro Bonnecarrere charge each other with divorce; case still going on in 1875; AGN, TC, 1, M, 5, 1871, Ramón Heredia case.

53. AGN, TC, 2, C, 1, 1870, case against Pascual Castro Echeverría for homicide of his wife, Eusebia Arrascaete.

54. AGN, TC, 1, M, 5, 1871, Ramón Heredia case.

55. AGN, TC, 1, B, 5, 1871, Juan Solari against Luisa Bisso for divorce and adultery.

56. *RJ* 12 (1895): 343–44. The references are to Lola Montez (1818–61), an Irish adventuress and "Spanish" dancer, and Messalina (A.D. 22–48), third wife of the Roman emperor Claudius, who were known for their power over men.

57. J. J. Díaz Arana, "Naturaleza del feminismo," *RJ* 16 (1899): 11; Lombroso and Ferrero, *Female Offender*, 147–91 passim.

58. AGN, TC, 1, U, 2, 1882, against Graciana Urrutigarray by her husband, Juan Bautista Bonnement, for calumny and serious injuries (including divorce).

59. AGN, Trib. Civil, Index no. 116, A, 347, 1892, Dionisio Anglada against his wife, Ana Arrix, and request to put her in a convent.

60. *PBT* 4, 112 (1907): 90; 117 (1907): 144; 116 (1907): 88; 125 (1907): 102.

61. AGN, TC, 1, M, 5, 1871, Ramón Heredia case.

62. Escriche, Diccionario, s.v. "Adulterio."

63. AGN, TC, 2, A, 48, 1900, Paula Ventura de Arzeno against José Arzeno and Catalina Marini, for adultery.

64. Drago, *Poder marital*, 12; Argentine Constitution of 1853, article 18.

Chapter 2: Social Responsibility and Free Will

1. AGN, TC, 1, L, 2, 1871, case against Juana Larramendia for infanticide.

2. For the debate on free will and birth, see Drago, *Hombres de presa*, 66, who supported the positivist position that people lacked free will, and Prack, "Escuela antropológica criminal," 109–13, 254–64, 298–306, who upheld the existence of free will. Cases where women were analyzed as not having had free will are CC, 1875, 366, 6, against Carmen Astudio for attempted infanticide and CC, 1890, 3, 2, against Delfina Moyano for attempted infanticide.

3. AGN, TC, 2, A, 54, 1903, case against Cesarina Almada for infanticide.

4. AGN, TC, 2, B, 78, 1899, case against Luisa Bernal for infanticide (in which Luisa, an Amerindian, received a sentence of four and a half years prison); C, 113, 1898, case against Juana Castro for infanticide (in which Juana, also an Amerindian, was acquitted). In both cases, the status of "indigenous" was used as an extenuating circumstance for the women.

5. Escriche, *Diccionario*, vol. 3, s.v. "Infanticidio."

6. CC, 1897, 6, 10, case against Ramona Funes for infanticide; her lawyer quoting Jeremy Bentham.

7. AGN, TC, 1, I, 2, 1873, case against María Iguerra and Pedro Danglá for infanticide.

8. Dr. Mauenaghton, "Las funciones sexuales, la locura e el delito en la mujer," lecture given at the British Gynocological Society, *APCCA* 1 (1902): 58–59 passim; D. J. G. d J. Pérez, *Nueva medicina doméstica, o sea arte de conservar la salud, de conocer las enfermedades, sus remedios y aplicación, al alcance de todos* (Buenos Aires: Revista, 1854), 162–64.

9. CC, 1850, 223, 14, case against Marquosa Solares for infanticide; Escriche, *Diccionario*, vol. 3, s.v. "Infanticidio."

10. Argentine Penal Code, 1886, 2.1.1.2.100–101. Argentine law also included the parents of the mother as able to be charged with infanticide, rather than the more severe homicide. For interesting comparisons of infanticide in Chile and Mexico, see Nara Milanich, "'Entrañas mil veces despreciables e indignas': Infanticide in Rural Nineteenth-Century Chile" (MS, 1995), and Elisa Guerra Speckman, "Las flores del mal: Mujeres criminales en el porfiriato," *Historia Mexicana* 47, 1 (1997): 212–13.

11. Kristin Ruggiero, "Honor, Maternity, and the Disciplining of Women: Infanticide in Late Nineteenth-Century Buenos Aires," *Hispanic American Historical Review* 72, 3 (1992): 356.

12. CC, 1880, 422, 6, against Higinia Pereyra for infanticide.

13. Escriche, *Diccionario*, s.vv. "Infanticidio" and "Aborto." For the continuation of

the principle of dishonor in late twentieth-century Latin American law codes, see Ernesto García Maañón and Alejandro Antonio Basile, *Aborto e infanticidio: Aspectos jurídicos y médico-legales* (Buenos Aires: Universidad, 1990), 18, 49, 60.

14. Princesa María Isenburg, "La reforma del traje femenino," *RDHL* 4, 11 (1901): 97.

AGN, TC, 2, A, 55, 1903, against Felipa Arce for infanticide; B, 79, 1899, against Teresa Bishop de Bennecke for infanticide; C, 154, 1904, against Catalina Costa for attempted infanticide; B, 28, 1886, against Juana Baret for infanticide; C, 70, 1902, against Inés Coria for infanticide; A, 52, 1902, against María Luisa Antoniana for infanticide; D, 57, 1899, against Teresa De Michelli for infanticide.

15. AGN, TC, 1, L, 2, 1871, Juana Larramendia case.

16. CC, 1897, 6, 10, Ramona Funes case; M. F. Rodríguez, "Adulterio," 237 on socioeconomic class and sense of honor.

17. CC, 1875, 363, 5, case against Micaela Barrera and Rufina Farías for infanticide; CC, 1880, 422, 6, Higinia Pereyra case; AGN, TC, 1, L, 2, 1871, Juana Larramendia case.

18. AGN, TC, 2, D, 57, 1899, Teresa De Michelli case.

19. AGN, TC, 2, A, 55, 1903, Felipa Arce case.

20. Ruggiero, "Honor," 356.

21. AGN, SB, leg. 101, Casa de Expósitos, 1887–1892, 62; Susan Migden Socolow, *The Women of Colonial Latin America* (New York: Cambridge University Press, 2000), 77.

22. AGN, SB, leg. 104, Casa de Expósitos, 1904–7.

23. AGN, TC, 2, B, 44, 1890, against Juana Barragan for homicide of a minor María Muriello, and attempted homicide of Luisa Sosa de Barragan, Agustina Barragan, and Manuela Suarez.

24. AGN, SB, leg. 103, Casa de Expósitos, 1900–1904; AGN, SB, leg. 181, Defensoría de Menores, 1904–7.

25. "Derecho civil," *RLJ* 5 (1870): 14–38 passim.

26. Ibid.

27. AGN, SB, leg. 179, Defensoría de Menores, 1824–95.

28. Ibid.

29. AGN, SB, leg. 51, Asilo del Buen Pastor, 1855–1891, 116–17, citing article from *La Pampa*, Oct. 20, 1882.

30. Emilio Gouchon, "La ordenanza reglamentaria del servicio doméstico," *RJ* 5 (1888): 86, 90–95.

31. Lino Ferriani, *La infanticida nel Codice Penale e nella vita sociale: Considerazioni* (Milan: Fratelli Dumolard Editori, 1886) 151–52.

32. J. C. Llames Massini, *La partera de Buenos Aires y la Escuela de Parteras* (Buenos Aires: Flaiban & Camilloni, 1915) 308; Socolow, *Women*, 157, 171 on colonial midwives.

33. Llames Massini, *Partera*, 309–13.

34. Ibid., 313–14.

35. Ibid., 178–79, 185.

36. Ibid., 317–19.

37. Pedro Barbieri, "El curanderismo en la República Argentina," *APCCA* 4 (1905): 718–19.

38. AGN, SB, leg. 103, Casa de Expósitos, 1900–1904.

39. Llames Massini, *Partera*, 325–27.

40. CC, 1873, 342, 17, case against María Bolazzini, for provoked abortion.

41. Escriche, *Diccionario*, vol. 1, s.v. "Aborto": Argentine Penal Code, 1886, 2.1.1.2.102–6, "Aborto."

42. AGN, TC, 2, C, 153, 1904, against María Lorenza Cabral, Juana Gay de Laserna, and Juana Sacco de Conterno for provoked abortion.

43. Ibid.

44. AGN, TC, 2, B, 19, 1882, against María Baby and Federico Hering for causing an abortion in Antonia Schotler.

45. M. Mujica Farías, "Curso de derecho penal," *RP* 2, 45 (Apr. 1, 1899): 757–59 passim.

46. AGN, 1904, María Lorenza Cabral et al. case.

47. AGN, 2, C, 64, 1891, and AGN, 2, C, 68, 1891, against Juan Lucio Cascallares Paz and Susana Breuil de Conderc for abortion; AGN, TC, 2, B, 22, 1883, against Susana Breuil de Conderc for violent abortion.

48. CC, 1897, 6, 10, against Ramona Funes for infanticide.

49. Ibid., Funes's lawyer quoting Jeremy Bentham.

Chapter 3: Social Poisons and Contagion

1. Carlos Olivera, "Venenos sociales," *RDHL* 2, 5 (1899): 216–17.

2. Diego Armus, "Salud y anarquismo: La tuberculósis en el discurso libertario argentino, 1890–1940," in *Política, médicos y enfermedades: Lecturas de historia de la salud en la Argentina*, ed. Mirta Zaida Lobato et al. (Buenos Aires: Biblos, 1996), 112.

3. Jan Goldstein, "'Moral Contagion': A Professional Ideology of Medicine and Psychiatry in Eighteenth- and Nineteenth-Century France," in *Professions and the French State, 1700–1900*, ed. Gerald L. Geison (Philadelphia: University of Pennsylvania Press, 1984), 201; Alain Corbin, *The Foul and the Fragrant: Odor and the French Social Imagination* (French ed., 1982; Cambridge, Mass.: Harvard University Press, 1986), 13; Jorge Salessi, *Médicos, maleantes y maricas* (Rosario: Beatriz Viterbo, 1995), 52, on the concept of separation.

4. Llames Massini, *Partera*, 133, 139.

5. *PBT* 4 (135): 1907 "Informes útiles" (reverse side of front cover).

6. Llames Massini, *Partera*, 162.

7. Dorothy Porter, *Health, Civilization and the State: A History of Public Health from Ancient to Modern Times* (New York: Routledge, 1999), 34, 81–87; Aisenberg, *Contagion*, 119–20, 15, 66, 71, 106, 166.

8. Julyan G. Peard, *Race, Place, and Medicine: The Idea of the Tropics in Nineteenth-Century Brazilian Medicine* (Durham, N.C.: Duke University Press, 1999), 107.

9. Llames Massini, *Partera*, 151, quoting Alfredo Parodi and Emilio Ramón Coni.

10. Wilde, *Obras*, pt. 1, *Científicas*, 3: 91, 30, 272. There are no dates given for this volume, but the sections were most likely written in the late 1870s.

11. Ibid., vol. 6, "Los cementerios" (Wilde's letter to *La Nación*, Jan. 14, 1882), 195.

12. Ibid., 3: 194.

13. Ibid., 3: 227, 201, 209–10.

14. Ibid., 3: 112.

15. Ibid., 3: 101.

16. Ibid., 3: 108, 104–5, 109.

17. Ibid., 106.

18. Ibid., 3: 135.

19. Ibid., vol. 6, "1880: Obras de salubridad" (Wilde's letter to *La Nación*, Feb. 13, 1880), 111.

20. *PBT* 3, 85 (1906): 87; 4, 150 (1907): 33; 3, 105 (1906): 66.

21. Benigno Trigo, "Crossing the Boundaries of Madness: Criminology and Figurative Language in Argentina (1878–1920)," *Journal of Latin American Cutlural Studies* 6, 1 (1997): 9, quoting Sarmiento; Goldstein, "Moral Contagion," 187–88; Corbin, *Foul and Fragrant*, 13.

22. Victor Arreguiné, "El suicidio," *CM* 1, 1 (Nov. 20, 1898): 7–8; Lucas Ayarragaray, *La imaginación y las pasiones como causas de enfermedades* (thesis, Buenos Aires, 1887); Eduardo A. Zimmermann, *Los liberales reformistas: La cuestión social en la Argentina, 1890–1916* (Buenos Aires: Sudamericana and Universidad de San Andrés, 1995), ch. 5.

23. Ricardo González Leandri, "La profesión médica en Buenos Aires: 1852–1870," in *Política, médicos y enfermedades*, ed. Zaida Lobato et al., 19–53.

24. Corbin, *Foul and Fragrant*, 13, 46, 62, 113–14; Goldstein, "Moral Contagion," 204–5, 208–9.

25. Eusebio Gómez, *Estudios penitenciarios* (Buenos Aires: Penitenciario Nacional, 1906), 16 (it is not clear whether Gómez is quoting Laurent, Gautier, and others here); Ruibal, "Honor y delito," 35–44 passim.

26. Wilde, *Obras*, pt. 1, *Científicas*, 3: 267 ; Drago, *Hombres de presa*, 119–20; José Ingenieros, "Fetichista con hermafrodismo psíquico activo y alucinaciones eróticas del olfato," *APCCA* 1 (1902): 618.

27. AGN, TC, 2, C, 64, 1891, and AGN, TC, 2, C, 68, 1891, against Juan Lucio Cascallares Paz and Susana Breuil de Conderc for abortion.

28. Lila Caimari, "Remembering Freedom: Life as Seen from the Prison Cell (Buenos Aires Province, 1900–1950)" (MS; see for women in prison in general); María Soledad Zárate C., "Mujeres viciosas, mujeres virtuosas: La mujer delincuente y la Casa Correccional de Santiago, 1860–1900," in *Disciplina y desacato: Construcción de identidad en Chile, siglos XIX y XX* (Santiago de Chile: SUR-CEDEM, 1995), 149–80.

29. *El Diario*, Aug. 24, 1891; AGN, SB, 51, Asilo del Buen Pastor, 1855–91: Juan Díaz to the inspectors of the Buen Pastor, Apr. 3, 1882; 51, 129ff.; *El Diario*, Oct. 12 and Dec. 10, 1891; Zárate, "Mujeres viciosas," 167, 169.

30. AGN, TC, 2, C, 64, 1891, and AGN, TC, 2, C, 68, 1891, against Juan Lucio Cascallares Paz and Susana Breuil de Conderc for abortion.

31. Fernández, "Reforma universitaria," *RDHL* 1 (1898): 411–12.

32. Moyano Gacitúa, *Curso de ciencia criminal*, 280.

33. Ernesto Quesada, *Comprobación de la reincidencia: Proyecto de ley presentado al señor ministro de justicia é instrucción pública, doctor don Osvaldo Magnasco* (Buenos Aires: Coni, 1901), 121; Fernández, "Reforma universitaria," *RDHL* 1, 3 (1899): 345; Rafael Huertas García-Alejo, *El delincuente y su patología: Medicina, crímen y*

sociedad en el positivismo argentino (Madrid: Consejo Superior de Investigaciones Científicas, 1991), 9.

34. AGN, SB, leg. 103, Casa de Expósitos, 1900–1904; Benjamin T. Solari, "La defensa de la raza por la castración de los degenerados: Las ideas profilácticas de Zuccarelli," *APCMLP* 1 (1902): 388; José Gregorio Rossi, "La criminalidad profesional en Buenos Aires," *APCMLP* 2 (1903): 169–76 passim, on the linking of Latin immigration to crime in Buenos Aires. Ferri's remark that "Latins have tendencies toward general homicide, assassination, and infanticide" was repeated by Eusebio Gómez in 1908.

35. R. J. Bunge, "Emigración," 251–52; José C. Moya, *Cousins and Strangers: Spanish Immigrants in Buenos Aires, 1850–1930* (Berkeley: University of California Press, 1998), 349–50, on the superiority of Spanish blood and anti-positivism.

36. Andrew R. Aisenberg, *Contagion: Disease, Government, and the "Social Question" in Nineteenth-Century France* (Stanford: Stanford University Press, 1999), 119–20; Fernández, "Reforma universitaria," *RDHL* 1, 3 (1899): 350.

37. I have not found the actual transcript of this case in the National Archives, but it is included as one of Argentina's most famous cases in secondary works. See Andrés I. Flores, *Casos famosos de la crónica policial argentina* (Buenos Aires: Orión, ca. 1975), "El Caso Farbos Tremblié: Ambición, cinismo y estupidez," 65–75; Albert Bataille, "Proceso Tremblié," *RP* 1, 13 (Dec. 1, 1897): 198–204, taken from Bataille's *Causes criminelles et mondaines* 17 (1896); Carlos Olivera, "Psicología del derecho penal," *RJ* 18 (1900): 363. Dates in Flores and Bataille differ slightly.

38. Bataille, "Proceso Tremblié," 199–200.

39. Flores, *Casos famosos*, 65–75 passim.

40. Bataille, "Proceso Tremblié," 201–2.

41. Flores, *Casos famosos*, 65–75 passim; Bataille, "Proceso Tremblié," 202.

42. "Identificación de cadáveres," *RP* 4, 85 (1900): 202–3 passim; Flores, *Casos famosos*, 68–69; Bataille, "Proceso Tremblié," 202.

43. Samuel Gache, "Congreso penitenciario: Antropología criminal," *RJ* 3 (1886): 1028–36 passim.

44. Brusa, "Derecho penal," 1051–74 passim.

45. Adolfo Enrique Rodríguez, *Cuatrocientos años de policía en Buenos Aires* (Buenos Aires: Editorial Policial, ca. 1981), 161.

46. Quesada, *Comprobación de la reincidencia*, 97; Ernesto Quesada, "La oficina antropométrica," *RP* 1, 6 (Aug. 15, 1897): 93; Francisco Luis Romay, *Historia de la Policía Federal Argentina*, vol. 6: 1880–1916 (Buenos Aires: Editorial Policial, 1975), 40.

47. Quesada, "Oficina antropométrica," 93.

48. Ibid., 94; "Oficina antropométrica, alcaidía y archivos criminales," *RP* 4, 81 (Oct. 1, 1900): 131–33 passim; 82 (Oct. 16, 1900): 149–51 passim; Quesada, *Comprobación de la reincidencia*, 127.

49. Quesada, *Comprobación de la reincidencia*, 102–3.

50. Quesada, "Oficina antropométrica," 94.

51. Quesada, *Comprobación de la reincidencia*, 113; Quesada, "Oficina antropométrica," 94; Horacio G. Piñero, "Psicología," *RJ* 19 (1900–1901): 342.

52. H. G. Piñero, "Psicología," 113, 119; Rossi, "Criminalidad profesional," 171.

53. AGN, TC, 2, A, 58, 1904, case against Agustín Acre for the homicide of his wife, Cristina Malagrini; Luis Reyna Almandos, *Dactiloscopía argentina: Su historia é influencia en la legislación* (La Plata: J. Sesé, 1909), 71–75; Rodríguez, *Cuatrocientos años,* 162.

54. Reyna Almandos, *Dactiloscopía argentina,* 23–24; Quesada, *Comprobación de la reincidencia,* 159, 106–7.

55. *PBT* 3, 37 (1906): 76; 4, 151 (1907): 45, 47.

56. Reyna Almandos, *Dactiloscopía argentina,* 20.

57. Ibid., 66, 71–75; "Interview with Juan Vucetich," *El Argentino,* Sept. 1, 1924, n.p.; Quesada, *Comprobación de la reincidencia,* 145; Jacqueline Urla and Jennifer Terry, "Introduction: Mapping Embodied Deviance," in *Deviant Bodies: Critical Perspectives on Difference in Science and Popular Culture,* ed. Jennifer Terry and Jacqueline Urla (Bloomington: Indiana University Press, 1995), 6.

58. Sislán Rodríguez, "Vucetich y la dactiloscopía (sintesis enumerativa de las principales fechas)," *RP* 1, 10 (Feb. 1942): 12.

59. Federico Quevedo Hijosa, "Cómo resolvió Vucetich el problema de la identificación personal," *El Hogar,* Feb. 13, 1925, 7; Reyna Almandos, *Dactiloscopía argentina,* 7–8, 16.

60. Maria Margaret López and Irina Podgorny, "The Shaping of Latin American Museums of Natural History, 1850–1990," in *Nature and Empire: Science and the Colonial Enterprise,* ed. Roy MacLeon, *Osiris,* 2d ser., vol. 15 (Chicago: University of Chicago press, 2000), 113, on the museum.

61. Jürgen Thorwald, *The Century of the Detective* (German ed., 1964; English trans., New York: Harcourt, Brace, 1965), 51–52; Federico Quevedo Hijosa, "La cuestión dactiloscópica: Necesidad impostergable de reparar una injusticia. ¿Se pretende negar a Vucetich o despojarle de su invento?" *La Argentina,* Jan. 17, 1925, 2.

62. Simon Ablon Cole, "Manufacturing Identity: A History of Criminal Identification Techniques from Photography through Fingerprinting" (diss., Cornell University, 1998), 228; Thorwald, *Century,* 53–55; Sislán Rodríguez, "Vucetich y la dactiloscopía," 11–12; Thorwald, *Century,* 56.

63. Sislán Rodríguez, "Vucetich y la dactiloscopía," 13; Vucetich interview in *El Argentino;* Reyna Almandos, *Dactiloscopía argentina,* 55–58.

64. Juan Vucetich, *Proyecto de ley de registro general de identificación* (La Plata: Impresiones Oficiales, 1929), 97; Vucetich interview in *El Argentino;* Reyna Almandos, *Dactiloscopía argentina,* xlv.

65. Vucetich, *Proyecto,* 99, 101–2.

66. *Encyclopedia of the Social Sciences,* ed. Edwin R. A. Seligman and A. Johnson (New York: Macmillan, 1932), s.v. "Identification"; Luis Reyna Almandos, "The Personal Number and the National Book of Personality" (in English), in *Biblioteca de la Revista de Identificación y Ciencias Penales,* no. 22 (La Plata: Impresiones Oficiales, 1936), 6–7, 13–14.

67. The "language of the Brahmans" is Sanskrit, but there is no Sanskrit noun *yu.* There are two verb roots *yu,* but roots are not words. The first root *yu* means "to separate, drive away, ward off, be or remain separated from"; the second means "to unite, tie, harness, yoke, bind, draw towards oneself, take possession of." The first *yu* belongs to the third-class conjugation (*yuyoti,* "he separates") and the second *yu* to the second-

class conjugation (*yauti*, "he unites"). However, *yu* is the Chinese term for the Sanskrit *dharma*, which does mean 'law.'"

68. Reyna Almandos, "Personal Number," 8.

69. Ibid., 11–13.

70. Vucetich interview in *El Argentino*.

71. Reyna Almandos, "Personal Number," 19–20.

72. Ibid., 18.

73. Wilde, *Obras*, pt. 1, *Científicas*, 3: 194, 195, 225.

Chapter 4: Modern Diseases in the National Identity

1. Rafael Huertas García-Alejo, *Locura y degeneración: Psiquiatría y sociedad en el positivismo francés* (Madrid: Consejo Superior de Investigaciones Científicas, 1991), 20.

2. Ibid., 34–36; Huertas, *Delincuente*, 18.

3. Huertas, *Delincuente*, 58.

4. Francisco de Veyga, "De la regeneración como ley opuesta a la degeneración mórbida," APCCA 4 (1905): 31–44 passim.

5. Drago, *Hombres de presa*, 119, quoting Max Nordau.

6. Richard L. Dugdale, *The Jukes: A Study in Crime, Pauperism, Disease, and Heredity* (1877; 4th rev. ed., reprint, New York: Putnam, 1910).

7. Drago, *Hombres de presa*, 119–20; Charles Féré, *Degeneración y criminalidad* (Paris, 1888; Madrid: Jorro, 1903); Gabriel Tarde, *La Criminalité comparée* (1886; 2d ed., Paris: F. Alcan, 1890).

8. Drago, *Hombres de presa*, 99, 113–18, 123.

9. Veyga, "Regeneración," 31–44 passim.

10. On race in Argentina and in Latin America, see George Reid Andrews, *The Afro-Argentines of Buenos Aires, 1800–1900* (Madison: University of Wisconsin Press, 1980); Richard Graham, *The Idea of Race in Latin America, 1870–1940* (Austin: University of Texas Press, 1990).

11. Zimmerman, *Liberales reformistas*, 109–10; Teresa A. Meade, *"Civilizing" Rio: Reform and Resistance in a Brazilian City 1889–1930* (University Park, Pa.: Pennsylvania State University Press, 1997), 27–29, on the Brazilian/Argentine context.

12. Miguel Romero, "Política interna: Estudio psicológico," *RJ* 20 (1901): 217–29, 222, 231.

13. Victor R. Pesenti, "Influencia de la civilización en la criminalidad," in *RJ* 20 (1901): 140–43 passim.

14. José Ingenieros, *Obras completas* (Buenos Aires: Mar Oceano, 1962), vol. 8, "Cronicas de viaje," 168–72.

15. Ibid.

16. Ibid.

17. Ingenieros, *Obras*, vol. 6, "La evolución sociológica argentina" (1904), 148, 195, 246.

18. Ibid., partly quoting E. Echeverría.

19. Robert M. Buffington, *Criminal and Citizen in Modern Mexico* (Lincoln: University of Nebraska Press, 2000), 157 on the negative effect of "Indians" on national progress in Mexico.

20. Ingenieros, *Obras*, vol. 6, "Evolución sociológica" (1904), 245–65 passim.

21. Víctor Mercante, *La crisis de la pubertad y sus consecuencias pedagógicas* (Buenos Aires: Cabaut, 1918), 300.

22. Víctor Mercante, "Peología: La voz en los niños y la degeneración," *CM* 2 (13–14) (Nov.-Dec. 1899): 433–39 passim.

23. Ibid.

24. Ibid.

25. Víctor Mercante, "Estudios de criminología infantil," *APCCA* 1 (1902): 463–68 passim.

26. Ibid.

27. Ibid.

28. Ingenieros, *Obras*, vol. 2, "Histeria y sugestion" (1904), 14–16.

29. E. M. Thornton, *Hypnotism, Hysteria and Epilepsy: An Historical Synthesis* (London: Heinemann, 1976), 116–19.

30. Ibid.; J. Alba Carreras and N. Acuña, "Curanderismo y locura: El caso de la 'Hermana María,'" *APCCA* 2 (1903): 649–53 passim on a case of hysteria.

31. Thornton, *Hypnotism*, 126; Pérez, *Nueva medicina doméstica*, 156–57.

32. Wilde, *Obras*, pt. 1, *Científicas*, 1: 209–10.

33. AGN, TC, 2, D, 53, 1898, against María Cristina D'Ambrosio for the homicide of Antonio Bobe.

34. AGN, TC, 2, D, 67, 1901, Santiago Morrone against Marcelina David and Edgardo Servich for adultery. At first they were absolved and then each was sentenced to one year.

35. Gómez, *Pasión y delito*, 49–50.

36. Owsei Temkin, *The Falling Sickness: A History of Epilepsy from the Greeks to the Beginnings of Modern Neurology*, 2d ed. (Baltimore: Johns Hopkins University Press, 1971), 354, 357, 359.

37. Ibid., 318.

38. Ibid., 292.

39. Ibid., 366–67.

40. AGN, TC, 1, M, 8, 1886, against Ignacio Monges for his attack on the president of the republic, Julio A. Roca. Additional material on this case is found in Ismael Bucich Escobar, *El atentado contra Roca, 10 de mayo de 1886, perspectiva semisecular de una histórica agresión* (Buenos Aires: Americana, 1935).

41. David Rock, *Argentina 1516–1987: From Spanish Colonization to Alfonsín* (Berkeley: University of California Press, 1987), 123.

42. This contrasts oddly with a modern definition of larval epilepsy: "unerupted epileptic seizures, represented only by characteristic waves in the electroencephalogram."

43. Allan Kardec, *The Spirits' Book* (French ed., 1859; English trans., Boston: Colby & Rich, 1875); David J. Hess, *Spirits and Scientists: Ideology, Spiritism, and Brazilian Culture* (University Park, Pa.: Pennsylvania State University Press, 1991), 61, 76, 77; Augusto Ruiz Zevallos, *Psiquíatras y locos: Entre la modernización contra los andes y el nuevo proyecto de modernidad, Perú, 1850–1930* (Lima: Pasado & Presente, 1994), 52, on the arrest of spiritists in Peru in the 1880s.

44. G. Sittoni, "La epilepsia en América: Sus causas y manifestaciones (contribución a la antropología criminal)," *CM* 2, 12 (Oct. 1899): 356–59.

45. H. G. Piñero, "Psicología," 346–47.

46. *PBT* 3, 85 (1906): 87; 4, 150 (1907): 33; 3, 105 (1906): 66.

47. *PBT* 3, 70 (1906): 101; 104 (1906): 70; 99 (1906); 2, 58 (1905): 40.

48. AGN, TC, 2, A, 42, 1898, against Luis Agote for firing a weapon at Francisco N. Viñas. See interesting series of articles on *"Fastidio"* in *RJ* 20 (1901–2), and Ruiz Zevallos, *Psiquíatras*, 123–24, on José Carlos Mariátegui's discussion of the *mal de siglo*, i.e., a "strange fatigue with life."

49. Ayarragaray, *Imaginación y pasiones*, 11.

50. Wilde, *Obras*, pt. 1, *Científicas*, 3: 247.

51. Rodolfo Benuzzi, "Sobre criminología," *APCCA* 1 (1902): 439; Ayarragaray, *Imaginación y pasiones*, 9.

Chapter 5: Eliminating Threats to the State

1. José Ingenieros, "Sobre enfermedades simuladas: Notas médico-sociológicas," *RDHL* 4, 12 (1902): 380.

2. Olivera, "Psicología," 367–69.

3. Rodolfo Benuzzi, "Sobre criminología," *APCCA* 1 (1902): 437–39 passim.

4. Solari, "Defensa de la raza," 388; Giuseppe Sergi, *La decadenza delle nazioni latine* (Turin: Bocca, 1900); Raimundo Nina Rodrigues, *As raças humanas e a responsibilidade no Brasil*, ed. Afrânio Peixoto (1894; Rio de Janeiro: Editora Nacional, 1938).

5. The actual case, if it is still extant, is in a section of the judicial archives that was not organized for consultation when the author was there. For the accounts of the Pedro Castro Rodríguez case, see José María Ramos Mejía, Florentino Ortega, and Marcelina Aravena, "El asesino de Olavarría: Su estado mental al cometer el crímen y despues de él. Responsibilidad. Interesante estudio médico legal," *RJ* 5 (1888): 428–52; Moyano Gacitúa, *Curso de ciencia criminal*; "Siguen los crímenes," *RJ* 5 (1888): 386–88; Drago, *Hombres de presa*, 162–76 (strangely Drago reported that Pedro had been killed by hanging).

6. Ingenieros, *Obras*, vol. 8, "Crónicas de viaje," 90–138, section on "La justicia de Bertoldo" (Turin, 1905) on criminal vanity.

7. AGN, TC, 2, C, 46, 1888, against Luis Castruccio for poisoning of Alberto Bouchot Constantín; Manuel Obarrio, "De los seguros sobre la vida," *RDHL* 1 (1898): 491–93.

8. Hugo Vezzetti, *La locura en la Argentina* (Buenos Aires: Folios Ediciones, 1983), 104–5.

9. Obarrio, "Seguros," 491–93.

10. Pérez, *Nueva medicina doméstica*, 162–64.

11. Drago, *Hombres de presa*, 58–59.

12. Ibid., 172.

13. Ibid., 115.

14. Pérez, *Nueva medicina doméstica*, 169–70.

15. Mercante, *Crisis de la pubertad*, 187; J.-P. Falret, *De l'hypochondrie et du suicide* (Paris: Société de Médecine, 1822), 28.

16. AGN, TC, 2, C, 46, 1888, Luis Castruccio case, defense lawyer quoting Leuret.

17. José Ingenieros, "El envenenador Luis Castruccio," *APCCA* 8 (1909): 5–29 passim.

18. Ibid., 13, 17–19.

19. Ibid., 4 (quoting Drago), 21, 24–29.

20. Víctor Arreguiné, "El suicidio," *APCCA* 4 (1905): 701, 703; Ruiz Zevallos, *Psiquíatras*, 89–95, 124, on suicide in Peru and elsewhere in Latin America, and suicide's connection to modernism.

21. Fermín Rodríguez, "Influencia del alcoholismo sobre el suicidio en Buenos Aires," *APCCA* 4 (1905): 544; id., "Influencia del estado civil sobre el suicidio en Buenos Aires," *APCCA* 4 (1905): 390, 396; id., "Estudios sobre el suicidio en Buenos Aires: La influencia de la edad y del sexo," *APCCA* 3 (1904): 8.

22. Arreguiné, "Suicidio," 6.

23. José Ingenieros, "El suicidio en las campañas argentinas," *APCCA* 1 (4) (1902): 247, review of article by L. Ayarragaray.

24. José Martínez Pérez, "El suicidio como indicador del bienestar de un Estado: Algunos problemas en torno al origen de su empleo por la psiquiatría francesa (1800–1856)," in *La salud en el estado de bienestar: Análisis histórico*, ed. Luis Montiel (Madrid: Complutense, 1993), 89.

25. Maurice Halbwachs, *The Causes of Suicide*, trans. Harold Goldblatt (French ed., 1930; New York: Free Press, 1978), 27.

26. Barbara T. Gates, *Victorian Suicide: Mad Crimes and Sad Histories* (Princeton: Princeton University Press, 1988), xiv, 151.

27. Halbwachs, *Causes of Suicide*, 311; Miguel A. Lancelotti, *La criminalidad en Buenos Aires: Al margen de la estadística (1887–1912)* (Buenos Aires, 1914), 104–5.

28. Martínez Pérez, "Suicidio," 92.

29. Gates, *Victorian Suicide*, 83; Paul Aubry, *La contagion du meurtre: Étude d'anthropologie criminelle*, 2d ed. (Paris: Félix Alcan, 1894); Martínez Pérez, "Suicidio," 95.

30. Enrico Morselli, *Suicide: An Essay on Comparative Moral Statistics* (New York: Appleton, 1882), 291–92; Martínez Pérez, "Suicidio," 80, 85, 86.

31. Havelock Ellis cited in Gates, *Victorian Suicide*, 150.

32. Halbwachs, *Causes of Suicide*, 84; Martínez Pérez, "Suicidio," 86, 94, 100.

33. Arreguiné, "Suicidio," *CM*, 6.

34. Ibid., 8. The 1897 rate only covers up to December 15, that is, it does not cover the whole year; F. Rodríguez, "Influencia del estado civil," 396.

35. Arreguiné, "Suicidio," *CM*, 8.

36. AGN, TC, 2, C, 21, 1881, attempted suicide of María Carnevale.

37. AGN, TC, 2, B, 18, 1882, attempted suicide of the minor María Bidú.

38. F. Rodríguez, "Influencia del estado civil," 392.

39. AGN, TC, 2, C, 23, 1882, attempted suicide of Teresa Cardeviola; F. Rodríguez, "Influencia del estado civil," 392.

40. F. Rodríguez, "Influencia del estado civil," 391, citing Samuel Jean Pozzi, *Traité de gynécologie clinique et opératoire* (Paris: G. Masson, 1890).

41. Ibid.; id., "Estudios sobre el suicidio," 12.

42. Octavio Ramón Amadeo, *Vidas argentinas* (Buenos Aires: Emecé, 1965), 39, 42.

43. Carlos Quirós, *Guia Radical* (Buenos Aires: Galerna, 1986), 103–9; Scobie, *City and a Nation*, 197–203.

44. Amadeo, *Vidas argentinas*, 39, 43, 44; Rivero Astengo, *Hombres*, 115–19; Sandra Gayol, "Violencia honorable, crímenes y justicia pública del estado: Argentina en el recambio de siglo" (MS, Latin American Studies Association, Sept. 2001), 11.

45. AGN, TC, 1, S, 4, 1871–77, summary of events in the parish of Balvanera, Apr. 1877; AGN, TC, 2, A, 2, 1876–77, antecedents relative to the sequester of arms ordered by the Supreme Court in several houses of the parish of Balvanera.

46. Carlos Quirós, *Guia Radical* (Buenos Aires: Galerna, 1986), 103–9; Scobie, *City and a Nation*, 197–203.

47. Rivero Astengo, *Hombres*, 115; Quirós, *Guia*, 103–9; Amadeo, *Vidas argentinas*, 45–46; Pedro Mario Degregori, *El austero silencioso* (Buenos Aires: Negri, 1982), 17.

48. Quirós, *Guia*, 103–9.

49. Degregori, *Austero silencioso*, 23–24.

50. Amadeo, *Vidas argentinas*, 44; Rock, *Argentina*, 184–85.

51. Estanislao Severo Zeballos, "Los jueces," *RDHL* 5, 13 (1902): 617; AGN, TC, 2, B, 47, 1891, case against José Bacco for adultery, and Julia Frigerio, for complicity. Mexican criminal cases reportedly do not contain these types of references.

52. AGN, TC, 2, C, 64, 1891 and AGN, TC, 2, C, 68, 1891, case against Juan Lucio Cascallares Paz and Susana Breuil de Conderc for abortion. The so-called La Roncière affair was often cited by legal experts who doubted the testimony given by women in court. In 1834, a cavalry cadet named Émile de la Roncière had been accused of writing menacing letters to Marie de Morell, the teenage daughter of his commanding officer. He was expelled from the École de Cavalerie, charged with assaulting the girl, and sentenced to ten years in prison. La Roncière insisted that he was innocent, and experts disagreed about the handwriting of the letters: some said it was La Roncière's, but others identified it as Marie's own writing. See Stéphane Arnoulin, *L'Affaire La Roncière: Une Erreur judiciaire en 1835* (Paris: Librairie Paul Ollendorff, 1899).

53. AGN, TC, 2, C, 64, 1891 and AGN, TC, 2, C, 68, 1891, case against Juan Lucio Cascallares Paz and Susana Breuil de Conderc for abortion.

54. Aldao, "Consideraciones," 362; Ernesto Quesada, "¿Tiene la Cámara de Apelaciones de la Capital la facultad de graciar procesados?" (review of Quesada's pamphlet) *RJ* 16 (1899): 174; A. Gancedo, "Justicia y eleciones," *RDHL* 4, 10 (1901): 62; Zeballos, "Los jueces," 611 quoting President Roca, May 1899; Homer Greene, "¿Pueden ser honrados los abogados?" *RDHL* 1 (1898): 53, n. 1; Zeballos, "Los jueces," 611, 612, 615, 616.

55. Zeballos, "Los jueces," 617.

56. AGN, TC, 2, A, 18, 1890, Dr. Don Abraham Arce against Don Rómulo Sarmiento, the author of an article published in *El Nacional*, for calumny, Sept. 26, 1890.

57. F. M. Herrera, "Correspondencia: Necesidad de reglamentar el ejercicio de la procuración y la abogacía," *RJ* 17 (1899): 312.

58. Emilio Daireaux, *Vida y costumbres en ei Plata*, vol. 1: *La sociedad argentina* (Buenos Aires: Lajouane, 1888), 43.

Chapter 6: Passion in a State of Reason

1. Gómez, *Pasión y delito*, 69.
2. Ingenieros, *Obras*, vol. 8, "Crónicas de viaje," 151–52.
3. Joaquín Francisco Pacheco, *Código penal*, 2d ed., vol. 1 (Madrid: Perinat, 1856), 131; Matthieu Joseph Bonaventure Orfila, *Medicina legal*, 4th ed., vol. 1 (Paris: Renouard, 1848), 336; Jean-Baptiste-Félix Descuret, *La medicina de las pasiones, ó las pasiones consideradas con respecto á las enfermedades, las leyes y la religion* (Barcelona: Oliveres, 1849), 1.
4. José Luis Peset, *Las heridas de la ciencia* (Madrid: Junta de Castilla y León, 1993), 132–33; Ann-Louise Shapiro, *Breaking the Codes: Female Criminality in Fin-de-Siècle Paris* (Stanford: Stanford University Press, 1996), 175.
5. Gómez, *Pasión y delito*, 44. For the earlier philosophical background of passion, see Peset, *Heridas de la ciencia*. Jean-Jacques Rousseau, although he understood passion as preserving life, also held that it could be altered through excess or perversion, and thus needed to be controlled (ibid., 144–45). On passion, see Ruibal, "Honor y delito," 35–44 passim.
6. Pérez, *Nueva medicina doméstica*, 26–30.
7. Ayarragaray, *Imaginación y pasiones*, 24.
8. Ingenieros, *Obras*, vol. 8, "Crónicas," 151–52; Gómez, *Pasión y delito*, 21 (quoting Ingenieros), 71.
9. Pacheco, *Código penal*, 171; Orfila, *Medicina legal*, 336.
10. Argentine Penal Code, 1886, 1.2.3.81.1, 5, 12, and art. 83.6; Pérez, *Nueva medicina doméstica*, 26–30.
11. Olivera, "Psicología," 363–64.
12. Gómez, *Pasión y delito*, 45–51.
13. Prack, "Escuela antropológica criminal," 109–13, 254–64 passim.
14. Ibid.; Lozano, "Reforma," 375; Gache, "Congreso penitenciario," 1028–36 passim.
15. Kristin Ruggiero, "The Devil and Modernity in Late Nineteenth-Century Buenos Aires," *Américas* 59, 2 (2002): 221–33.
16. Gómez, *Pasión y delito*, 166.
17. AGN, TC, 1, L, 2, 1871, case against Juan Lagourdette for the homicide of Aristides Bodiet.
18. Argentine Penal Code, 1886, 1.2.3.81.12; Escriche, *Diccionario*, vol. 1, s.v. "Adulterio"; Argentine Penal Code, 1886, 1.2.6.94.1.
19. Escriche, *Diccionario*, s.v. "Adulterio"; Gómez, *Pasión y delito*, 19.
20. Abelardo Levaggi, *Historia del derecho penal argentino* (Buenos Aires: Perrot, 1978), 134, on the case of Clorinda Sarracán de Fiorini, 1856, homicide of her husband, death penalty. Carlos Cúneo and Abel González, *La delincuencia* (Buenos Aires: América Latina, 1971), 101, on the case against Carmen Guillot, wife of Frank Carlos Livingston, member of Jockey Club, crime of passion, July 19, 1914.
21. Gómez, *Pasión y delito*, 156, quoting R. J. N. Rivarola's *Derecho penal argentino* of 1910; Argentine Penal Code of 1886, art. 83.6; art. 81.12; art. 27.
22. Gómez, *Pasión y delito*, 156.
23. Ibid., 145, 147.
24. Gómez, *Pasión y delito*, 184–85. Two cases in which the judge explained this well are AGN, TC, 2, B, 9, 1877, case against James Barret for the homicide of his wife

Brigida Barret, and AGN, TC, 2, A, 13, 1886, case against Daniel Alzerano for the homicide of his wife María Canforterio.

25. Gómez, *Pasión y delito*, appendix D, on Rivarola.

26. Ibid., appendix D, on Norberto Piñero.

27. AGN, TC, 2, C, 1, 1870, against Pascual Castro Echeverría for homicide of his wife Eusebia Arrascaete. Ricardo Salvatore points out that the crime of beheading with a knife, *degüello*, was viewed as a particularly dastardly form of homicide because of its association with the dictator Rosas. Ricardo Salvatore, "Death and Liberalism: Capital Punishment after the Fall of Rosas," in *Crime and Punishment in Latin America: Law and Society since Late Colonial Times*, ed. Ricardo D. Salvatore, Carlos Aguirre, and Gilbert M. Joseph (Durham, N.C.: Duke University Press, 2001), 311.

28. The following is a sample of cases from different time periods in which the victim-wives were judged to have provoked their husbands' violence: AGN, TC, 2, A, 1, 1875, against José Alberti for wounds to his wife Catalina Escola (Alberti received two years' *presidio*); AGN, TC, 2, C, 22, 1881, against José Cayolla for suspected homicide of his wife Filomena Conti (Cayolla was absolved); AGN, TC, 2, B, 43, 1890, against Siro Boso for attempted homicide of his wife Margarita Dalio (Boso's original sentence was three years' imprisonment, which was changed to ten years' *presidio*); AGN, TC, 2, D, 63, 1900, against Bautista Daguero for homicide of his wife María Grattone (Daguero's original sentence was three years' imprisonment, which was changed to *presidio* for an undetermined time; he received a *gracia* after fifteen years); and AGN, TC, 2, B, 91, against Gaudencio Borgna for attempted homicide of his wife Dominga Pancro (Borgna received two years and ten months' imprisonment).

29. AGN, TC, 2, C, 84, 1894, against Enrique Campanelli for attempted homicide of Juan, María, Margarita, Victoria, and Pedro Barat.

30. It was also argued, however, that the act of reprisal did not have to follow immediately the act of witnessed adultery. See, e.g., the defense attorney's explanation in AGN, 1904, Agustin Acre case.

31. Gómez, *Pasión y delito*, 61, 166.

32. AGN, TC, 2, B, 31, 1887, Club "Sud América" against Mariano Beascochea, policeman, for violation of domicile.

33. AGN, TC, 2, A, 24, 1892, case against Dr. Pedro N. Arata, brought by Dr. Atanasio Quiroga, for calumny and injury.

34. AGN, TC, 2, B, 91, 1901, against Antonio Ballvé for contempt and abuse of authority, brought by Judge Ernesto Madero.

35. Salvatore, "State Legal Order," 6–7; Laudelino Vázquez, "La reforma en la justicia criminal: El jurado," *RDHL* 2 (4) (1899): 521, quoting Rivarola on Argentina.

36. José Luis Muratore, "Cuestiones penales de actualidad," *APCCA* 1 (1902): 12–13; Raimundo Wilmart, "El jurado," *RJ* 11 (1895): 20–26 passim.

37. Muratore, "Cuestiones penales," 13.

38. Rodolfo Juan Nemesio Rivarola, "Origenes y evolución del derecho penal argentino," *RJ* 18 (1900): 305–6; Ingenieros, *Obras*, vol. 8, "Crónicas de viaje," 104–10.

39. AGN, TC, 2, B, 19, 1882, case against María Baby and Federico Hering for causing an abortion in Antonia Schotler.

40. Escriche, *Diccionario razonado* vol. 3, s.v. "Pena," 523–53.

41. Levaggi, *Historia*, 130–32.

42. AGN, TC, 2, D, 70, 1902, against Santiago Danella for homicide of Pedro Rescca.

43. José Mármol, "La pena de muerte," *RJ* 14 (1897–98): 217.

44. Alfredo M. Gándara, "La pena de muerte," *RJ* (1884): 493; Mármol, "Pena de muerte," 217–18.

45. Mármol, "Pena de muerte," 223; AGN, TC, 1, G, 5, 1873, against Francisco Guerri, Pedro Guerri, and Luis Casimiro, for attempted homicide against Domingo F. Sarmiento, president of the republic.

46. Gándara, "Pena de muerte," 492–94; Muratore, "Cuestiones penales," 16.

47. Sicardi, "Vida del delito," 11, 13.

48. Mármol, "Pena de muerte," 220; Olivera, "Psicología," 369.

49. R. M. Fraga, *Memoria de la Penitenciaría Nacional 1901* (Buenos Aires: 1902); Eusebio Gómez, *Memoria descriptiva de la Penitenciaría Nacional de Buenos Aires* (Buenos Aires: Penitenciaría Nacional, 1914); Guglielmo Ferrero, "La Penitenciaría Nacional de Buenos Aires juzgada en el extranjero," *APCCA* 7 (1908); G. Lombroso, "Instituciones americanas," 236.

50. Cúneo and González, *Delincuencia*, 33; Francisco Netri, "Sobre la reincidencia criminal específica reiterada," *APCCA* 1 (1902): 284–89 passim.

51. Osvaldo M. Piñero, "Criminalidad y represión," *RJ* 5 (1888): 300.

52. AGN, TC, 2, C, 46, 1888, case against Luis Castruccio for poisoning of Alberto Bouchot Constantín; the prosecutor quoting the French prosecutor in the Tremblié case.

53. Gándara, "Pena de muerte," 503; CC, 1860, 268, 4, case against Ramona Vergara for infanticide.

54. Gori, "Estudios carcelarias," 179.

55. Luis Castruccio case, 1888.

56. Estanislao Severo Zeballos, "Analecta," *RDHL* 3, 9 (1901): 151; AGN, TC, 2, B, 19, 1882, case against María Baby and Federico Hering for causing an abortion in Antonia Schotler, defense lawyer for María Baby.

57. Carlos Octavio Bunge, "El caracter nacional y la educación," *RJ* 19 (1900–1901): 75–76; Estanislao Severo Zeballos, "Analecta," *RDHL* 3, 8 (1901): 479.

58. Estanislao Severo Zeballos, "*Revista de Derecho, Historia y Letras*," *RDHL* 1 (1898): 7.

59. Estanislao Severo Zeballos, "Analecta," *RDHL* 3, 7 (1900): 160; Romero, "Política interna," 220; Zeballos, "Crisis del gobierno," 453.

60. Zeballos, "Analecta," 7.

61. "Nuestros propósitos," *RJ* 8 (1891): 5–8 passim; *RJ* 19 (1900–1901): 71–72, review of Uladislao F. Padilla's law thesis.

62. Estanislao Severo Zeballos, "La reunión de los peritos," *RDHL* 1, 3 (1898): 256.

Conclusion

1. C. O. Bunge, "Caracter nacional," 75; Romero, "Política interna," 218.

2. Zeballos, "Crisis del gobierno," 456; AGN, TC, 2, C, 64, 1891, and AGN, TC, 2, C, 68, 1891, case against Juan Lucio Cascallares Paz and Susana Breuil de Conderc for abortion.

Select Bibliography

Primary Works Cited

Aguirre, Julián L. *Autos y sentencias del Juez del Crímen . . . (departamentos del Sud y capital de la provincia de Buenos Aires, 1875–1881; capital, 1882–1885)*. Buenos Aires, 1885.

Alba Carreras, J., and N. Acuña. "Curanderismo y locura: El caso de la 'Hermana María.'" *APCCA* 2 (1903): 649–53.

Aldao, Carlos A. "Consideraciones sobre la justicia argentina." *RDHL* 1 (1898): 350–64.

Arreguiné, Victor. "El suicidio." *CM* 1, 1 (Nov. 20, 1898): 5–10.

———. "El suicidio." *APCCA* 4 (1905): 695–706.

"Asilo de Mujeres 1899." *RP* 3, 64 (Jan. 16, 1900): 260–61.

Aubry, Paul. *La Contagion du meurtre: Étude d'anthropologie criminelle*. 2d ed. Paris: Félix Alcan, 1894.

Ayarragaray, Lucas. *La imaginación y las pasiones como causas de enfermedades*. Thesis. Buenos Aires, 1887.

Barbieri, Pedro. "El curanderismo en la República Argentina." *APCCA* 4 (1905): 707–25.

Bartolo da Sassoferrato. *Commentaria in corpus iuris civilis (codice e istituzioni)*. Venice, 1567.

Bassi, Aurelio. "El Proyecto de Código penal: Su exámen." *RJ* 9 (1892): 405–16.

Bataille, Albert. "Proceso Tremblié." *RP* 1, 13 (Dec. 1, 1897): 198–204.

Batiz, Adolfo. *Buenos Aires, la ribera y los prostíbulos en 1880: Contribución a los estudios sociales (libro rojo)*. Buenos Aires: AGA-TAURA, n.d. Published in Paris, 1908.

Benuzzi, Rodolfo. "Sobre criminología." *APCCA* 1 (1902): 437–39.

Bravo, Mario. *Derechos civiles de la mujer: El código, los proyectos, la ley*. Buenos Aires: El Ateneo, 1927.

Brusa, Emilio. "Derecho penal: El tercer Congreso internacional penitenciario y el antropológico-criminal." *RJ* 3 (1886): 1051–74.

Bucich Escobar, Ismael. *El atentado contra Roca, 10 de mayo de 1886, perspectiva semisecular de una histórica agresión*. Buenos Aires: Americana, 1935.

"Buen Pastor." *El Diario* (Oct. 12, 1892) n.p.

Bunge, Carlos Octavio. "El caracter nacional y la educación." *RJ* 19 (1900–1901): 75–101.

Bunge, Roberto J. "Emigración é inmigración." *RJ* 19 (1900–1901): 235–63.

Campos Urquizi, Luis M. "Solicitud." *RJ* 20 (1901): 61–66.

Cantilo, José Luis. "El gran problema." *RDHL* 1, 2 (1898): 299–307.

Carette, Augusto, ed. *Diccionario de la jurisprudencia argentina, ó sintesis completa de las sentencias dictadas por los tribunales argentinos.* 2 vols. Buenos Aires: Lajouane, 1917–21.

Carlés, Manuel. "Atavismo pampa." *CM* 1, 2 (1898): 57–58.

——. "Atavismo pampa." *CM* 2, 5 (1899): 143–44.

Catalina del Amo, Severo. *La mujer: Apuntes para un libro.* 2d ed. Madrid: San Martin, 1861.

Coni, Emilio Ramón. *Patronato y asistencia a la infancia en la Capital de la República.* Buenos Aires: El Censor, 1892.

Daireaux, Emilio. *Vida y costumbres en el Plata.* Vol. 1: *La sociedad argentina.* Buenos Aires: Lajouane, 1888.

Darwin, Charles. *On the Origin of Species by Means of Natural Selection; or, The Preservation of Favoured Races in the Struggle for Life.* London: John Murray, 1859.

Dellepiane, Antonio. "Nuestros propósitos." *RJ* 12 (1895–96): 5–7.

"Derecho civil." *RLJ* 5 (1870): 5–40; 10 (1876): 246–99.

Descuret, Jean-Baptiste-Félix. *La Médecine des passions, ou les Passions considérées dans leurs rapports avec les maladies, les lois et la religion.* Paris: Béchet jeune & Labé, 1841. Translated as *La medicina de las pasiones, ó las pasiones consideradas con respecto á las enfermedades, las leyes y la religion* (Barcelona: Oliveres, 1849).

Díaz Arana, J. J. "Naturaleza del feminismo." *RJ* 16 (1899): 5–24.

Drago, Luis María. *Los hombres de presa: Antropolojía criminal.* Buenos Aires: F. Lajouane, 1888. 2d ed. Buenos Aires: Cultura Argentina, 1921.

——. *El poder marital.* Thesis, Facultad de Derecho y Ciencias Sociales. Buenos Aires: El Diario, 1882.

Duffy, José Luis. "Curiosidades fiscales: Otro dictámen del Dr. Quesada." *RP* 3, 57 (Oct. 1, 1899): 139–42.

——. "Curiosidades fiscales: Sentencia del doctor Barrenecha." *RP* 3, 58 (Oct. 16, 1899): 151–52.

Dugdale, Richard L. *The Jukes: A Study in Crime, Pauperism, Disease, and Heredity.* 1877. 4th rev. ed. Reprint. New York: Putnam's, 1910.

Encyclopedia of the Social Sciences. Edited by Edwin R. A. Seligman and Alvin Johnson. New York: Macmillan, 1932.

Escalada, Marcelino. "Matrimonio civil y divorcio." *RJ* 5 (1888): 401–15.

Escriche y Martín, Joaquín. *Diccionario razonado de legislación y jurisprudencia.* 4 vols. Madrid: Cuesta, 1874–76.

Estrada, José Manuel. "El patriotismo." *RJ* 13 (1896–97): 65–82.

Falret, J.-P. *De l'hypochondrie et du suicide.* Paris: Société de Médicine, 1822.

"Fastidio." *RJ* 20 (1901–2).

Féré, Charles. *Dégénérescence et criminalité.* Paris: F. Alcan, 1888. Translated as *Degeneración y criminalidad* (Madrid: Jorro, 1903).

Fernández, Juan Ramón. "Reforma universitaria." *RDHL* 1 (1898): 406–30; 1 (1899): 329–59.

——. "Reforma universitaria: Concepto filosófico del plan de instrución pública proyectado." *RDHL* 2, 6 (1899): 212–26.

Ferrero, Guglielmo. "La Penitenciaría Nacional de Buenos Aires juzgada en el extranjero." *APCCA* 7 (1908): 217–23.

Ferriani, Lino. *La infanticida nel Codice Penale e nella vita sociale: considerazioni.* Milan: Fratelli Dumolard Editori, 1886.

Fraga, R. M. *Memoria de la Penitenciaría Nacional 1901.* Buenos Aires: 1902.

Gache, Samuel. "Congreso penitenciario: Antropología criminal." *RJ* 3 (1886): 1028–36.

Gancedo, A. "Justicia y eleciones." *RDHL* 4, 10 (1901): 61–66.

Gándara, Alfredo M. "La pena de muerte." *RJ* (1884): 451–56, 489–506.

Gómez, Eusebio. *Estudios penitenciarios.* Buenos Aires: Penitenciaría Nacional, 1906.

———. *Memoria descriptiva de la Penitenciaría Nacional de Buenos Aires.* Buenos Aires: Penitenciaría Nacional, 1914.

———. *Pasión y delito.* Buenos Aires: J. Roldán, 1917.

Gonzáles Roura, O. "Delitos contra la honestidad." *APCCA* 1 (1902): 659–69.

Gori, Pedro. "Estudios carcelarios: Una visita a la Penitenciaría de Sierra Chica." *CM* 2, 6 (1899): 176–82.

———. "La ortodoxia antropológica en el derecho penal." *RJ* 15 (1898–99): 73–78.

Gouchon, Emilio. "La ordenanza reglamentaria del servicio doméstico." *RJ* 5 (1888): 82–98.

Greene, Homer. "¿Pueden ser honrados los abogados?" *RDHL* 1 (1898): 53–64.

"¡Guerra al delito!" *CM* 1 (1) (1898): 1–2.

Herrera, F. M. "Correspondencia. Necesidad de reglamentar el ejercicio de la procuración y la abogacía." *RJ* 17 (1899): 311–13.

Iberlucea, Enrique del Valle. "Fundamentos científicos del divorcio." *APCCA* 1 (1902): 469–89.

"Identificación de cadáveres." *RP* 4, 85 (1900): 202–3.

Ingenieros, José. "El envenenador Luis Castruccio." *APCCA* 8 (1909): 5–29.

———. "Fetichista con hermafrodismo psíquico activo y alucinaciones eróticas del olfato." *APCCA* 1 (1902): 616–21.

———. *Obras completas.* 8 vols. Buenos Aires: Mar Oceano, 1962.

———. "Sobre enfermedades simuladas: Notas médico-sociológicas." *RDHL* 4, 12 (1902): 376–88.

———. "El suicidio en las campañas argentinas." *APCCA* 1, 4 (1902): 247.

"Interview with Juan Vucetich." *El Argentino,* Sept. 1, 1924.

Isenburg, Princesa María. "La reforma del traje femenino." *DHL* 4, 11 (1901): 96–101.

Kardec, Allan [Denizard Hippolyte-Léon Rivail]. *The Spirits' Book.* English translation of *Le Livre des esprits* (1859). Boston: Colby & Rich, 1875.

Lancelotti, Miguel A. *La criminalidad en Buenos Aires: Al margen de la estadística (1887–1912).* Buenos Aires: V. Abeledo, 1914.

Llames Massini, J. C. *La partera de Buenos Aires y la Escuela de Parteras.* Buenos Aires: Flaiban and Camilloni, 1915.

Llerena, Baldomero. "Discurso." *RDHL* 1 (1898): 226–37.

Logan, Walter S. "Tribunales sajones y latinos." *RDHL* 1 (3) (1899): 78–91.

Lombroso, Cesare. *L'uomo delinquente; studiato in rapporto alla antropología, alla medicina legale ed alle discipline carcerarie.* Milan: Hoepli, 1876.

Lombroso, Cesare, and Guglielmo Ferrero. *La donna delinquente, la prostituta e la donna normale.* Turin: Roux, 1893. Translated as *The Female Offender* (New York: Appleton, 1898).

Lombroso, Gina. "Instituciones americanas: La Penitenciaría Nacional de Buenos Aires." *APCCA* 7 (1908): 236.

Lozano, Godofredo. "La reforma del Código penal argentino." *RDHL* 3, 8 (1901): 374–94.

Magnan, Valentin. *Des Anomalies, des aberrations et des perversions sexuelles, par Magnan . . . (Communication faite à l'Académie de médecine dans la séance du 13 janvier 1885)*. Paris: A. Delahaye & E. Lecrosnier, 1885.

Magnan, Valentin, and Paul-Maurice Legrain. *Les Dégénérés (état mental et syndromes épisodiques), par le Dr Magnan et le Dr Legrain*. Paris: Rueff, 1895.

Mármol, José. "La pena de muerte." *RJ* 14 (1897–98): 213–23.

Mauenaghton, Dr. "Las funciones sexuales, la locura y el delito en la mujer." *APCCA* 1 (1902): 58–59.

Mercante, Victor. *La crisis de la pubertad y sus consecuencias pedagógicas*. Buenos Aires: Cabaut, 1918.

———. "Estudios de criminología infantil." *APCCA* 1 (1902): 463–68.

———. "Peología: La voz en los niños y la degeneración." *CM* 2, nos. 13–14 (Nov.–Dec. 1899): 433–39.

Molinario, Alfredo J. "La desincriminación del adulterio en el Proyecto de Código penal argentino." *Anales de la Sociedad Argentina de Criminología* 5 (1939): 17–32.

Montes de Oca, Juan José. "Derecho criminal." *RLJ* 7 (1872): 421–32.

Morache, G. "La responsabilidad criminal de la mujer diferente de la del hombre." *RDHL* 4, 11 (1901): 592–604.

Morel, Benedict-Auguste. *Traité des dégénérescences physiques, intellectuelles et morales de l'espèce humaine. . . .* Paris: J. B. Baillière, 1857.

———. *Traité des maladies mentales*. Paris: V. Masson, 1860.

Morselli, Enrico. *Suicide: An Essay on Comparative Moral Statistics*. New York: Appleton, 1882.

Moyano Gacitúa, Cornelio. *Curso de ciencia criminal y derecho penal argentino*. Buenos Aires: Lajouane, 1899.

Mujica Farías, M. "Curso de derecho penal." *RP* 2, 45 (Apr. 1, 1899): 757–59.

Muratore, José Luis. "Cuestiones penales de actualidad." *APCCA* 1 (1902): 12–16.

Netri, Francisco. "Sobre la reincidencia criminal especifica reiterada." *APCCA* 1 (1902): 284–89.

Nina Rodrigues, Raimundo. *As raças humanas e a responsibilidade no Brasil*. Edited by Afrânio Peixoto. 1894. Rio de Janeiro: Editora Nacional, 1938.

Nordau, Max. *Entartung*. 2 vols. Berlin: C. Duncker, 1892–93. Translated as *Degeneration* (1895; Lincoln: University of Nebraska Press, 1993).

"Nuestros propósitos." *RJ* 8 (1891): 5–8.

Obarrio, Manuel. "Derecho penal." *RLJ* 11 (1878): 5–29.

———. "Familia." *RJ* 4 (1888): 143–58.

———. "De los seguros sobre la vida." *RDHL* 1 (1898): 489–504.

"Oficina antropométrica, alcaidía y archivos criminales." *RP* 4, 81 (Oct. 1, 1900): 131–33; 4, 82 (Oct. 16, 1900): 149–51.

Olivera, Carlos. "Psicología del derecho penal." *RJ* 18 (1900): 353–69.

———. "Venenos sociales." *RDHL* 2, 5 (1899): 204–17.

Orfila, Matthieu Joseph Bonaventure. *Medicina legal*. 4th ed. Vol. 1. Paris: Renouard, 1848.

Pacheco, Joaquín Francisco. *Código penal.* 2d ed. Vol. 1. Madrid: Perinat, 1856.

Padilla, Uladislao F. Review of his law thesis. *RJ* 19 (1900–1901): 71–72.

Pérez, D. J. G. de J. *Nueva medicina doméstica, o sea arte de conservar la salud, de conocer las enfermedades, sus remedios y aplicación, al alcance de todos.* Buenos Aires: Revista, 1854.

Pesenti, Victor R. "Influencia de la civilización en la criminalidad." *RJ* 20 (1901): 140–43.

Piñero, Horacio G. "Psicología." *RJ* 19 (1900–1901): 335–52.

Piñero, Osvaldo M. "Criminalidad y represión." *RJ* 5 (1888): 289–303.

Prack, Enrique B. "Escuela antropológica criminal." *RJ* 8 (1891): 109–13, 254–64, 298–306.

Quesada, Ernesto. *Comprobación de la reincidencia: Proyecto de ley presentado al señor ministro de justicia é instrucción pública, doctor don Osvaldo Magnasco.* Buenos Aires: Coni, 1901.

———. "Identificación dactiloscópica: ¿Se trata de un sistema argentino ó inglés? Exámen de la cuestión de prioridad: Vucetich versus Henry." *Renacimiento* 1, 1 (1909): 189–222.

———. "La oficina antropométrica." *RP* 1, 6 (Aug. 15, 1897): 93–94.

———. "Tiene la Cámara de Apelaciones de la Capital la facultad de graciar procesados?" *RJ* 16 (1899): 174–76.

Quevedo Hijosa, Federico. "Cómo resolvió Vucetich el problema de la identificación personal." *El Hogar,* Feb. 13, 1925, 7.

———. "La cuestión dactiloscópica: Necesidad impostergable de reparar una injusticia. ¿Se pretende negar a Vucetich o despojarle de su invento?" *La Argentina,* Jan. 17, 1925, 2.

———. "El 'Vucetichismo' reconocido universalmente, es negado por la policía de Buenos Aires." *La Argentina,* Jan. 10, 1925, 2.

Ramos Mejía, José María, Florentino Ortega, and Marcelian Aravena. "El asesino de Olavarría: Su estado mental al cometer el crímen y despues de él. Responsibilidad. Interesante estudio médico legal." *RJ* 5 (1888): 428–52.

"Reforma de la Constitución de la Provincia de Buenos Aires." *RLJ* 5 (1870): 394–447.

Reyna Almandos, Luis. *Dactiloscopía argentina: Su historia é influencia en la legislación.* La Plata: J. Sesé, 1909.

———. "The Personal Number and the National Book of Personality" (in English). In *Biblioteca de la Revista de identificación y ciencias penales,* no. 22. La Plata: Impresiones Oficiales, 1936.

Reynal, Gualberto. "Juan Vucetich en la anécdota: Ensayo." MS. N.d.

Rivarola, Rodolfo Juan Nemesio. *Derecho penal argentino.* Madrid: Reus, 1910.

———. "Origenes y evolución del derecho penal argentino." *RJ* 18 (1900): 277–308.

Rivero Astengo, Agustín. *Hombres de la organización nacional: Retratos literarios.* 1st ser. Buenos Aires: Coni, 1936.

Rodríguez, Fermín. "Estudios sobre el suicidio en Buenos Aires: La influencia de la edad y del sexo." *APCCA* 3 (1904): 1–21.

———. "Influencia del alcoholismo sobre el suicidio en Buenos Aires." *APCCA* 4 (1905): 531–47.

———. "Influencia del estado civil sobre el suicidio en Buenos Aires." *APCCA* 4 (1905): 385–404.

Rodríguez, Miguel F. "El adulterio: Contribución al estudio de nuestra legislación penal." *RDHL* 3, 7 (1900): 233–39, 391–404.

Rodríguez, Sislán. "Vucetich y la dactiloscopía (síntesis enumerativa de las principales fechas)." *RP* 1, 10 (Feb. 1942): 9–19.

Romero, Miguel. "Política interna: Estudio psicológico." *RJ* 20 (1901): 217–33.

Rosa, José María. "Derecho civil: ¿Puede pedirse judicialmente el reconocimiento de filiación natural, á una mujer casada?" *RLJ* 10 (1876): 225–44.

Rossi, José Gregorio. "La criminalidad profesional en Buenos Aires." *APCMLP* 2 (1903): 169–76.

Sergi, Giuseppe. *La decadenza delle nazioni latine.* Turin: Bocca, 1900.

Sicardi, Francisco A. "La vida del delito y de la prostitución: Impresiones médico-literarias." *APCCA* 2 (1903): 11–21.

"Siguen los crimenes." *RJ* 5 (1888): 386–88.

Sittoni, G. "La epilepsia en América: Sus causas y manifestaciones (contribución a la antropología criminal)." *CM* 2, 12 (Oct. 1899): 356–64.

Solari, Benjamin T. "La defensa de la raza por la castración de los degenerados: Las ideas profilácticas de Zuccarelli." *APCMLP* 1 (1902): 385–91.

Tarde, Gabriel. *La Criminalité comparée.* 1886. 2d ed. Paris: F. Alcan, 1890.

Vázquez, Laudelino. "La reforma en la justicia criminal: El jurado." *RDHL* 2, 4 (1899): 521–35.

Veyga, Francisco de. "Los auxiliares del vicio y del delito." *APCCA* 3 (1904): 289–313.

——. "De la regeneración como ley opuesta a la degeneración mórbida." *APCCA* 4 (1905): 31–44.

Vucetich, Juan. *Dactiloscopía comparada, el nuevo sistema argentino; trabajo hecho expresamente para el 2. Congreso médico latino-americano, Buenos Aires, 3-10 de abril de 1904.* La Plata: Peuser, 1904.

——. *Proyecto de ley de registro general de identificación.* La Plata: Impresiones Oficiales, 1929.

Wilde, Eduardo. *Obras completas.* 14 vols. Buenos Aires: Peuser, 1914.

Wilmart, Raimundo. "El jurado." *RJ* 11 (1895): 20–26.

——. "Nuestro poder judicial." *RJ* 17 (1899): 14–23.

Zeballos, Estanislao Severo. "Analecta." *RDHL* 3, 7 (1900): 149–60; 8 (1901): 473–80; 9 (1901): 147–60.

——. "La crisis del gobierno y del país." *RDHL* 2, 5 (1899): 448–57.

——. "Discurso." *RDHL* 5, 13 (1902): 457–66.

——. "El Instituto de Criminología de la República Argentina." *APCCA* 7 (1908).

——. "Los jueces." *RDHL* 5, 13 (1902): 611–19.

——. "La reunión de los peritos." *RDHL* 1, 3 (1898): 256–65.

——. "*Revista de Derecho, Historia y Letras.*" *RDHL* 1, 1 (1898): 5–7.

Secondary Works Cited

Aisenberg, Andrew R. *Contagion: Disease, Government, and the "Social Question" in Nineteenth-Century France.* Stanford: Stanford University Press, 1999.

Amadeo, Octavio Ramón. *Vidas argentinas.* Buenos Aires: Emecé, 1965.

Andrews, George Reid. *The Afro-Argentines of Buenos Aires, 1800–1900.* Madison: University of Wisconsin Press, 1980.

Armus, Diego. "Salud y anarquismo: La tuberculósis en el discurso libertario argenti-no, 1890–1940." In *Política, médicos y enfermedades: Lecturas de historia de la salud en la Argentina*, ed. Mirta Zaida Lobato et al., 91–116. Buenos Aires: Biblos, 1996.

Borges, Dain. *The Family in Bahia, Brazil, 1870–1945.* Stanford: Stanford University Press, 1992.

Buffington, Robert M. *Criminal and Citizen in Modern Mexico.* Lincoln: University of Nebraska Press, 2000.

Caimari, Lila. "Remembering Freedom: Life as Seen from the Prison Cell (Buenos Aires Province, 1900–1950)." Unpublished paper.

Cole, Simon Ablon. "Manufacturing Identity: A History of Criminal Identification Techniques from Photography Through Fingerprinting." Thesis, Cornell University, 1998.

Corbin, Alain. *The Foul and the Fragrant: Odor and the French Social Imagination.* Cambridge, Mass.: Harvard University Press, 1986. Originally published as *Le Miasme et la jonquille: L'Odorat et l'imaginaire social, XVIIIe–XIXe siècles* (Paris: Aubier Montaigne, 1982).

Cúneo, Carlos, and Abel González. *La delincuencia.* Buenos Aires: América Latina, 1971.

Degregori, Pedro Mario. *El austero silencioso.* Buenos Aires: Negri, 1982.

Findlay, Eileen J. Suárez. *Imposing Decency: The Politics of Sexuality and Race in Puerto Rico, 1870–1920.* Durham, N.C.: Duke University Press, 1999.

Flores, Andrés I. *Casos famosos de la crónica policial argentina.* Buenos Aires: Orión, ca. 1975.

García Maañón, Ernesto, and Alejandro Antonio Basile. *Aborto e infanticidio: Aspectos jurídicos y médico-legales.* Buenos Aires: Universidad, 1990.

Gates, Barbara T. *Victorian Suicide: Mad Crimes and Sad Histories.* Princeton: Princeton University Press, 1988.

Gayol, Sandra. "Duelos, honores, leyes y derechos: Argentina, 1887–1923." *Anuario Iehs* (Instituto de Estudios Histórico-sociales, Universidad Nacional del Centro, Tandil, Argentina) 14 (1999): 313–30.

Goldstein, Jan. "'Moral Contagion': A Professional Ideology of Medicine and Psychiatry in Eighteenth- and Nineteenth-Century France." In *Professions and the French State, 1700–1900*, ed. Gerald L. Geison. Philadelphia: University of Pennsylvania Press, 1984.

González Leandri, Ricardo. "La profesión médica en Buenos Aires: 1852–1870." In *Política, médicos y enfermedades: Lecturas de historia de la salud en la Argentina*, ed. Mirta Zaida Lobato et al., 19–53. Buenos Aires: Biblos, 1996.

Graham, Richard. *The Idea of Race in Latin America, 1870–1940.* Austin: University of Texas Press, 1990.

Guy, Donna J. *Sex and Danger in Buenos Aires: Prostitution, Family, and Nation in Argentina.* Lincoln: University of Nebraska Press, 1991.

———. *White Slavery and Mothers Alive and Dead: The Troubled Meeting of Sex, Gender, Public Health, and Progress in Latin America.* Lincoln: University of Nebraska Press, 2000.

Halbwachs, Maurice. *The Causes of Suicide.* Translated by Harold Goldblatt. New York: Free Press, 1978. Originally published as *Les Causes du suicide* (Paris: F. Alcan, 1930).

Hess, David J. *Spirits and Scientists: Ideology, Spiritism, and Brazilian Culture*. University Park, Pa.: Penn State University Press, 1991.

Huertas García-Alejo, Rafael. *El delincuente y su patología: Medicina, crímen y sociedad en el positivismo argentino*. Madrid: Consejo Superior de Investigaciones Científicas, 1991.

————. *Locura y degeneración: Psiquiatría y sociedad en el positivismo francés*. Madrid: Consejo Superior de Investigaciones Científicas, 1991.

Hunefeldt, Christine. *Liberalism in the Bedroom: Quarreling Spouses in Nineteenth-Century Lima*. University Park, Pa.: Pennsylvania State University Press, 2000.

Johnson, Lyman L., and Sonya Lipsett-Rivera. Introduction to *The Faces of Honor: Sex, Shame, and Violence in Colonial Latin America*, ed. id. Albuquerque: University of New Mexico Press, 1998.

Lavrin, Asunción. *Women, Feminism, and Social Change in Argentina, Chile, and Uruguay, 1890–1940*. Lincoln: University of Nebraska Press, 1995.

Levaggi, Abelardo. *Historia del derecho penal argentino*. Buenos Aires: Perrot, 1978.

Lipsett-Rivera, Sonya. See Johnson, Lyman L.

Martínez Pérez, José. "El suicidio como indicador del bienestar de un Estado: algunos problemas en torno al origen de su empleo por la psiquiatría francesa (1800–1856)." In *La salud en el estado de bienestar. Análisis histórico*, ed. Luis Montiel. Madrid: Complutense, 1993.

Masiello, Francine. *Between Civilization and Barbarism: Women, Nation, and Literary Culture in Modern Argentina*. Lincoln: University of Nebraska Press, 1992.

Meade, Teresa A. *"Civilizing" Rio: Reform and Resistance in a Brazilian City, 1889–1930*. University Park, Pa.: Pennsylvania State University Press, 1997.

Milanich, Nara. "'Entrañas mil veces despreciables e indignas': Infanticide in Rural Nineteenth-Century Chile." Unpublished manuscript, 1995.

Moya, José C. *Cousins and Strangers: Spanish Immigrants in Buenos Aires, 1850–1930*. Berkeley: University of California Press, 1998.

Muriel, Josefina. *Los recogimientos de mujeres: Respuesta a una problemática social novohispana*. Serie de Historia Novohispana, no. 24, Mexico City: Universidad Nacional Autónoma de México, Instituto de Investigaciones Históricas, 1974.

Peard, Julyan G. *Race, Place, and Medicine: The Idea of the Tropics in Nineteenth-Century Brazilian Medicine*. Durham, N.C.: Duke University Press, 1999.

Peset, José Luis. *Las heridas de la ciencia*. Madrid: Junta de Castilla y León, 1993.

Peset, José Luis, and Mariano Peset. *Lombroso y la escuela positivista italiana*. Madrid: Junta de Castilla y León, 1975.

Piccato, Pablo. *City of Suspects: Crime in Mexico City, 1900–1931*. Durham, N.C.: Duke University Press, 2001.

————. "La política y la tecnología del honor: El duelo en México durante el porfiriato y la revolución." *Anuario Iehs* (Instituto de Estudios Histórico-sociales, Universidad Nacional del Centro, Tandil, Argentina) 14 (1999): 273–94.

Pitt-Rivers, Julian. "La enfermedad del honor." *Anuario Iehs* (Instituto de Estudios Histórico-sociales, Universidad Nacional del Centro, Tandil, Argentina) 14 (1999): 235–45.

Plotkin, Mariano Ben. *Freud in the Pampas: The Emergence and Development of a Psychoanalytic Culture in Argentina, 1910–1983*. Stanford: Stanford University Press, 2001.

Porter, Dorothy. *Health, Civilization and the State: A History of Public Health from Ancient to Modern Times*. New York: Routledge, 1999.

Quirós, Carlos. *Guia radical*. Buenos Aires: Galerna, 1986.

Rock, David. *Argentina, 1516–1987: From Spanish Colonization to Alfonsín*. Berkeley: University of California Press, 1987.

Rodríguez, Adolfo Enrique. *Cuatrocientos años de policía en Buenos Aires*. Buenos Aires: Editorial Policial, ca. 1981.

Romay, Francisco Luis. *Historia de la Policía Federal Argentina*. Vol. 6: 1880–1916. Buenos Aires: Editorial Policial, 1975.

Ruggiero, Kristin. "Dactiloscopy and Other Identification Techniques in Turn-of-the-Century Argentina." In *Documenting Individual Identity: The Development of State Practices Since the French Revolution*, ed. Jane Caplan and John Torpey. Princeton: Princeton University Press, 2001.

———. "The Devil and Modernity in Late Nineteenth-Century Buenos Aires." *Américas* 59, 2 (2002): 221–33.

———. "Honor, Maternity, and the Disciplining of Women: Infanticide in Late Nineteenth-Century Buenos Aires." *Hispanic American Historical Review* 72, 3 (1992): 353–73.

———. "Houses of Deposit and the Exclusion of Women in Turn-of-the-Century Argentina." In *Isolation: Places and Practices of Exclusion*, ed. Carolyn Strange and Alison Bashford. New York: Routledge, 2003

———. "Not Guilty: Abortion and Infanticide in Nineteenth-Century Argentina." In *Reconstructing Criminality in Latin America*, ed. Carlos A. Aguirre and Robert Buffington. Wilmington, Del.: Scholarly Resources, 2000.

———. "Passion, Perversion, and the Pace of Justice in Argentina at the Turn of the Last Century." In *Crime and Punishment in Latin America: Law and Society Since Late Colonial Times*, ed. Ricardo D. Salvatore, Carlos Aguirre, and Gilbert M. Joseph. Durham, N.C.: Duke University Press, 2001.

———. "Wives on 'Deposit': Internment and the Preservation of Husbands' Honor in Late Nineteenth-Century Buenos Aires." *Journal of Family History* 17, 3 (1992): 253–70.

Ruibal, Beatriz Celina. "El honor y el delito: Buenos Aires a fines del siglo XIX." *Entrepasados* 6, 11 (1996): 35–44.

Ruiz Zevallos, Augusto. *Psiquíatras y locos: Entre la modernización contra los andes y el nuevo proyecto de modernidad, Perú, 1850–1930*. Lima: Pasado & Presente, 1994.

Salessi, Jorge. *Médicos, maleantes y maricas*. Rosario: Beatriz Viterbo, 1995.

Salvatore, Ricardo D. "Death and Liberalism: Capital Punishment After the Fall of Rosas." In *Crime and Punishment in Latin America: Law and Society Since Late Colonial Times*, ed. Ricardo D. Salvatore, Carlos Aguirre, and Gilbert M. Joseph. Durham, N.C.: Duke University Press, 2001.

———. "Positivist Criminology and State Formation in Argentina." Forthcoming.

———. "State Legal Order and Subaltern Rights: The Modernization of the Justice System in Argentina (1870–1930)." MS.

Salvatore, Ricardo D., and Carlos Aguirre, eds. *The Birth of the Penitentiary in Latin America: Essays on Criminology, Prison Reform, and Social Control, 1830–1940*. Austin: University of Texas Press, 1996.

Scarzanella, Eugenia. *Italiani malagente: Immigrazione, criminalità, razzismo in Argentina, 1890–1940*. Milan: FrancoAngeli, 1999.

Scobie, James R. *Argentina: A City and a Nation*. New York: Oxford University Press, 1964.

———. *Buenos Aires: Plaza to Suburb, 1870–1910*. New York: Oxford University Press, 1974.

Shapiro, Ann-Louise. *Breaking the Codes: Female Criminality in Fin-de-Siècle Paris*. Stanford: Stanford University Press, 1996.

Socolow, Susan Migden. "Women and Crime: Buenos Aires, 1757–97." In *The Problem of Order in Changing Societies: Essays on Crime and Policing in Argentina and Uruguay*, ed., Lyman L. Johnson. Albuquerque: University of New Mexico Press, 1990.

———. *The Women of Colonial Latin America*. New York: Cambridge University Press, 2000.

Speckman, Elisa Guerra. "Las flores del mal: Mujeres criminales en el porfiriato." *Historia Mexicana* 47, 1 (1997): 183–229.

Temkin, Owsei. *The Falling Sickness: A History of Epilepsy from the Greeks to the Beginnings of Modern Neurology*. 2d ed. Baltimore: Johns Hopkins University Press, 1971.

Terán, Oscar. *Positivismo y nación en la Argentina*. Buenos Aires: Puntosur, 1987.

Thornton, E. M. *Hypnotism, Hysteria and Epilepsy: An Historical Synthesis*. London: Heinemann, 1976.

Thorwald, Jürgen. *The Century of the Detective*. New York: Harcourt, Brace, 1965. Originally published as *Das Jahrhundert der Detektive: Weg und Abenteuer der Kriminalistik* (Zurich: Droemer, 1964).

Trigo, Benigno. "Crossing the Boundaries of Madness: Criminology and Figurative Language in Argentina (1878–1920)." *Journal of Latin American Cultural Studies* 6, 1 (1997): 7–20.

Twinam, Ann. *Public Lives, Private Secrets: Gender, Honor, Sexuality, and Illegitimacy in Colonial Spanish America*. Stanford: Stanford University Press, 1999.

Urla, Jacqueline and Jennifer Terry. "Introduction. Mapping Embodied Deviance." In *Deviant Bodies: Critical Perspectives on Difference in Science and Popular Culture*, ed. Jennifer Terry and Jacqueline Urla. Bloomington: Indiana University Press, 1995.

Van Deusen, Nancy E. "Determining the Boundaries of Virtue: The Discourse of *Recogimiento* Among Women in Seventeenth-Century Lima." *Journal of Family History* 22, 4 (1997): 373–89.

Vezzetti, Hugo. *La locura en la Argentina*. Buenos Aires: Folios Ediciones, 1983.

Zárate C., María Soledad. "Mujeres viciosas, mujeres virtuosas: La mujer delinquente y la Casa Correccional de Santiago, 1860–1900." In *Disciplina y desacato: Construcción de identidad en Chile, siglos XIX y XX*, 149–80. Santiago de Chile: SUR-CEDEM, 1995.

Zimmermann, Eduardo A. *Los liberales reformistas: La cuestión social en la Argentina, 1890–1916*. Buenos Aires: Sudamericana and Universidad de San Andrés, 1995.

———. "El poder judicial, la construcción del estado, y el federalismo: Argentina, 1860–1880." In *In Search of a New Order: Essays on the Politics and Society of Nineteenth-Century Latin America*, ed. Eduardo Posada-Carbó. London: Institute of Latin American Studies, University of London, 1998.

Index

In this index an "f" after a number indicates a separate reference on the next page, and an "ff" indicates separate references on the next two pages. A continuous discussion over two or more pages is indicated by a span of page numbers, e.g., "57–59."